Developing a Successful Soccer Program

George Hageage
Stephenie Jordan

©2006 Coaches Choice. All rights reserved. Printed in the United States.

No part of this book may be reproduced, stored in a retrieval system, or transmitted, in any form or by any means, electronic, mechanical, photocopying, recording, or otherwise, without the prior permission of Coaches Choice. Throughout this book, the masculine shall be deemed to include the feminine and vice versa.

ISBN: 1-58518-963-4
Library of Congress Control Number: 2006921720
Cover design: Studio J Art & Design
Book layout: Studio J Art & Design
Text photos: Tamara Hageage
Front cover photo: Tamara Hageage

Coaches Choice
P.O. Box 1828
Monterey, CA 93942
www.coacheschoice.com

Acknowledgments

I would like to thank all the coaches I have played for, coached with, or coached against who have helped me develop and continue to develop as a coach. I would like to especially recognize my father, Dr. George Hageage, Jr., Lazlo Koltay, and Dr. Maurice Manning for not only being great teachers of the game of soccer but for also helping me develop the passion and desire to coach. What a tremendous impact you have had—and still have—on my life.

To Rj Anderson—Thank you for starting me on this journey. I owe you more than I could give you.

To all my players (past and present)—I hope I have taught you as much as you have taught me. You truly are my extended family.

To all my family and friends, especially Jeff, Dave, and Dan—Your support has meant so much. Thanks for being there for me!

To my mom and dad—What an incredible journey! I can't express to you how much you mean to me. Your support of me has been unwavering. I love you very much!

To my wife, Tamara—I honestly can't believe how lucky I am. You are always there to keep me going both as my wife and as my colleague. You have helped me in all facets of my life and made me stronger than I could ever be alone. Soccer is great, but you are my life.

To my son George—What a wonderful gift God has bestowed on Tamara and me. You have changed my life in more ways than I can count. I love you so much!

—George Hageage

I offer sincere thanks and appreciation to my Lord and Savior, Jesus Christ; to my husband Jody, who is the greatest football coach, husband, and daddy; to my parents, Roger and Claire Scott, who do so much for us; to our children, Scott and Rebekah, who are the greatest joy and blessing in our lives; to Trevor White, whose passion has always been the game of soccer; and to Dr. Jim Peterson and Kristi Huelsing for their patience and guidance.

—Stephenie Jordan

Preface

Developing a Successful Soccer Program is a resource-packed, comprehensive handbook that touches on more than the X's and O's of the sport. Many areas left untouched by other soccer books are covered here, including a preseason checklist, scouting, job descriptions for your assistants, game-day considerations, and much more.

Chapter 1 is a season timeline that highlights important issues that need to be addressed before the season, when practice begins, and at the midseason point. Chapter 2 gives insight into planning the season, beginning with assessing your players through a tryout system and then choosing the teams, assigning players to their positions, and choosing a game plan. The next two chapters give you a well-rounded list of drills for specific skills and then practice-planning help utilizing those drills. Chapters 5 through 8 are related specifically to the X's and O's of coaching soccer and include basic offensive and defensive principles, set pieces for every situation, and detailed information about the different systems of play. Chapter 9 is dedicated to the position of goalkeeper, including techniques, skills, drills, and sample training sessions. Chapter 10 includes five important checklists to use when assessing your upcoming opponent and tips for developing a game plan based on your assessment. Chapter 11 is dedicated to game-day considerations, including what to take to an away game, what to do during the pregame, and what to do after the game. Chapter 12 summarizes the season-ending responsibilities in an easy checklist. Chapter 13 explains how to plan your off-season and provides activities for field players as well as the goalkeepers.

Finally, the appendices provide detailed information about planning your own tournament, terminology, fundraising ideas, and club team information. The tournament and fund-raising sections are presented in a timeline format and take you from the planning stages to the day of the event and after.

Developing a Successful Soccer Program is intended for use as a reference. Pick and choose what you need when you need it. We hope you find it gives you the added edge you need to be a successful coach.

Contents

Acknowledgments 3

Preface 4

Chapter 1: Season Planning Checklist 9
- Before the First Day of Practice
- After Practice Begins
- Midseason Responsibilities

Chapter 2: Planning the Season 43
- Player Assessment
- Choosing the Teams
- Assigning Players to Positions
- Choosing Your Game Plan
- A Checklist of Skills
- Putting it all on a Timeline

Chapter 3: Drills 63
- Basic Dribbling Skills
- Dribbling—General Coaching Points
- Dribbling Activities
- Passing/Striking—General Coaching Points
- Passing/Striking Activities
- Combination Play Activities
- Receiving—General Coaching Points
- Receiving Activity
- Heading—General Coaching Points
- Heading Activities
- Turning—General Coaching Points
- Types of Turns While Receiving a Ball
- Turning Activities
- Tackling—General Coaching Points
- Tackling Activities
- Shooting/Finishing—General Coaching Points
- Shooting/Finishing Activities
- Throw-Ins—General Coaching Points
- Throw-In Activity
- Conditioning
- Conditioning Activities
- Game Situations—Possession Games

Chapter 4: Planning a Practice 94
- General Practice Guidelines
- General Practice Outline

Assessing Your Practice Session
Master Practice Outline
Sample Coaching Outline
Sample Practice Plans
Sample Week for High School
Other Practice Concerns

Chapter 5: Offensive Strategy 114
Basic Offensive Principles
Offensive Principles Within Each Third of the Field

Chapter 6: Set Pieces 119

Chapter 7: Defensive Strategy 125
Basic Principles of Defense
Defensive Principles Within Each Third of the Field

Chapter 8: Systems of Play 128
1-3-5-2
1-4-4-2
1-4-3-3
1-3-4-3
1-4-5-1

Chapter 9: Goalkeeping 136
Characteristics of the Goalkeeper
Goalkeeping Techniques
Basic Communication Skills Required for the Goalkeeper
Training Focal Points for Goalkeepers
Drills
Fun Games for Two Goalkeepers
Sample Training Sessions

Chapter 10: Scouting 152
General Checklist
Offensive Checklist
Set Pieces
Defensive Checklist
Goalkeeper Checklist
Developing a Practice Plan

Chapter 11: Game-Day Considerations 155
  Away-Game Preparation
  Home-Game Procedures
  Pregame Routine
  Keeping Stats During the Game
  Statistical Analysis for Individual Skills
  During the Game
  Halftime
  After the Game
  The Next Day

Chapter 12: Season Ending Responsibilities 160

Chapter 13: Off-Season Training 167
  Off-Season Activities
  Setting Individual Goals
  Off-Season Scoring Charts
  A Sample Off-Season Conditioning Program

Appendix A: Planning a Tournament 182

Appendix B: Terminology 192

Appendix C: Fundraising Ideas 204

Appendix D: Club Team Information 219

About the Authors 221

1

Season Planning Timeline

Before the First Day of Practice

- Inventory current equipment
- Check the fund balance
- Make a needs and wants list for the athletic director
- Request field improvements
- Fill out a purchase request form
- Order equipment
- Order booster material
- Make personal calls to players
- Send letters to athletes
- Schedule the season
- Schedule officials
- Fill out travel requests
- Request checks for tournaments
- Develop a team website
- Make a recruiting video
- Make signs for businesses
- Meet with civic groups
- Distribute goodwill gifts to administration and VIPs
- Schedule a college trip or clinic
- Arrange for substitutes for clinics/trips
- Get a commercial driver's license (CDL) and bus-driving certification
- Develop team standards and expectations
- Secure coaching positions
- Get a coaches' packet ready
- Meet with coaches
- Order coaches' shirts
- Meet with prospective team members
- Have a kick-off-the-season BBQ

- Host a parents meeting
- Issue equipment
- Organize yourself
- Join coaches associations and organizations
- Schedule a photographer
- Read the rule book

Inventorying Equipment

To develop a list of needs and wants, you'll first need to know what you've got. If you are new on the job, don't rely on the list left by the previous coach. Figure 1-1 illustrates a sample form that can be used to record the equipment.

Sample Inventory Sheet					
Item Description	New	Usable	Old	Total	Needed

Figure 1-1. Sample inventory sheet

Checking the Fund Balance

See where you stand at the beginning of the season so you know how much money you have to work with. The amount in your budget will also dictate how many fundraisers (if any) you will need to plan.

Making a Needs and Wants List

If you want some items that may be out of the ordinary, then do what you can to make a professional presentation to your athletic director. For example, if you think you can't live without a specific rebound goal, find three companies that make them, find the best price, and show you've done your homework. If your athletic director rejects the idea, then begin thinking about a fundraiser (Appendix C).

Among the items you should include in your needs list are the following:

Shoes—Order new shoes for your high school squads. It is important that they are comfortable for each athlete so offer a choice of several different brands of shoes. Some shoe brands don't fit everyone the same way.

Uniforms—Make sure you have enough uniforms to fit everyone, not just clothe everyone. You want your team to look good and feel comfortable. You will need to order uniforms for your goalkeeper as well. It must be different from the other team and the referee.

Practice uniforms—Issue these the first day you meet and require that everyone wear them. When everyone dresses the same, you have a sense of team.

Pennies/bibs—Order three sets of 11 in different colors to use for possession games.

Corner flags

Ankle braces—Issuing braces to everyone can be preventative medicine. Or, if you prefer, you can issue them only to those with chronic problems. If an injury occurred within the last month or two, taping or requiring a brace is recommended.

Shin guards—Shin guards are mandatory, so order enough for your entire team.

Head gear—Order bands to help cushion the impact when heading balls. The bands may help lessen the severity of concussions.

Soccer balls and an air pump—Order one ball and small pump for each player and set aside several new balls to use for games.

Ball bags—The type of bags you order will depend on how much money you have to spend. Try to order ball carts and at least one ball bag for travel.

Video equipment—You will need a camera, two good VCRs, and plenty of tapes.

Whistles and lanyards—Get two or three, as they are easy to misplace.

Nets—Order nets for your goals and double-check the measurements to get a proper fit.

Chalk and paint—Check with your athletic director to find out how much you will need to purchase. Chalk and paint may be bought in bulk when the head football coach, head baseball coach, or field maintenance director places an order, so you may be able to pick some up from one of them as you need it.

Chalker—If you have enough funds, consider purchasing one of your own. If not, you could probably share with the baseball program.

Athletic training supplies—Among the items that you should consider ordering for your travel kit are the following:
- Adhesive tape
- Prewrap material
- Bandages/Band-Aids (assorted sizes)
- Butterfly strips
- Contact solution
- Elastic knee sleeves (small, medium, and large)
- Elastic thigh sleeves (small, medium, and large)
- Eyewash
- Feminine napkins
- Gauze (one-inch and two-inch rolls)
- Heel cups (plastic)
- Instant cold packs
- Internal agents (acetaminophen, ibuprofen, and aspirin)
- Peroxide
- Safety pins
- Scissors
- Sterile pads (2 x 2 and 3 x 3)
- Tape adherent (spray can)
- Tape cutters
- Tweezers

Optional equipment includes the following:

Score books—One per season per team is sufficient.

KICKBACK™—Optimally, you would want two.

Portable/mini goals—Purchase four portable goals that are smaller than regulation size.

Medicine balls—Order a set of balls to improve stability, strength, jumping power, and arm acceleration for the goalie.

Agility ladder—The agility ladder develops coordination and position-specific foot quickness. A cost-effective alternative would be to paint several of these on the field.

Hurdle sets—Hurdle sets develop coordination and foot speed. The sets are six inches or higher off the ground and set up the same way as an agility ladder.

Coaching sticks/slalom—These tools are used for agility and improvement in lateral movements similar to those of a skier.

Bench cover—For inclement weather, a bench cover is a nice addition to the field. A portable carport would be a good investment.

Requesting Field Improvements

Providing an enjoyable place for soccer should be a priority. Try to make one or two improvements each year to your field. Additions to your field could include:
- Flag pole
- Sound system with speakers
- Covered benches
- Wind screen
- Signage (e.g., championship titles, retired numbers, field name)
- Scoreboard
- Extra bleachers

Filling Out Purchase Request Forms

If your business office doesn't already have a purchase order form that it employs, Figure 1-2 offers an example of a form that you could use.

Ordering Equipment

When ordering equipment, write down the sales representative's name, phone number, and the date and time of your order, so you will know who to contact in case of an error. Make copies of the purchase order requests and compare invoices of shipped items with your list. Highlight items as they arrive.

Ordering Booster Material

Having shirts, sweatshirts, hats, and other items with your team logo is a great way to promote your team and the sport they play. Sell the apparel at all home games, as well as other team functions. The team logo items also make great gifts for administration, people who donate their time or supplies to your field or program, or other support staff. What you have printed on the shirts could correlate with the motivational theme

PURCHASE REQUEST FORM				
Date:				
Requested By:				
Approved By:				
Purchase Order #:				
Quantity	Catalogue #	Description	Unit Price	Total
			REQUISITION TOTAL :	

Figure 1-2. Purchase request form

you've chosen, or you might purchase ready-made shirts. Have pencils made in team colors with your logo on them. They make great little gifts that you can send with letters to your players.

Making Calls to Players

Get a list from your school's administrative office with the telephone numbers of your prospective athletes, and call every one of them. Be sure to personally speak to the athlete instead of getting information from the parents. Simply ask him if he will be participating this year. If he says "no," then just encourage him to at least come out and see if he likes it and let him know you would enjoy seeing him participate.

Sending Letters

An effective and easy way to communicate with your athletes before the season is through letters. The letters should include information and important dates that occur before the first day of practice. Figure 1-3 is an example of such a letter.

It is that time of year again! I can't believe that we are now entering our fourth year here as coaches, and the changes, not only in talent but in commitment, have been staggering.

Coming in to preseason camp, we have 16 players who have earned varsity letters in their career. Nine players have been recognized as either an All-Big Sky and/or All-Tournament Team player. Add a handful of return players who are primed to step up and win positions and the numerous freshmen, at least six of whom could have an immediate impact on our team, and we are set for a competitive fall!

To make sure that you put yourself in the position of making the travel team, you must take care of one thing—fitness! As we have continued our evolution into a committed D-I program, our expectations for our athletes' fitness has increased. It is no longer acceptable to just compete. We are set up to succeed and all of you who were here in the spring know that this team can become the best soccer team in Eagle history if we commit to being fit and embrace each of our roles on this team.

The first day of preseason will be fitness day. To be eligible to dress varsity you must complete seven laps in the cooper test (12-minute run) or accumulate a total of 40 points at the end of all the fitness tests. The tests we will conduct this year are as follows:
- Cooper test (12 minute run, as far as you can go)
- Illinois agility test (average of two runs is used)
- 300-yard shuttle (average of three runs is used)
- 10-30s
- Vertical jump
- 20 lateral test
- Two points will be awarded for benching 85% of your body weight or 120 lbs
- Three points will be awarded for benching 135 lbs +

To prepare, run the cooper, but at least once a week you must run 120s—sprint 120 yards in 18 to 20 seconds with 60 seconds rest before going again. Repeat 10 times and try to complete all of the runs in the specified time. As you know, soccer involves a lot of sprint and recovery. This type of training is just as important as your aerobic conditioning. Running 30 minutes a day or three miles a day without doing sprint work will not help you in the long run.

Remember, we are only as good as our weakest link. Push each other to work hard. We have the talent to compete with anyone. If we raise our fitness standards, we will not only compete—we will win.

If you have any questions, give me a call.

George Hageage

Figure 1-3. Sample letter

Send a welcome back letter to your returning players with a quick note at the beginning of school as well. Include reminders to them about their commitment to class work, to keeping in shape, etc.

Scheduling the Season

If you have an experienced team, find tougher opponents for your predistrict or preconference play. Playing top-level teams can give your team the confidence to say, "No one in our district is better than (whoever), but we played with them." On the other hand, if your team is struggling or young, find some weaker teams or teams with equal ability to build some confidence as you approach district or conference play. Remember to designate one game as parents' night and another as an interleague youth night (preferably at games where you need extra support). Once you have your schedule in place, print a clean copy and distribute it to everyone who needs it (players, principals, officials, athletic director, etc.).

Scheduling Officials

Send a completed schedule to the secretary of the official's chapter you have chosen. At least one day before each game, confirm that you have officials for the game. If it is your responsibility to fill out official's pay sheets after each game, get them from the athletic director or use the form in Figure 1-4.

ANYWHERE INDEPENDENT SCHOOL DISTRICT
INVOICE FOR FEES
PAID TO SOCCER REFEREES

Date: _____ Number of Games: _____

___ Varsity ___ Jr. Varsity ___ 9th Grade ___ 8th Grade ___ 7th Grade

OFFICIAL INFORMATION:

Name: _____ SS# _____

Address: _____

PAY SCALE		NUMBER OF GAMES WORKED
1 game	$17.00	☐ 1 game
2 games	$35.00	☐ 2 games
3 games	$60.00	☐ 3 games

Total mileage _____ @ $0.32 per mile = $ _____

Fee due for officiating = $ _____

Total due = $ _____

Figure 1-4. Official's pay sheet

If you coach for a club, officials are either paid at the field or from your league entrance fee. Make sure you know if you need to have a check ready on game day.

Filling Out Travel Paperwork and Requests

Under normal circumstances, the transportation director at your school will insist on having at least three days' notice to provide transportation for your team. Get as many forms as you'll need for all of your out-of-town games and fill them all out at once. Before each trip, confirm with the director a few days in advance that your bus/van will be ready.

Club coaches should check with the state association before traveling from state to state. Most associations require travel permits for any event or contest for which you leave the state. Check with your association for proper procedures.

Requesting Checks for Tournaments

Simply fill out a check request form (obtained from your business office or athletic office) and submit it to your athletic director as soon as possible.

Developing a Team Website

Communication with parents is crucial and the perfect way to provide information about your program is through a website. If you are not familiar with how to develop one, ask someone else to do it for you (e.g., the technology coordinator or a student). Include the following information:
- Calendar of events
- Schedule with links to maps for out-of-town games
- Game results
- Newsletter
- Team records
- Individual records
- Handouts
- Pictures from games

Making a Recruiting Video

Use highlights from the previous season and assemble a video to be shown to the physical education departments and junior high schools.

Making Signs for Businesses

To generate some excitement within the community, make signs that say "I'm a Fighting (*Mascot*) Soccer Backer!" or something similar. This step may give you an opportunity to personally meet prominent people in the community.

Meeting with Civic Groups

Take the time to meet with your local civic groups. Take some of your players with you and be sure to hand out schedules, media guides, or anything else that will promote your program. Invite the groups to your games, preview your goals for the upcoming season, and inform them about any fundraisers you might be putting together.

Distributing Goodwill Gifts to Administration and VIPs

The gifts should include media guides and coaches' game shirts, if your program budget will allow.

Scheduling a College Trip or Clinic

Contact a successful college coach and arrange to go watch a practice and spend some time visiting with the coach afterwards. Try to attend at least one clinic a year as well.

Arranging for Substitutes for Clinics/Trips

Alert the secretary in charge of getting substitutes as soon as you know the dates you will be gone for a trip or a clinic. Then verify that you have a substitute a few days before you leave.

Getting a Commercial Driver's License (CDL) and Bus-Driving Certification

Though not a requirement for everyone, this requires mentioning. Your state's Department of Motor Vehicles or Department of Public Safety will issue your commercial driver's license (CDL). The bus-driving certification can be obtained through a local school district and is usually offered during the summer. For example, initial certification in Texas is a 20-hour course. A refresher is necessary every three years to maintain certification.

Developing (or Updating) Team Standards and Expectations

The athletic director will probably have guidelines for the entire athletic program. You will certainly have to adhere to those policies, but if you are given the liberty to create your own, consider the following fundamental areas that may need clarification, and address them to fit your personal situation:

- Classroom expectations
- Alcohol and drug violations
- Stealing
- Lettering
- Travel to and from games
- Attendance
- Excused and unexcused absences
- Profanity
- Quitting the team

- Injury or illness
- Unsportsmanlike conduct
- Dress code
- Equipment management
- Multiple extracurricular athletes
- Use of technology (cell phones, headphones, etc.)
- Suspension from school
- Disrespect to teachers and coaches
- Locker room behavior
- Demerit system
- Merit system
- Commitment to the program

Demerit System

The demerit system can be very useful for an athletic program. Assign point values for violations of the team policies and time-based point totals for further disciplinary action. For example, once an athlete receives five points (or demerits), the athlete incurs a one-game suspension. However, if an athlete goes one week without getting any points, one point is deducted from his total. If the athlete accumulates 15 points during the season, he is suspended from the team.
- Some examples of how points may be assigned include:
- Suspension from school = five points
- Cheating or any other academic dishonesty = four points
- Unexcused absence from practice = three points
- Unexcused absence from leadership council meeting = three points
- Unexcused absence from class = three points
- Unexcused absence from tutorials = two points
- Dress code violation = one point
- Dressing room violation = one point
- Failure to follow instructions = one point

Merit System

Instituting a merit system can give extra incentive to your team during the season. The team can accumulate points by doing some of the following:
- Everyone being dressed and ready on the field at 3:00 pm
- Sending a verbal message to a teammate as you pass the ball
- Going in hard at practice for every 50/50 ball
- Never letting a ball in the air hit the ground before touching it
- Achieving a team GPA of 3.0 or better

At a predetermined point total, the team is rewarded with a day off, a fun practice, T-shirts, etc.

Commitment Page

The last page of your policies should be a summary of what you expect. Include a line for the athlete's signature and the signature of the athlete's parents, as illustrated in Figure 1-5.

THE COMMITMENT TO EXCELLENCE

I have read the handbook and understand the policies of the soccer program and the athletic program.

In addition to keeping the aforementioned policies, I will:
- Follow all school, district, and UIL rules
- Strive to excel academically
- Not lie or steal
- Not use alcohol, illegal drugs, tobacco, or other harmful substances
- Give my best effort at all times

I hereby state that I have received, read, and understand the policies and agree to abide by these policies in all respects.

Student signature: _____

Parent/Guardian signature: _____

Date: _____

Figure 1-5. Commitment page

Securing Coaching Positions

If your state requires that only certified teachers who are employed by the school can coach, then the coaching positions will need to be arranged at the end of the previous school year. If your assistants are not employed by the school, get a commitment from them by at least two months before the start of the season.

Getting a Coaches' Packet Ready

Include the following items in your coaches' packet:
- Agenda for meeting
- Job descriptions
- Program policies
- Academic plan

Agenda for Meeting

7:30	Introductions of coaches
7:40	Philosophy of coaching

   ✓ expectations
   ✓ discipline of athletes
   ✓ attitude

8:00	Job descriptions
8:20	Training and philosophy discussion
10:00	Break
10:10	Training and philosophy discussion (cont.)
11:30	Staff discussion

   ✓ Missed practices
   ✓ Leadership
   ✓ Motivation
   ✓ Grades
   ✓ Attendance
   ✓ Team policies
   ✓ Other

12:00 Dismiss

Job Descriptions

The following examples illustrate some possible assigned duties for a typical staff of three high school coaches (head coach, junior varsity coach, and freshman coach) and two junior high coaches. Some duties can be easily delegated to the team managers as well.

❑ Coach #1
- Assist the varsity head coach with practices and in games.
- Call in scores and stats after games.
- Prepare the end-of-season report for all levels.
- Post computer printout of individual and team stats after each game.
- Coordinate academic and tutorial programs.
- Coordinate off-season workout program.
- Put a player list in teachers' boxes three days prior to out-of-town trips.
- Compile a needs list for purchasing.
- Oversee maintenance of the field.
- Manage travel-request and return-travel forms.
- Develop in-season and off-season weight programs.
- Schedule officials.
- Keep scouting reports during each game.
- Lock up in the evenings and after games.

- ❏ Coach #2
  - Act as the head junior varsity coach.
  - Give out locker and lock assignments.
  - Maintain all lists (e.g., telephone, locker combinations, ID numbers).
  - Coordinate use of equipment.
  - Submit completed inventory sheets and keep up-to-date records on all equipment.
  - Maintain a neat and orderly equipment room.
  - Make sure that players do not wear equipment home.
  - Submit inventory of equipment two weeks after the season is over.
  - Manage roll check board and send attendance record to office.
  - Supervise team managers (grades, duties during practices and games, out-of-town checkout).
  - Assist with academics.
  - Supervise the locker room.

- ❏ Coach #3
  - Act as head freshman coach.
  - Coordinate scouting.
  - Coordinate recruitment of young players.
  - Make and print team rosters (include number, name, position, and classification).
  - Manage the care and prevention of injuries.
  - Keep files on all athletes (physicals, medical history, emergency numbers, etc.).
  - Submit a needs list of medical items at the end of the season.
  - Manage all strength testing, charts, workout cards, and motivational record boards.
  - Assist with academics.
  - Supervise the locker room.

- ❏ Junior High Coaches
  - Plan the daily practice schedule for junior high athletes.
  - Monitor academics of junior high athletes.
  - Maintain attendance list, including ID numbers.
  - Take care of early dismissals for out-of-town trips; put lists in teachers' boxes three days prior to each trip.
  - Type team rosters and have them ready to distribute at games.
  - Provide a game-summary report to the high school varsity coach by 8:00 am the following day.
  - Manage roll check board and attendance records; report to high school varsity coach daily.
  - Oversee equipment issue and inventory records; coordinate needs with the high school program.
  - Organize junior high parent meeting; notify high school varsity coach when it will be held.
  - Supervise the locker room.

Meeting with All Coaches

It is very important to meet with all your coaches from all levels prior to every season. You will find it very helpful if the junior high and high school coaches are all teaching the same techniques and using similar approaches. The packets you have compiled should cover every aspect of your program. At the meeting, ask coaches for their shirt, shoe, and hat sizes so you have the information for ordering.

Ordering Coaches' Shirts

When ordering the shirts, be sure to order additional items for administrators and VIPs.

Meeting with Prospective Team Members

Pass out the program handbook and go over each item in detail. Among the items the handbook should include are the following:
- School history—Include team records, individual records, names of players who went on to play collegiate ball, and former award winners
- Season schedule
- Maps to schools for out-of-town games (www.mapquest.com is a good place to start)
- School requirements for participation
- Team rules and policies
- Information on equipment—For example, what is issued by the school and what the athlete should provide
- Criteria for earning a varsity letter
- Phone numbers and e-mail of school, coaching staff, and teammates. Also make a laminated, wallet-sized card with everyone's number on it for players to keep in their wallets.
- Academic expectations—Have your athletes set a goal for a specific GPA they would like to achieve. Also, have them list their course schedule and pinpoint any courses that might be considered "problem courses." A sample questionnaire is illustrated in Figure 1-6.
- Practice rules
    - ✓ Always be on time to class and get dressed quickly.
    - ✓ The training room is never an excuse for being late. Get there as early as necessary so you can be on the field in a timely manner.
    - ✓ Wear the appropriate practice gear unless otherwise instructed.
    - ✓ Do not wear jewelry during practice time.
    - ✓ Be detail-oriented. Learn the drill and the name of the drill. Ask questions if you do not fully understand…but listen! Do not ask questions just to be asking questions.
    - ✓ Accept criticism as constructive. No criticism is personal or meant for embarrassment. The coaches are trying to help you become the best player possible.

ANYTOWN HIGH SCHOOL SOCCER

Player Questionnaire

Name: _____ Grade: _____
Address: _____ City: _____ Zip: _____
Telephone: _____ Counselor: _____

Guardians' Names:
Name: _____ Relation: _____
Name: _____ Relation: _____

Brothers and sisters and their ages:
_____
_____
_____
_____

Class Schedule:

Period	Subject	Teacher	Room#
_____	_____	_____	_____
_____	_____	_____	_____
_____	_____	_____	_____
_____	_____	_____	_____
_____	_____	_____	_____
_____	_____	_____	_____
_____	_____	_____	_____

What level do you plan on playing? (freshman, JV, varsity): _____
What positions do you play? _____
What team do you play for in the summer? _____
What other sports do you play at AHS? _____
Born (date and city): _____
Shoe size: _____ T-shirt size: _____
Height: _____

Biggest sports thrill: _____
Career plans/goals: _____
Few people know this about me: _____
Hobbies: _____
School activities (government, clubs, etc): _____
Role model and why: _____
Awards won at AHS (athletic or academic): _____
Favorite movie: _____
Favorite food: _____
Favorite TV show _____

Write a paragraph describing what you like about Anytown High School soccer:

Figure 1-6. Academic expectations questionnaire

- ✓ Be helpful to your teammates.
- ✓ Look your coaches in the eyes during instructions. "Listen" with your eyes.
- ✓ Do not argue with your teammates, coaches, etc. at any time.
- ✓ Respect your coaches and teammates and earn their respect as well.
- ✓ Hustle from one drill to another and shag balls if necessary.
- ✓ Use appropriate language and address your teammates and coaches with respect at all times.
- ✓ Strive to work to your fullest potential during practice time; eliminate wasted time.
- ✓ Leave all problems out of the locker room; certainly do not take them to the field.
- ✓ Do not gossip or plan social events during practice.
- ✓ Be intense and enthusiastic about each day of practice. Practice is what makes the difference in your ability to succeed.

- Player information sheet—Have the players fill out a general information sheet to be passed out to fans during home games. Highlight one player during each home game. If you have a short season, highlight more than one. Have players fill in the following information:
  - ✓ Nickname
  - ✓ Favorite food
  - ✓ Favorite music artist(s)
  - ✓ Favorite sports team
  - ✓ Favorite place to hang out
  - ✓ Favorite book
  - ✓ Favorite class
  - ✓ Favorite hobby
  - ✓ Favorite video game
  - ✓ Favorite movie
  - ✓ Favorite TV show
  - ✓ Favorite athlete
  - ✓ Favorite nonsoccer activity
  - ✓ One word that describes you
  - ✓ If you were going on a road trip and could only take one CD, which one would you take?
  - ✓ Best vacation or trip you have ever taken
  - ✓ Opponent you would most like to beat
  - ✓ If you could play another sport, what would it be?
  - ✓ Best thing about being a student-athlete
  - ✓ Best part about your game
  - ✓ What is the best sporting event you have ever attended as a spectator?

Having a Kick-off-the-Season BBQ

A BBQ is a good way to informally introduce your incoming freshmen, newcomers, and their parents to the veterans and coaches. Have lunch and play horseshoes, sand volleyball, or whatever is available at a nearby park and then have a welcome-to-the-season talk. Answer any questions parents might have and remind them that a much more informative parent meeting will take place at a later date.

Hosting a Parents Meeting

Include the date of your meeting in your letters to the athletes. Your parent meeting should address the following subjects:
- Introduction
    - ✓ Background
    - ✓ Success you've had as a coach (or anticipated success)
- Explanation of your philosophy
    - ✓ Conduct of athletes
        - o Class, character, and commitment to excellence
        - o Train hard to become active contributors to society
        - o Alcohol and drug violations; punishment involved
    - ✓ Academics
        - o Tutoring program
        - o Grade checks
    - ✓ Keys to success
        - o Mental attitude
        - o Developing winning potential
        - o Athletes will be prepared
    - ✓ Multiple extracurricular athletes
        - o Athletes will be involved in extracurricular activities
        - o Conflicting schedules will be resolved by coach, teacher, and student
- Discipline
    - ✓ Disrespect to teachers and coaches
        - o Players who are disrespectful to teachers and coaches will be entered into a disciplinary conditioning program.
        - o Behavior agreement (Figure 1-7)
    - ✓ Alcohol and drug violations
        - o First offense
        - o Second offense
        - o Third offense

- ✓ Missed practices
    - ○ Excused
    - ○ Unexcused
- Closing—question and answer time

BEHAVIOR AGREEMENT

Date: _____

Dear _____,

I want to apologize for the way I've been acting in your class. Because of my poor behavior, Coach Jordan has put me in a reminder program until you decide my behavior has improved. Once you feel it has improved, please sign this sheet and return it to Coach Jordan.

Thank you very much,

_____

Instructor: _____   Date: _____
         (signature)

Figure 1-7. Behavior agreement form

Issuing Equipment

Use a checkout chart to keep track of equipment (Figure 1-8).

Organizing Yourself

Keep a notebook dedicated only to soccer and divide it into the following sections. You could also establish a system by keeping each in its own notebook:
- Schedules—Include your team's schedule and a copy of each conference/district opponent's schedule.
- Student information sheets—Before the season begins, have each athlete fill out an information card with his name, address, phone numbers (cell, home, work), e-mail address, birth date, shoe size, pant size, shirt size, class schedule, and emergency contact information. After your manager types it in alphabetically, put your copy in the notebook.
- Eligibility forms—These forms can be acquired from your athletic director's office. Check on the requirements for your state and school.

EQUIPMENT CHECKOUT SHEET

Name	Shirt #	Shorts #	Shoe Sz.	Ret?

Figure 1-8. Equipment checkout sheet

- Inventory sheet
- Transportation requests—Put a copy of each completed bus request in this section, so you'll have documentation in case of a mix-up.
- Purchase orders—Use your purchase orders to check off equipment as it arrives. These forms can be used to help with inventory as well.
- Important phone numbers—List the name and phone number of the athletic director, principal, coaches in your district, and the transportation director.
- Workout schedules

- Articles—As you find articles from magazines, the Internet, journals, or clinics, make copies and put them in your folder for easy reference. You may want to categorize the articles into subsections (e.g. nutrition, leadership, etc.).
- District/conference notes and rules—Once a week, the chairperson of the district usually sends results to each coach with team standings and scores. Include any rule changes or other pertinent information about the district or conference.
- Workout notes—Compile a master list of skills and situations for your sport. Keep your workout notes so that every area is covered. These notes can be a valuable tool for the next year as well.
- Drills—As you find drills you like, from this book, other books, the Internet, journals, or clinics, make copies and put them in your folder for easy reference. You may want to categorize your drills into subsections.
- Stat sheets—The day after a game, the managers should enter all statistics into the computer and print a copy for you and a copy to post for the athletes to see.

Joining Coaching Organizations

Join the National Soccer Coaches Association of America (www.nscaa.com) as well as your state coaches association. Membership in these organizations allows you to nominate your players for All-Region, All-American, and Academic All-American status. You will also get a monthly newsletter that contains drills, instruction, and clinic dates. The dues paid to be a member of the organization usually include admission to their convention, where you can hear notable speakers, be informed of rule changes, browse the products sold by a variety of vendors, and see an all-star game.

Scheduling a Photographer

After the season begins, you will be hosting a media day. Schedule a photographer well in advance for this day and have individual pictures of each athlete taken. Take a team picture at the end of the season and ensure all who participated are in it.

Reading the Rule Book

Before the season begins, you should study the rules (also known as the Laws of the Game). It should be noted that high schools, club leagues, tournaments, and colleges may have slightly different rules on substitutions, so be sure you are aware of the rules for your level of competition. Go to www.fifa.com for a comprehensive look at the Laws of the Game.

After Practice Begins

- Choose a motivational theme
- Order team shirts
- Prepare themes for the week
- Plan and schedule a team retreat
- Vote on a unity council

- Check varsity players' schedules
- Make an attendance board
- Contact media
- Take pictures for the media guide
- Begin work on the media guide
- Get an academic plan ready
- Choose a manager
- Train a videographer
- Check video equipment
- Pick music for the dressing room
- Visit the elementary schools
- Talk with clubs and organizations
- Verify scrimmage date and times
- Plan for team special days
- Post goal charts
- Have a team dinner
- Send thank you notes to parents
- Have an intrasquad scrimmage
- Verify transportation in athletic office
- Send out a newsletter
- Create itineraries for trips

Choosing a Motivational Theme

Motivation can be an integral part of the success of your team. Choose a theme or have your captains choose a theme (or team motto) that can be represented by something tangible and give that tangible item to each athlete. Whatever tangible item you use, decide how it relates to your team as a motivational tool and introduce it at your initial team meeting or at a team retreat. Put a slogan on the back of T-shirts as well. Some examples include:

- Paperclip—Make a long chain of two-to-three-inch clips. Explain that each clip represents each athlete's link to the team. Distribute the clips to the players to hang on their purses, backpacks, etc., as a constant reminder that they are a part of the team.
- Boomerang—Find inexpensive boomerangs and paint them using school colors. Ask the team, "What does a boomerang do?" Explain that, in life, what you put in to something comes back to you.

Ordering Team Shirts

What you have printed on the shirts could correlate with the motivational theme you've chosen, or you might purchase ready-made shirts.

Preparing Themes for the Week

In addition to creating a special theme, spend some time each week emphasizing a certain character trait (e.g., courage, loyalty, boldness, decisiveness, dependability) and decorate the locker room with quotes that correspond to that trait. The signs can be done on a computer by your managers and can be posted on lockers, doors, and bulletin boards.

Planning a Team Retreat

If you cannot afford to dedicate an entire day to a team retreat, then combine some of the following activities to fit your schedule.

- 10:30–10:45—Welcome and brief introductions
  Use a good icebreaker to get things started.

- 10:45–11:30—Bookshelf activity
  These 45 minutes are for reflection on how each individual can put aside anything that could disrupt the team. In the bookshelf activity, explain that we all have a certain amount of "dead weight" that can hinder or hurt us individually or as a team. Say, "As you come into this season, what do you need to leave on the 'bookshelf' as you come into the room?"

- 11:30–12:00—Refrigerator magnets
  Choose an activity that will give everyone more insight on each teammate and coach. For example, explain that refrigerator magnets are fun and descriptive, and then ask, "What magnets would I see on your refrigerator if I came over for a visit?"

- 12:00–2:00—Lunch
  Order pizza and have the players bring their own drinks.

- 2:00–4:00—Team-building activities
  Use this time to go through a ropes course, or go to a park, split the team into two groups, give them a map and a compass, and select an ending point to meet at. Look at team-building books for other ideas. If you don't feel comfortable with this type of team building activity, hold a practice instead.

- 4:00–4:45—Pass out uniforms
  Receiving team uniforms will help the players get excited about the upcoming season.

- 4:45–5:15—"What can you bring to the table?"
  Ask athletes to reflect on what they can contribute to the team. Make a simple one-page form with questions that will get your players thinking about what they can "bring to the table." For example: What specific skills can you bring to the team that will help us be successful?

- 5:15–5:30—Preparation for dinner

  Invite parents and the athletic director to eat a potluck dinner with the team. Assign dishes by position. For example, goalies and forwards bring pastas, midfielders bring salads, and defensive players bring desserts.

- 5:30–6:30—Dinner and clean-up

- 6:30–7:30—Introduce the theme

  Explain your tangible item and how it relates to the theme for the season. If using the boomerang, for example, use this time to have each athlete personalize his boomerang, listing the things he wants to come back to him.

Voting on a Unity Council

As an adult and coach, you are more knowledgeable than your athletes. At the same time, you still need to listen to them. A good way to listen to your players is to have your team vote for members of a unity council that will meet with you on a weekly basis to just talk about "things." This council should not only include your team captains, but also a fair number of representatives from the team. Although they may or may not have legitimate gripes, the council is a good way to stay in touch with your team. During the off-season, take this unity council to visit other schools that have successful programs and let your athletes see what other teams are doing to prepare for the next season. Let them see how hard those teams are working, and then your athletes will realize that they can work harder or that what they are doing now will pay off later.

Checking Varsity Players' Schedules

If you travel a great distance to away games, you might consider moving all of your varsity players into a nonacademic class (e.g., PE) during the last period of the day.

Make an Attendance Board

A simple method of keeping track of a large number of athletes is to make an attendance board out of plywood, nails, and tags. Write each athlete's name on both sides of a round tag—one side in black and the other in red (or a school color). Put an appropriate number of nails on the plywood and hang the tags. Each athlete simply turns his tag over according to the day (black or red). Station a manager or coach by the board so the athletes don't flip someone else's tag. Attendance can then be taken via a glance at the board.

Contacting Media

Contact the local newspaper in your area and provide them with information about your team. Include a list of returning athletes, remind them how the varsity team did the previous year, note any promising newcomers, and give them a schedule. Request an e-mail address and cell phone number so you can send your results within a day of the game. Let your contact know about your team website and the date of team picture day as well.

Taking Pictures for the Media Guide

Invite the local media out to take both posed and action shots. Also, ask your school newspaper to send a photographer to take some action shots for use on your team website. You might also consider taking a team picture at the end of the season to ensure you have a picture that includes all of the players that finished the season.

Making a Media Guide/Banquet Program

The media guide can be as simple or elaborate as you like and can be given at the end-of-season banquet. Consider obtaining a media guide from a college nearby that highlights the soccer team and use it as a template for your own media guide.

Assembling the media guide can be very time consuming, so you should start early in the season. The following items are examples of what you might include:
- Banquet program
- School information sheet
- Schedule
- Varsity letter winners
- Individual records
- Team records
- Junior varsity team records
- Freshmen team records
- Award winners
    - ✓ Fighting heart award
    - ✓ Most valuable player (Golden Eagle, for example)
    - ✓ Offensive MVP
    - ✓ Defensive MVP
    - ✓ Iron Eagle (most weight room improvement)
    - ✓ Silver Eagle (conditioning award)
    - ✓ Outstanding JV player
    - ✓ Scholar athlete
    - ✓ Most improved
    - ✓ Outstanding freshman player
- Scholarship award winners
- Championship season history
- History of previous teams
- Senior spotlight
- Career stats for seniors
- Game results
- Pictures taken throughout the season

Getting an Academic Plan Ready

Whether or not your state has a strict rule about passing classes before being eligible to play, teachers appreciate the interest you take in the academic success of your athletes. After all, without academics, extracurricular activities would not exist. Also, monitoring your players' grades from the start of the school year sends a message about what will be expected during your season. Grades are another way for players to strive for greatness. They give every player the opportunity to succeed. The following six-step procedure can be employed to monitor the academic progress of your athletes. If you have campus e-mail, these steps can be altered.

Step #1: Type a list of all participating athletes on one sheet, using columns and a smaller font if necessary (see Figure 1-9).

Teacher's Name: _____

Teachers,

I would like to implement a weekly grade check for the soccer players to ensure their academic success. As a coaching staff, we will work with you and help with discipline as well as tutoring, if necessary.

Please look over the following list, circle any soccer players you have in class, add any that aren't on this list, and return it to Coach Jordan's box by Friday afternoon. This will be the last time you will have to sort through the entire roster. You will have an individualized sheet starting Monday or Tuesday. Thanks for your help.

Coach Jordan

Anderson, Alice	Hogan, Christy	Sims, Holli
Arbuckle, LaDona	Janda, Theresa	Strickland, Holly
Beard, Vicki	Jordan, Rebekah	Talbert, Wegi
Bollman, Rachael	Milligan, Angela	Thompson, Christy
Booth, Cathy	Mulvaney, Stefanie	Welch, Ramey
Burch, Beverly	Noss, Ashleigh	White, Norma
Crawley, Allison	Noss, Kara	Wing, Jenna
Dinkler, Julie	Pilcik, Cindy	Wing, Lauren
Dickerson, Mindy	Poorman, DeeAnn	
Ford, Miriam	Scott, Claire	
Hill, Brianne	Shields, Tammy	

Figure 1-9. Teacher's list

Step #2: Distribute the list of players to the teachers. Ask them to circle the names of any players they have in class and then return the form to you (or your box). Keep a master list of all teachers who have turned in their sheets and track down those who haven't.

Step #3: Once you have each teacher's list, type individual reports for each teacher listing only the athletes in that teacher's classes. Making the individual lists requires some work, but it makes it easier on the teachers. Figure 1-10 shows an example of a sample weekly grade report form.

WEEKLY GRADE REPORT

Teacher: Talbert, Grover
Week of: August 21-25th

Please check the list and make necessary changes (add or delete names). Then, complete the form and return it to Coach Jordan's box by Thursday morning. We would like to meet with you if you have a student-athlete who is failing (or nearly failing) or has been a discipline problem. Thanks for your support.

NAME	GRADE	BEHAVIOR	COMMENTS
Burkhalter, Cindy	P F B	E S U	
Dinkler, Julie	P F B	E S U	
Draggoo, Rachelle	P F B	E S U	
Droog, Janet	P F B	E S U	
Jordan, Rebekah	P F B	E S U	
Reding, Tracy	P F B	E S U	
Ribardo, Kay	P F B	E S U	
	P F B	E S U	
	P F B	E S U	
	P F B	E S U	

KEY:
P - Passing
F - Failing
B - Borderline
E - Excellent
S - Satisfactory
U - Unsatisfactory

ADDITIONAL COMMENTS:

Figure 1-10. Weekly grade report

Step #4: After the first grade check, compile all the information into one report and divide the number of athletes with academic or behavioral problems among your coaches. Each coach should speak directly to the teacher and work on improving the student's situation. Figure 1-11 shows a sample summary report form that can be used.

| GRADE REPORT FOR WEEK OF: August 21-25th |||||
Teacher's Name	Student's Name	Beh.	Gr.	Comments
Dan Decker	Kara Noss	S	P	Needs to make up a test.
Seth Garcia	Lauren Wing	E	P	Hasn't turned in two papers.
Jeff Neal	Jenna Wing	S	P	Has been late several times.
Dave Prediger	Ashleigh Noss	S	P	Spends a lot of time talking.

Figure 1-11. Report summary

Step #5: Be sure to also keep up with the athletes that are doing well. Recognize honor roll students by posting a sign on their locker, on the bulletin board, or in the gym.

Step #6: Prepare a report to be presented to the school board during each grading period. Determine each player's grade point average for each team and then present the following information: number of A's, B's, C's, D's, and F's; team GPAs; A honor roll members; A and B honor roll members; and incompletes. If you want to get fancy, graph this information using Excel. Include a cover sheet as well. Figure 1-12 illustrates an example of how this information can be organized and presented.

Choosing a Manager

The most valuable people you can have on your staff are responsible, trustworthy, and willing student managers. After the season begins and some athletes realize that the sport is not for them, consider asking them to stay with the team and become managers. Give them a job description so they know exactly what is expected of them.

Manager Duties and Expectations

- General
  - Attend all practices and games.
  - Be willing and ready to do any tasks that are asked of you.
  - Stay positive and give that impression to the coach.
  - Be organized and efficient at the games.
  - Act like you know what you're doing and ask for help only when necessary.
  - Assist the team and coach whenever you can.

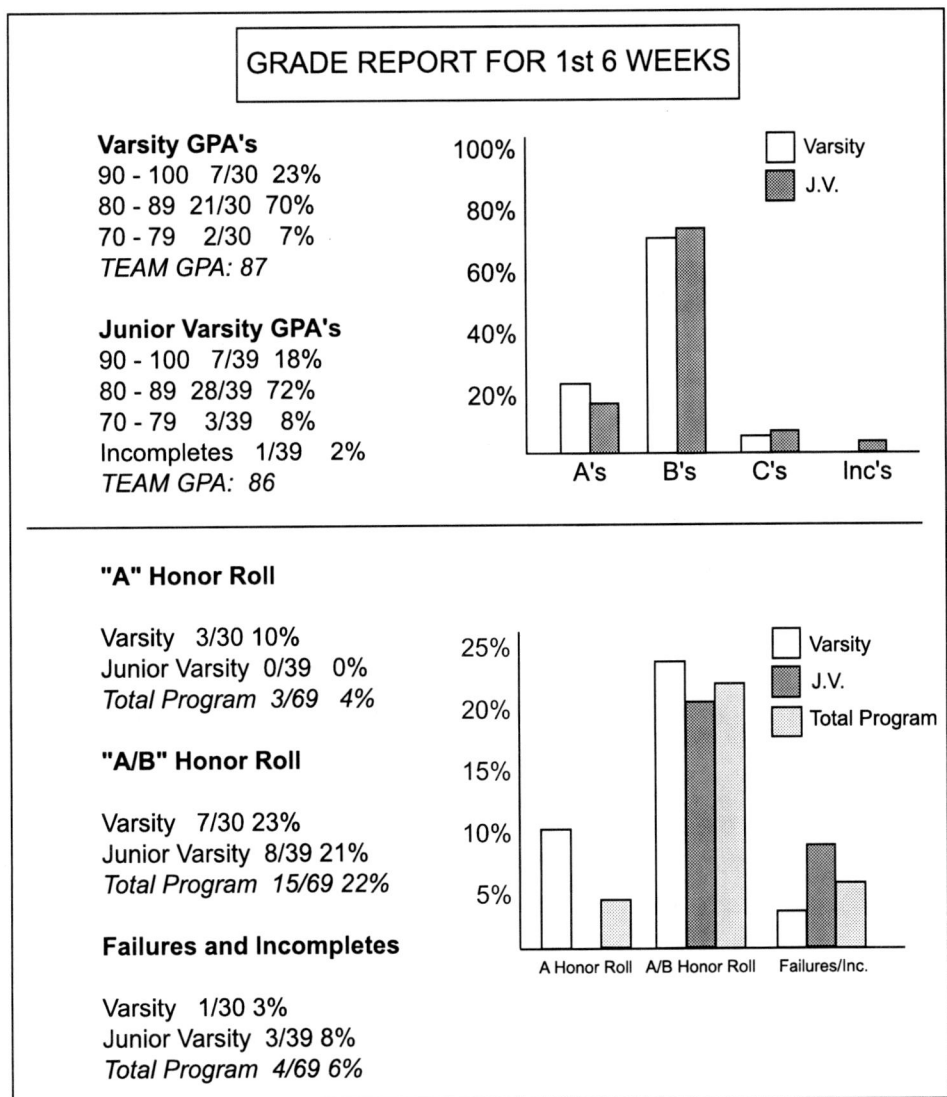

Figure 1-12. School board report

❑ At Games
- Fill out the scorebook and stat sheets and have them ready for the game.
- Shag for coaches during the warm-up.
- If you have any questions during the game, ask the opposing team's manager first. If that individual can't help and the matter can't wait, ask the coach.
- Make sure the scorebook is correct after the game. If needed, compare with the other team's book after the game to check assists, etc.
- Videotape the games.

❑ At Practices
- Shag for coaches.
- Summarize stats and put into the computer.

- Take stats as needed.
- Set up the field for daily drills prior to practice.
- Clean up the field following practice.
- Ask the coach if any specific jobs need to be done.
- Make inspiring signs for the locker room.
- If really bored, replace material on the bulletin boards.
- Help the team and coaches as needed.

Training a Videographer

One of the managers can be designated as videographer as long as he knows exactly how you'd like the game filmed. Give the following tips to your videographer, which will ensure a good videotape:

- Video cameras normally rewind a small amount each time the camera is turned off or even paused. Let at least three to five seconds run off the tape before you stop. This will prevent you from erasing good footage. It also takes about the same amount of time when beginning to record after the camera has been turned off. Since there is plenty of tape for the game, be liberal as you start and stop filming.
- Try to set up and film from a nice, high place in the middle of the field so you're out of everyone's way.
- Scan the field slowly using a wide-angle shot, occasionally zooming in on the action. If you have to move the camera to follow the ball, zoom back out.
- Keep the camera on a tripod to avoid shaking the camera. Don't talk while filming.
- Occasionally film the players individually, as well as the coaches, fans, and scoreboard so this footage can be used for the end-of-year video.
- Label the tape with the opponents' name, the date, and the final score.

Checking Video Equipment

Check on your equipment before the first game. You may have to check out a camera from the library if the athletic department doesn't have one for the soccer program.

Picking Music for the Dressing Room

Make a tape (or entrust this to your managers, who are way more hip than you are) to be played while the team is dressing before practice. If you're really creative, find a song that goes with your theme and make it the song of the season. Make sure you approve the songs.

Visiting the Elementary Schools

Take two or three representatives from the team and visit with the elementary school classes. Let the players promote the program, hand out information about upcoming games, camps, and club membership, and answer any questions the students might have. Promote club involvement and call it Little Eagles or whatever your mascot may be. Give these kids a "membership kit" that might include a magnetic schedule, passes to games, decals, and a T-shirt.

Talking with Clubs and Organizations

Find out when the clubs and organizations within your school meet and send players to visit with them about attendance at the soccer games. If you have a Fellowship of Christian Athletes chapter, for example, set aside an FCA night with free admission for any members and reserved seating as a group. Have the announcer acknowledge the group during breaks.

Verifying Scrimmage Date and Times

Although the season has already been scheduled, you should always verify the playing date, time, and location of a scrimmage.

Planning for Team Special Days

Have a meeting with your newly elected unity council and decide specific dates for the team special days, which may include trips to college games, playoff games, sleepovers, scavenger hunts, or laser tag. The idea behind these days is to break up the monotony of daily practices, to build team unity, and to give you an opportunity to get out of "coach mode" and have some fun with the team. Try to schedule one team day per month.

Posting Goal Charts

You might post several different goal charts according to your priorities. Some examples might include, win five games, win conference, or win state. Other goals could be more game-specific such as out-shooting the opponent or getting four to five corner kicks.

Having a Team Dinner

Have a "meet the team" dinner. This event will be a great fundraiser for the program and a way for the community to meet the players. Have a raffle, a silent auction, door prizes, and a table set up to sell booster wear.

Sending Thank You Notes to Parents

Take some time to handwrite personal notes to the parents of your players. Having a daughter on the team requires some sacrifices from parents and thanking them for their support is important.

Having an Intrasquad Scrimmage

Have an intrasquad scrimmage before your first scheduled "real" scrimmage. Consider promoting the event and having a family luncheon immediately following the game. Serve pizza and have the players supply side dishes, beverages, desserts, and snacks.

Verifying Transportation

Your travel paperwork should be in already. Take time to verify that you have transportation and a driver at least three days before each away game.

Sending Out a Newsletter

Sending out a newsletter is a great opportunity to relay information to parents and students. The first newsletter should be distributed after the first game and could include the following information:

- Upcoming game information
- Notes from the coach
- Special points of interest (dates of meetings and other events)
- Stats and game results
- Athletes of the week

This information should also be included on your website.

Making Itineraries for Trips

If you are fortunate enough to take an out-of-town trip to a tournament, you'll need to be well organized. Make out an itinerary and include the hotel address and phone number, van assignments, room assignments, a packing checklist (uniform and equipment), and a tournament schedule (Figure 1-13).

ROAD TRIP ITINERARY

Embassy Suites Hotel
122 Anywhere St.
Anywhere, TX 78999
903-555-1212

TUESDAY, MARCH 13th

3:30 - 4:00	Van check-in (see list)
4:00	VANS LEAVE SCHOOL
11:00	Arrive/ Check into hotel
12:00	In rooms for bed check

WEDNESDAY, MARCH 14th

9:00 - 10:00	Breakfast as a team
10:00 - 11:00	Study Hall
11:15	Leave for practice
11:30 - 1:00	Practice
1:00 - 3:00	Relax around the hotel (snack stop after practice)
3:00 - 4:00	Study Hall
4:00 - 6:00	Team activities
6:00 - 7:00	Dinner as a team (location to be announced)
7:00 - 8:00	Motivational talk (speaker to be announced)
8:00 - 10:00	Team activities
10:30	In rooms for bed check

THURSDAY, MARCH 15th

7:00	Breakfast as a team (location to be announced)
8:00 - 10:00	Relax around hotel
10:00	Leave for fields (white uniforms)
12:00	GAME VS. MT. PILOT (1:00)

Times to be announced

FRIDAY, MARCH 16th

Times to be announced (blue uniforms)

SATURDAY, MARCH 17th

8:00	Vans leave
5:00	ARRIVE

Van Assignments

Coach Noel	Coach Douglas	Coach Grisgby
H. Reed	Mr. Douglas	Coach Romy
N. Willis	J. Cervantez	M. Barr
J. Reynolds	B. Geary	A. Altamiran
J. Johnson	S. Johnson	C. Shackelford
D. Davila	B. Paillet	A. Castanon
N. Johnson		

Room Assignments

Room 1	Room 2	Room 3	Room 4
Reynolds	Johnson, N.	Shackelford	Johnson, J.
Geary	Cervantez	Reed	Castanon
Davila	Paillet	Johnson, S.	Altamiran
Willis	Barr		

Figure 1-13. Trip itinerary

Midseason Responsibilities

- Recognize honor roll students
- Order senior plaques
- Scout possible playoff opponents
- Prepare for playoffs

Recognizing Honor Roll Students

At each grading period, encourage the principal or athletic director to recognize the athletes that have done well in their academics. Promoting this idea may also encourage other athletes to do better in class.

Ordering Senior Plaques

During the last home game, have "Senior Night." Present each senior with a plaque. Their teammates might also choose to give them additional gifts. Figure 1-14 gives an example of a script to give the announcer.

> "Rebekah is a four-year varsity starter who has provided a great deal to her teammates on and off the field. On the field, Rebekah will finish her career at Anytown High School ranked in the career top five in games played and goals scored. Her ability on the field has led to many accolades including four First Team All-District honors, two First Team All-Area honors, and two First Team All-State honors.
>
> Off the field, Rebekah has been just as prolific. She has been named Academic All-American four times and will graduate in May with a GPA of 3.98.
>
> Rebekah will be remembered for her caring nature and hard-working attitude. Thank you, Rebekah, for everything you have given us.
>
> Rebekah is joined on the field by (*introduce her parents here*).
>
> Ladies and Gentlemen, Rebekah Jordan."

Figure 1-14. Senior Night script

Scouting Potential Playoff Opponents

Chapter 10 provides detailed information on how to scout your opponents. Arrange your schedule so you and some of your coaches can attend games of possible playoff opponents.

Preparing for the Playoffs

In addition to the obvious practice planning and preparation to play, you should also consider doing the following:

- Advertise the dates, times, and locations of your games at the school and in the community.
- If you are playing at home, provide extra seating at the field and schedule your announcer and National Anthem performances.
- If asked, rank the top five officials you'd like to call the games.
- Submit additional travel requests.
- Double-check grades to avoid playing an ineligible player.
- Have the players prepare in advance for missing any classes by meeting with their teachers and getting assignments.

2

Planning the Season

Player Assessment

While tryouts can be run in many ways, some things need to be done in soccer that may be different than other sports. If you have more than one day to make decisions on who should and should not make your team, then you may want to evaluate physical characteristics through some "nonsoccer" tests such as the Cooper test, agility tests, and sprints. If you have a limited time to pick your team (e.g., two to six hours), you need to focus on soccer-specific skills performed in game-related activities.

Some of the following drills and tests might be employed to evaluate performance:
- Cooper test
- 120s
- 300-yard shuttle
- 20/40-yard sprint
- Box agility drill
- "T" agility drill
- Finish first
- Passing circuit
- 1v1 (i.e., one-on-one)
- 1v1 to goal
- Heading competitions
- Bench press
- Subjective assessment

A Formula for Evaluation

Once you have determined the tests you will use to evaluate your players, set up a table that can be used to keep track of each player and his rank compared to the other athletes. This system was adapted from University of North Carolina head women's coach and former national team coach Anson Dorrance. A point system may be employed based exclusively on the ranking of the players in each test (Figure 2-1).

	Joe	John	Paul	Larry
Cooper	1	2	3	4
120s	2	1	3	4
20/40	2	1	4	3
Passing	4	1	2	3
Heading	3	1	2	4
1v1	4	1	2	3
Total	16	7	16	21

Figure 2-1. Evaluation chart

You may decide that it is more important for a player to be good at 1v1 rather than good at 20/40s. If you assign a value that gives more weight to this particular skill, the players' final totals will reflect the types of players you want on your team. For example, if 1v1s are more important than anything else you test, multiply the total in the 1v1 column by two, three, or more, depending on how critical you believe the skill is for a player on your team (Figure 2-2).

	Joe	John	Paul	Larry
Cooper	1	2	3	4
120s	2	1	3	4
20/40	2	1	4	3
Passing	4	1	2	3
Heading	3	1	2	4
1v1 (x2)	8	2	4	6
Total	20	8	18	24

Figure 2-2. Revised evaluation chart

You can see that in the first ranking, John would be ranked first with Paul and Joe tied for second and Larry fourth. After multiplying 1v1s by two, thereby giving them more weight, John is still first, but Paul is now ranked better than Joe.

In a high school or college environment, it may be desirable to have fitness standards and expectations defined before beginning the season. In the examples, Joe ranked first in the Cooper test. But, if Joe only runs four laps in the 12-minute Cooper test, that is not very good. Dedicated athletes should run about a six-minute mile. For collegiate females, the best players run seven-and-a-half laps in the 12-minute test while males run eight.

Whether or not you want to post the results of your evaluation efforts for the players to see is up to you. It may be a good motivational technique to use throughout the year, or you may choose to use this information in determining how to organize your teams. It may also become useful if a parent disagrees with where you have placed his child.

The following examples illustrate how you can organize the evaluative process and determine player rankings.

Agility

To score an agility test, take the best time for the event. Calculate 10% of this time and add the result back to the original best time. Use the best time and the result of this equation to determine an estimated range for each event. As the time for different events gets longer the ranges also get longer.

Example: 300-yard shuttle

Best time = 55 seconds

55.0 x 0.10 = 5.5 seconds

Add 5.5 to the best time (55.0 + 5.5 = 60.5). Anyone completing this event within the range of 55.0 to 60.5 seconds would receive 10 points. Use the 5.5-second differential to develop the rest of the chart. Figure 2-3 shows an example of the entire scale. By lowering the percentage used, you can set a tougher standard.

```
55.0 to 60.5 = 10 points
60.6 to 66.1 = 8 points
66.2 to 71.7 = 6 points
71.8 to 77.3 = 4 points
77.4 to 82.9 = 2 points
83.0 to 88.5 = 1 point
```

Figure 2-3. Sample timed event chart

Skill Events

Scoring skilled events is much simpler. The best attempt earns 10 points, The second-best attempt earns eight points, and so on. Another way to score skill events is simply to record the number of successful attempts. For example, in a shooting event, award one point for each goal scored. Figure 2-4 provides an example of how to assign points for skill events.

```
4 goals = 10 points
3 goals = 8 points
2 goals = 6 points
1 goal = 4 points
```

Figure 2-4. Sample skill event chart

Explanation of Events

Cooper Test

Players must run seven laps in 12 minutes. If a player runs fewer than seven laps, he receives points based on the chart in Figure 2-5.

6 laps + 200 m	6 laps + 250 m	6 laps + 300 m	6 laps + 350 m	7 laps	7 laps + 100 m	7 laps + 200 m	7 laps + 250 m	7 laps + 350 m	8 laps
1 point	2 points	3 points	4 points	5 points	6 points	7 points	8 points	9 points	10 points

Figure 2-5. Cooper test point chart

120s

Players run 10 120-meter runs. They must run each in 18 to 20 seconds with 54 to 60 seconds of rest to get back to the start. Players get an extra 15 seconds of rest after the third and seventh runs. If a player misses a run, he must make it up. Points are awarded for completed 120s. For example, if a player completes nine out of 10 120s in 18 to 20 seconds, he may receive nine points. You also may choose to award no points if fewer than seven 120s were completed. A sample chart is illustrated in Figure 2-6.

10 runs in 18-20 sec	9 runs in 18-20 sec	8 runs in 18-20 sec	7 runs in 18-20 sec
6 points	5 points	4 points	3 points
*No points awarded for less than 7 runs in 18-20 seconds			

Figure 2-6. Chart for recording 120s

300-yard Shuttle

Each player should run 300 yards three times. Players can be ranked by fastest run, total time for three runs, and percent change in the run. The percent change will help determine the fitness level of each athlete. The closer together the three times are, the more fit the athlete. For example, if Sue runs three 300s in 55 seconds, 58 seconds, and 60 seconds and Sally runs her three 300s in 57 seconds, 57 seconds, 59 seconds, then Sally is more fit. Break the entire team into four groups so that each group runs and then rests while the other three groups run, thereby creating a one work to three rest ratio.

20/40-yards Sprint

This drill is a 40-yard sprint with a time taken at the 20-yard mark and at the 40-yard mark. Each player should run this three times with complete rest.

Box Agility

The player starts on his stomach, sprints 10 yards around a cone, runs to the center and down through a series of four cones, then runs up and around the last cone in the opposite corner and back down through the finish line (Figure 2-7).

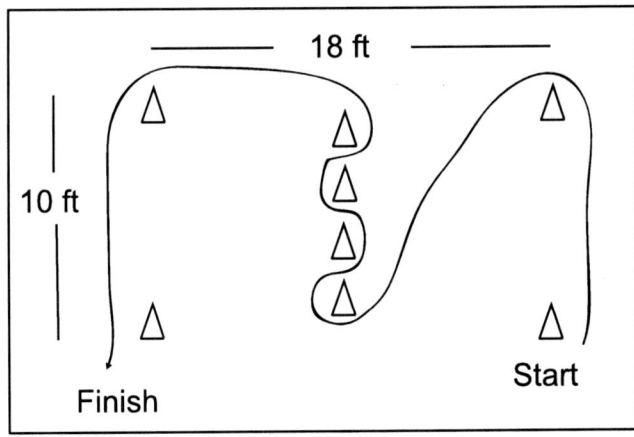

Figure 2-7. Box agility drill

"T" Agility

The player starts at the cone positioned at the center of a "T." He shuffles to the left cone five yards away, then shuffles to the right cone 10 yards away. He then shuffles back to the start and backpedals though the finish (Figure 2-8).

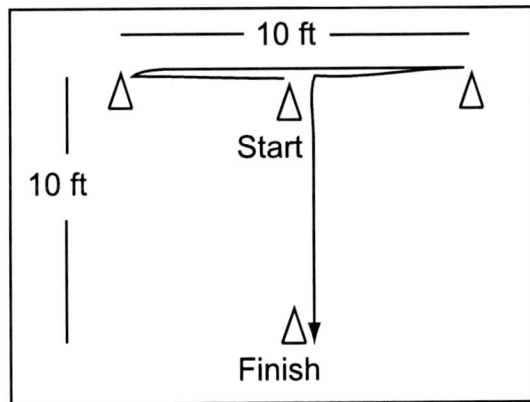

Figure 2-8. "T" agility drill

Finish First Shooting (Figure 2-9)

The three shots are as follows:
- Shot from outside the 18-yard box.
- Shot with the inside of the foot finishing a pass from the end line immediately following the shot from the 18.
- Recycle the run to the 18-yard box and finish a cross from outside the 18 on the flank.

The athlete then recycles the run and finishes a pass from the opposite end line. Passes from the end line should be on the ground and placed between the six-yard box and penalty mark. Keep track of shots faced by the keepers as well as saves and goals allowed using the sheet in Figure 2-10.

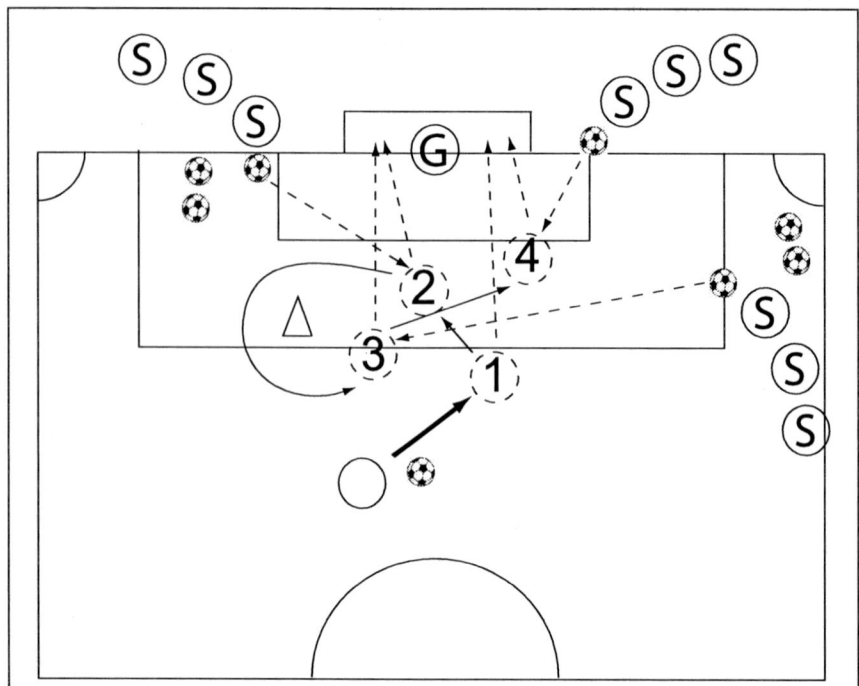

Figure 2-9. Finish first shooting

NAME	Long	Box	Cross
	1 2 3 4	1 2 3 4	1 2 3 4
1			
2			
3			
4			
5			

Figure 2-10. Finish first evaluation sheet

Passing Circuit

This circuit will test long balls, shooting the gaps, and a crossing circuit.

• Long balls. Players are ranked in order on the team by how far they can drive a ball to a teammate's thigh or chest with both the left and right foot individually. Players start at 10 yards as shown in Figure 2-11, and then move back in 10-yard increments until they are unsuccessful twice in a row. It is important to remember that this test is for ball-in-the-air skills. You may repeat this test for driven balls in the air or placed balls on the ground.

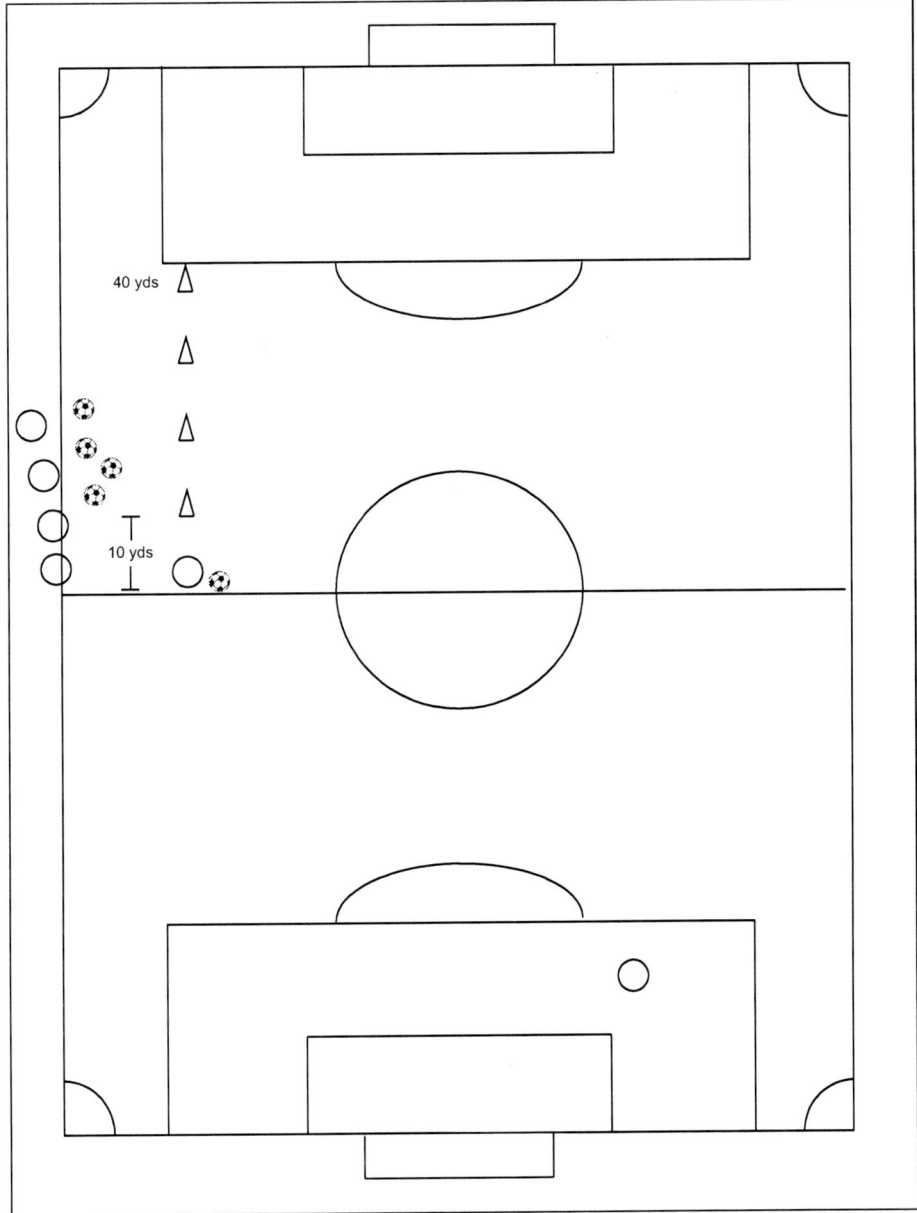

Figure 2-11. Passing circuit: long balls

• Shooting the gaps. Players are ranked in order on the team by how many through balls they can complete to a teammate, hitting them in stride with both a left-footed service on the ground or in the air and a right-footed service on the ground or in the air. The player receiving the pass gets a touch to settle into space for a shot. Keep track of goals scored. For goalkeepers, keep track of shots faced, saves, and goals against. See Figure 2-12.

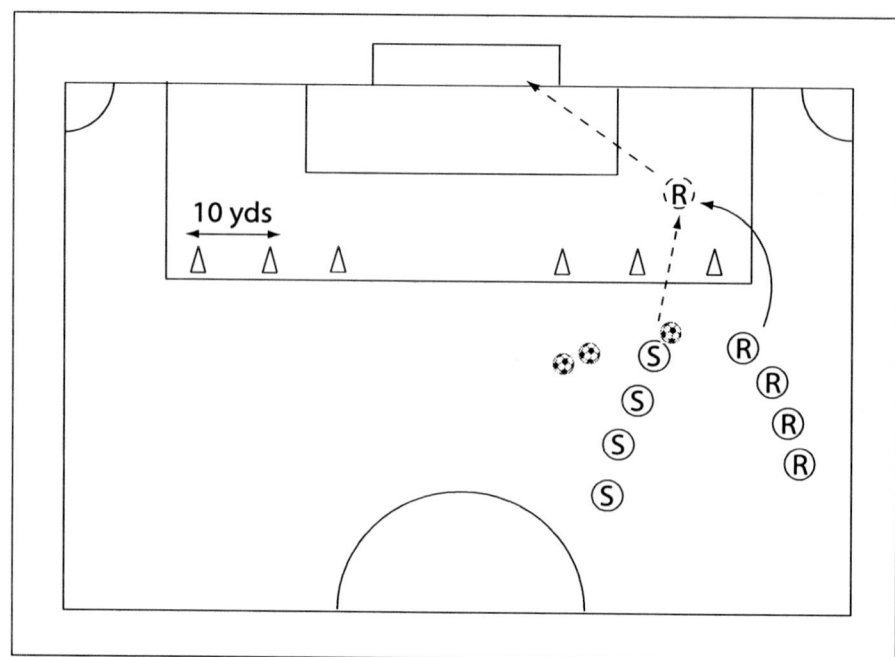

Figure 2-12. Passing circuit: shooting the gaps

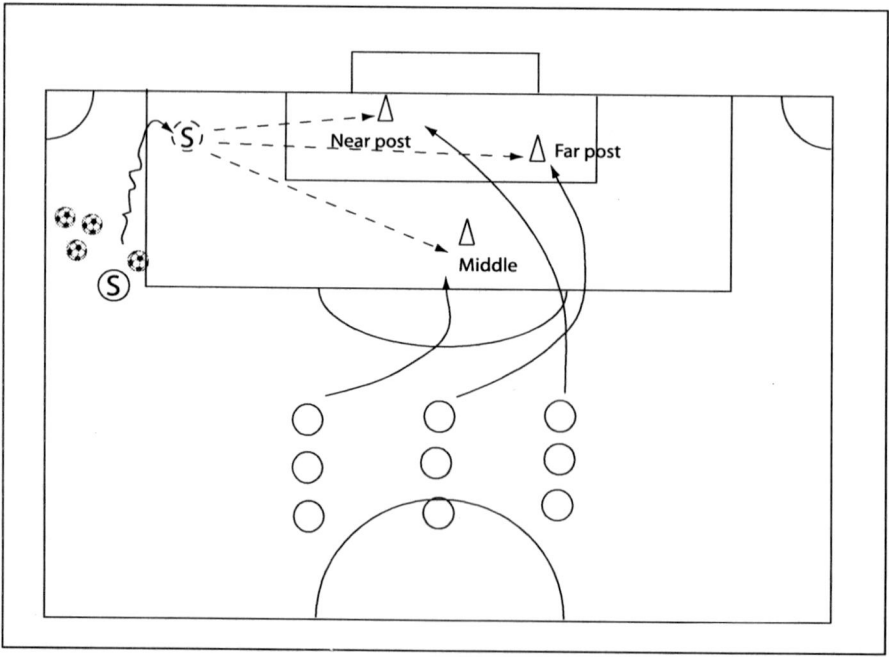

Figure 2-13. Crossing circuit

• Crossing circuit. This involves a series of three consecutive runs and crosses to targets, earning a point for each completed pass (Figure 2-13). Run the series four times. For a variation, change where players run and what targets they are looking for depending on your team's needs and style of play.

1v1

Players play 1v1 to a cone. The defender must stay within two to three yards of the player with the ball. Play five to seven games for evaluation. Keep track of wins, losses, and ties. This is useful to continue throughout the season. Time per game should range from one to two-and-a-half minutes.

1v1 to Goal (Version 1)

A defender serves a ball from the six-yard box toward the offensive player, who is located about 35 yards out. The offensive player earns five points for a goal and two points for getting around the defender. The defender earns three points for preventing a shot and one point for allowing a shot to the goalkeeper (Figure 2-14).

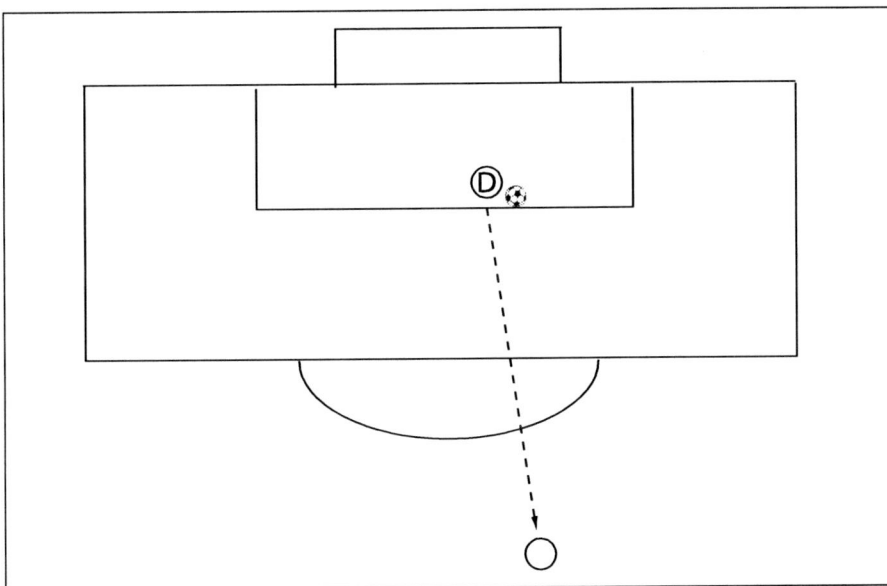

Figure 2-14. 1v1 to goal (version 1)

1v1 to Goal (Version 2)

The offensive player receives a pass from a server while making a run down the flank. The defender starts at the edge of the 18-yard box and tries to prevent the offensive player from getting around the corner or cutting toward the goal (Figure 2-15). The offensive player gets five points for a goal or for a cross leading to a one-touch goal, two points for a cross or for getting around the defender and shooting. The defensive player gets three points for winning the ball, two for knocking the ball away but not gaining possession, and one for allowing a poor cross. The defender gets zero points for a goal scored.

Heading Competition

This simple game focuses on winning balls in the air. The offensive player tries to win the header by flicking the ball toward the goal. The player behind tries to head the ball back in the direction of the service (Figure 2-16). Go through three services from each server. The ball can be thrown if your players have a hard time serving in the air.

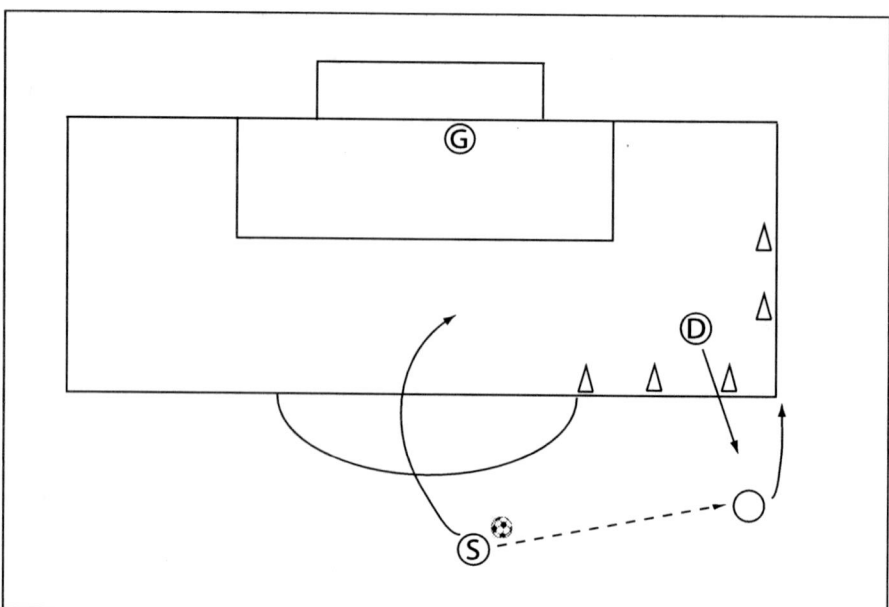

Figure 2-15. 1v1 to goal (version 2)

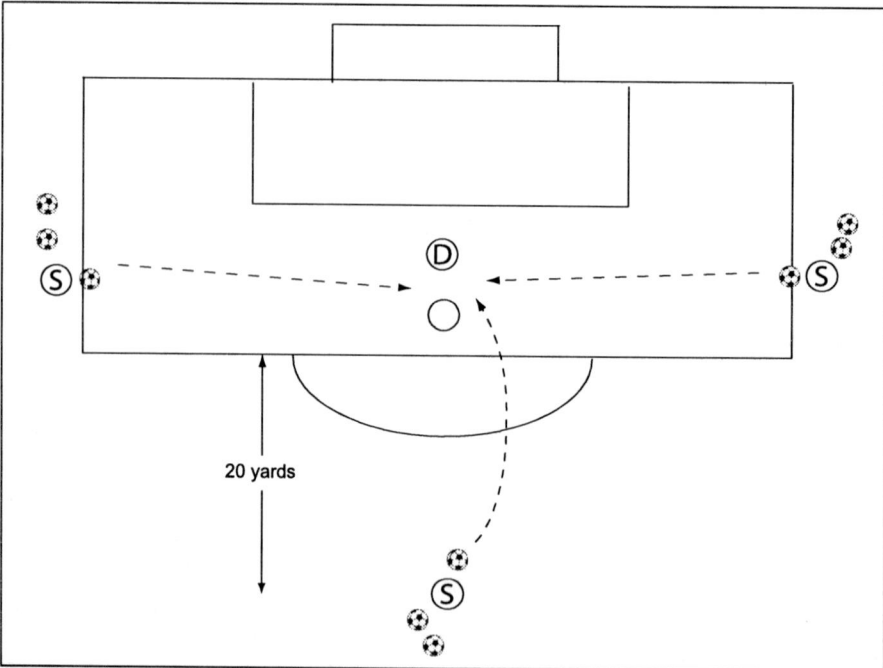

Figure 2-16. Heading competition

Bench Press

The bench press can be evaluated and assigned point values for extra credit points. The target weights will vary by gender and age. Following is one possible way to assign points:

- Two points for 120 lbs or 80% of body weight
- Three points for 135+ pounds
- Four points for 145+ pounds

Subjective Assessment

Watch each player and give a subjective score based on the answers to the following questions. To be consistent with other evaluations, assign one point for a strength, two points for average, and three points for a weakness. Obviously, the lower a player's score, the better.

- Can the player create space for himself or his teammates at the correct time?
- Can the player understand the visual cues to support a teammate or when to stretch the other team?
- Does the player display a high level of mobility?
- Can the player move from offense to defense quickly?
- Does the player make quick decisions with the ball?
- Can the player take people on 1v1 and defend 1v1?
- Does the player hold the ball well?
- Can the player defend in small groups?
- Does the player have any great physical or psychological qualities?
- Does the player make good decisions?
- Can the player turn with the ball quickly with one to two touches?
- Does the player recognize opportunities to combine with teammates (e.g., overlap, take-over, wall pass)?

Sample Evaluation Form

You'll need a form to record times and attempts for your entire team. Use the form in Figure 2-17 as an example. Each athlete should have his own evaluation form as well. This may seem like a lot of paperwork, but utilize your assistant coaches or managers to transfer information. Figure 2-18 shows a sample form that can be used for athletes. This form should not show the weights assigned to each skill, just the final ranks compared to their teammates.

Name	Cooper	120s	300	20/40	Box	"T"	3-Tier	Passing	1v1
Jordan, R.									
Scott, C.									
White, N.									

Figure 2-17. A sample team evaluation form

| Name: _____ | Grade: _____ |

1. Cooper Test
2. 120s
3. 300-yd Shuttle
4. 20/40-yd Sprint
5. Box Agility Drill
6. "T" Agility Drill
7. Three Tier Shooting
8. Passing Circuit
9. 1v1
10. 1v1s to Goal
11. Heading Wars
12. Bench Press
13. Subjective Assessment

Comments:

Final Rank: _____

Figure 2-18. A sample individual evaluation report

Choosing the Teams

After you have assessed everyone's skills and are ready to cut players, you will usually end up having a hard time with some that are on the fringe. By getting as much objective information as you can, you make explaining your decisions easier to both the player and parent if you are questioned. The skill information is to be used as supplemental information. Be careful not to fall into the trap of believing that just because one person ranked tenth and another seventeenth, that the player ranked tenth will be a better player on the field at game time.

As a coach, you know life is full of challenges and disappointments, but that's hard for most young people to understand. If you have to cut players, then bring each one in and talk to him personally rather than posting a list. Show him his evaluation form and talk to him about how he can improve in the off-season. Help him accept your decision and offer alternatives if possible.

Assigning Players to Positions

You want soccer players who can play the game and not just a particular position. Because soccer is a dynamic and fluid sport, players often find themselves in situations that require them to read space, shape, and movement. This is common and necessary for all positions and is the root of the game of soccer. You should expect all of your players to be able to play every position. You should, however, look for certain strengths and characteristics that may make one player more effective in filling a role for one position compared to another.

General Characteristics

Forwards

- Speed/pace with the ball
- Ability to finish (score)
- 1v1 offensive ability and willingness to attack

Center Midfielders

- Strong player (strong tackler, wins 50/50s and balls in the air)
- Able to play 360 degrees and does a good job running with the ball
- Good 1v1 and passes well

Wing Midfielders

- Fast with and without the ball
- Can serve balls consistently (crosses well)
- Good 1v1 player

Backs

- Good 1v1 defender
- Good tactically; understands how to support
- Has good speed

Sweeper

- Reads tactical cues well defensively and can initiate offense
- Understands support
- Has speed and is a good 1v1 defender

Stopper

- Strong tackler
- Good in the air
- Can push forward offensively

Goalkeeper

- Great communicator
- Strong tactically
- Strong technically
- Good with the ball at his feet

Characteristics of Players According to Systems of Play

When choosing a system of play, it is best to take your players' strengths and put them in positions that utilize those strengths. Below are some of the major characteristics each player should posses.

1-3-5-2

- ❏ Defenders (3)
  - Athleticism and speed are priorities.
  - Markers must be very good 1v1 defenders if playing with a sweeper and two man markers.
  - The central defender in any system must be a firm leader with a dominating personality. He must also be smart in reading space and solving defensive breakdowns, and be a dominate force in the air.
  - Defenders should have an accurate long ball service and be able to serve balls forward for penetrating runs.
  - All three defenders should be exceptional at understanding how to limit space behind them.

- ❏ Midfielders (5)
  - Stamina is a key factor because flanks must come back to balance the defense and/or take the first runner down on the weak side.
  - Flanks must also be responsible for penetrating runs on their side so speed is also necessary, along with good early services and crosses.
  - A defensive midfielder must be able to win 50/50 balls and be a solid and dominant tackler who is also good in the air.
  - An organizing midfielder, generally a very creative player and excellent with the ball at his feet, must have tremendous vision and technical ability. He must be able to turn quickly with the ball, play with his back to the goal, and step up to support when on attack. This is the player you try to play through.
  - The attacking midfielders should be a strong 1v1 player and be able to shoot from a distance. He also must be good at cutting out space defensively and be very proficient technically.

- ❏ Forwards (2)
  - One forward is responsible for stretching the defense and should have exceptional speed, the ability to take people on 1v1, and look for penetrating runs.
  - The linking forward must be good with his back to the goal and be able to hold the ball. Speed helps, but strength on the ball and in the air, as well as vision, are also needed.

1-4-4-2

- ❏ Defenders (4)
  - Each outside back must be a good 1v1 defender and possess speed, athleticism, and the patience to understand that he does not need to take the ball away, but instead can force the attacker to make a poor decision or force the attacker somewhere he does not want to go.
  - Flat four center backs should be able to read the game well and must understand the principle of cover. Players should be good in the air. Speed is great, but you can hide a slower player with good soccer sense in the middle.

- ❏ Midfielders (4)
  - The center midfielder needs to have good vision. A technical ability to play 360 degrees is a must.
  - Midfielders must be good at winning 50/50s.
  - Outside midfielders need speed and stamina to cover the area from the 18-yard box (penalty box) to your opponent's 18-yard box (penalty box).
  - Outside midfielders should be good at taking people on 1v1 and defending 1v1.

- ❏ Forwards (2)
  - One forward is responsible for stretching the defense. Exceptional speed, as well as the ability to take people on 1v1 and find penetrating runs, are musts. This forward must be able to play with his back to the goal he is attacking and hold/shield the ball long enough for the team to make runs forward.
  - The linking forward must be good with his back to the goal and be able to hold the ball. Speed helps, but strength on the ball and in the air, as well as vision, are also needed.

1-4-3-3

- ❏ Defenders (4)
  - Each flank must be a good 1v1 defender and possess speed and athleticism.
  - Center backs should be able to read the game well and must understand the principle of cover. These players should be good in the air. Speed is great, but you can hide a slower player with good soccer sense in the middle.

- ❏ Midfielders (3)
  - Size and strength, or the ability to win 50/50s, are musts for the center midfielder.
  - The center midfielder must understand when and where to provide support for the

three forwards. The center midfielder is an important link between defense and attack.
- The center midfielder must have a long shot.
- Outside midfielders need to be athletic with good work rates. They are generally pinched in and therefore don't provide width in this system.
- Excellent fitness is a must for all midfielders.

❑ Forwards (3)
- Work rate and athleticism are essential.
- Forwards must have the ability to break down defenses both 1v1 and by timing penetrating runs.
- They should have great speed and understand the concept of pressure.
- Forwards should be able to cover and balance defensively as they work to put pressure on the defenders and deny their service.

Choosing Your Game Plan

The system you choose must fit your players. It may seem that "everyone" is now playing a 1-3-4-3, but if you do not have the players to play that system, why do it? Every system has its strengths and weaknesses that you must understand to make appropriate changes during games and help place your players in a position to increase their chances of success. Detailed explanations of the systems of play are found in Chapter 8. If you have an inexperienced group, they will never perfect every aspect of the game. As a result, you must decide what is important and teach those things well.

Beginning players who are in junior high or are freshman will exhibit most technical and tactical skills at a level that is below age-appropriate, but will probably be physically and psychologically in their age group. Generally, an older beginner will present like an eight to 11 year old. Technically and tactically, an intermediate player will present similar to a 12 to 14 year old and an advanced player will be similar to a player 15 or older. A list of some of the more appropriate aspects of the game that generally need to be taught at the three different age levels includes the following.

Beginner

Technical

- Your teaching should be mostly foot-skill oriented with an emphasis on dribbling, receiving, and passing—in that order.
- Teaching should be done within small-sided games. (2v2 to 6v6).
- Try not to use games that eliminate players. Elimination games tend to push the players out who actually need the playing time while the better players continue to play and get more experience.
- Eliminate cones. No cones are used in soccer, so try to eliminate dribbling through cones or passing between cones as a technical, repetitive practice.
- *Fun*damentals should be emphasized.

Tactical

- Shape and space should be addressed to some degree.
- A system of play can be adopted but space and shape should take precedence.
- No man marking!
- Teach zonal defending using the ideas of pressure and cover.
    - ✓ Pressure: First person defense—delay, contain, force one way, tackle if presented with the ball
    - ✓ Cover: Second person defense—support first person by positioning 45 degrees off the inside shoulder; requires lots of communication
- Principals of attack should focus on 1v1 and 2v1 situations. Emphasize taking on a defender by beating him with a move first, then passing second.

Physical

- Fitness should be taught in the context of the game if you have limited practice opportunities. In a high school setting, fitness may be addressed as an addendum to your practice one or two times in every five or six practices.

Psychological

- Short-term goals should be addressed at this level. For example, pick technical skills to track for improvement during a game, such as completing passes or making dribbling moves, instead of focusing on just winning or losing the game.
- Use a lot of positive reinforcement.

Intermediate

The following aspects can be addressed once players master the beginning techniques.

Technical

- Emphasis is still on foot skills using both feet.
- Introduce shielding and 1v1 skills.
- Teaching should be done in small games.
- Emphasize increasing speed of play and decreasing the time and space for players to control a ball.
- Technical skills such as shooting with the instep, driving balls with the laces, crossing, and receiving a ball should be emphasized within game-like situations. Players need to be able to perform under increased defensive pressure.

Tactical

- Shape and space must be emphasized.
- Phase play practice should be used to paint exact pictures of spacing within one-third of the pitch. For example, how do you defend in your defensive third?

- Continue the development of zonal defending roles.
- Introduce some choreography/shadow play by playing against an imaginary team or against just the back four players. If you can field 11v11, shadow play can be done in this setting with neither team able to tackle or intercept the ball on defense. In other words, the offensive team is allowed to be successful in running your patterns of play without opposition but with the usual cues a moving opponent offers.
- Introduce more involvement of the supporting players in attack. The use of two-player combination passes set up by the dribble should now be emphasized (e.g., wall pass, overlap, takeover).

Physical

- Fitness needs to be emphasized.
- Fitness can still be done with the ball, but place more emphasis on nonball fitness.

Psychological

- Introduce team-building exercises.
- Goals, both long-term and short-term, should be outlined individually as well as for the entire team.
- Emphasize being a "student" of the game and being allowed to solve situations with little instruction from the coach.
- Teach players to take responsibility for themselves.

Advanced

The following areas, from a teaching standpoint, are most appropriate for your varsity-level athletes, who are proficient in their fundamentals and understand the game fairly well.

Technical

- Emphasis should shift to understanding how to read the game and use the correct technique.
- Continue individual skill development in small-sided games.
- Add larger games and continue to decrease space and time.

Tactical

- Emphasize continued understanding of space and shape.
- All players should be able to easily transition between different systems of play.
- Emphasize high- and low-pressure defending.
- Transition play is very important.
- How to attack bunker defenses and establish a rhythm in attack become important topics.

- Attacking and defending principles should be a major emphasis while adding the third person combinations in attack and the continued development of balance in defense.

Physical

- Continue to emphasize physical fitness. It should become a lifestyle, not a hobby.

Psychological

- Continue to develop goals.
- Make sure players understand that the only things you as a coach can control are fitness and foot skills.

A Checklist of Skills

To be successful, you need a master schedule so that all aspects of the game are covered. The following basic checklist should get you started. You have to decide what is important for your team to accomplish before the first game and throughout the season.

- Basic fundamentals (e.g., ball control, dribbling, screening, passing, trapping, crossing, heading, shooting, tackling)
- 1v1 ability/dribbling moves
- Ability to turn with the ball in one to two touches
- Tackling 1v1
- Finishing skills (i.e., the ability to score with either foot, inside/outside/toe)
- Offensive strategy (See Chapter 5)
- Set pieces (See Chapter 6)
- Defensive strategy (See Chapter 7)

Putting It All on a Timeline

Break your season down into phases and determine what your teaching emphasis will be during each phase. Then write down general areas you want to cover during each week so nothing is left out. Once the season begins, you should refer to this master plan and use it to write detailed practice plans. You will have to make changes according to the development of your team, but having a solid master plan to work from will be helpful.

Phase One (Preseason)

- Cover your checklist of skills.
- Develop a good conditioning base.
- Improve individual skills.
- Implement your offensive and defensive systems.

Phase Two (In-Season)

- Note team weaknesses and plan practices to target them.
- Increase game play eventually, from 1v1 to small-sided games to 11v11 as you build toward your game each week.
- Work on individual skills in small games.
- Continually emphasize fitness.
- Practice choreography/shadow play.

Phase Three (Off-Season)

- A detailed plan of action for off-season training is outlined in Chapter 13.

3

Drills

The number and variety of drills available to soccer coaches is too numerous to list. As a result, this chapter includes selected drills for improving each skill.

Basic Dribbling Skills

Three types of situations include the need for dribbling: dribbling to maintain possession, dribbling to beat an opponent, and dribbling with speed. Teach your athletes the following basic moves to build a solid foundation of ball control.

Feints

Feints are moves that rely on body fakes in one direction while taking the ball in the opposite direction.

Scissors Behind the Ball

While dribbling, the player fakes like he will go to the left by planting the left foot in a hard cut to the left of the ball, then takes the ball with the outside of his right foot as he pushes off with his left foot (Figures 3-1 through 3-3).

Figure 3-1

Figure 3-2

Figure 3-3

Scissors Around the Ball

While dribbling, the player takes his left foot and moves it around the ball from inside to outside, planting the left foot down behind the ball. He then takes the ball with the outside of his right foot to the right as he pushes off his left foot (Figures 3-4 through 3-7).

Figure 3-4   Figure 3-5

Figure 3-6   Figure 3-7

Double Scissors

In double scissors, the player combines two scissors, one with one foot followed by one with the other foot.

Fake Shot and Push to the Side

The player fakes as if he is going to shoot by bringing his leg back in a swift motion, stopping it just short of touching the ball. He then takes the ball with the outside of the foot he faked with and pushes off the other foot (Figures 3-8 and 3-9).

Figure 3-8

Figure 3-9

Step Over

With a defender on his back, the player steps over the ball with his right foot so that it lands to the left of the ball and takes the ball with the inside of his left foot to the right in a cutting motion (Figures 3-10 through 3-13).

Figure 3-10

Figure 3-11

Figure 3-12

Figure 3-13

Skilled Moves

Skilled moves are those that require pulling, pushing, cutting, or rolling the ball with some part of the foot.

"Pull the V"

This move can be done with or without a fake shot feint. The player puts the toe of his right foot on the top of the ball. As he pulls the ball back, he pivots on his left foot to the right while pushing the ball in that direction with the inside or outside of the right foot (Figures 3-14 through 3-17).

Figure 3-14

Figure 3-15

Figure 3-16

Figure 3-17

Basic Cut

While dribbling, the player takes the inside of his right foot and brings it down on the right side of the front of the ball. This forces the ball to go to the left. The more he gets his hips around the side, the more radical the cut will be.

Pull Across

This move requires that the player roll the ball with the bottom of his right foot across his body to the left. To do this, the player plants his right foot in a normal manner. He should be cross-legged with the left foot behind the right foot. He must quickly move the left leg to the left to stop the ball with the inside of the left foot (Figures 3-18 through 3-21).

Figure 3-18

Figure 3-19

Figure 3-20

Figure 3-21

Figure 3-22

Pull Behind

To do this move, the player places the sole of his right foot on the ball. As he pulls the ball back behind himself, he turns to his right and pushes the ball further with the inside of his right foot (Figures 3-22 through 3-25).

Figure 3-23

Figure 3-24

Figure 3-25

Pull Behind and Chop

This move (also called a Cruyff, named after the famous Dutch player who originated it) is the same as the pull behind, except when the player pulls the ball back under his body, he quickly takes his foot off the ball and then cuts the ball with the inside of his foot to push it to his left behind the left foot, which is planted on the ground (Figures 3-26 through 3-29).

Figure 3-26

Figure 3-27

Figure 3-28

Figure 3-29

Continuous Sole Roll

To perform this move, the player places the sole of his right foot on the ball and rolls the ball forward, stepping down when the foot reaches the end of his foot. As he puts his right foot down, he plants it so the toe is facing left. He then turns to the left and, as he turns, brings the left foot up with the toe pointed down so the sole of the foot contacts the ball. As he continues to turn, he continues to pull the ball with the sole until he is facing the way he was when he started (Figures 3-30 through 3-34).

Figure 3-30

Figure 3-31

Figure 3-32

Figure 3-33

Figure 3-34

Hip Swivel

While dribbling, the player pulls his hips around to briefly touch the front of the ball with the inside of his left foot as if he was going to cut the ball or stop it. He then quickly brings his hips back around and takes the ball with his right foot to continue (Figures 3-35 through 3-37).

Figure 3-35

Figure 3-36

Figure 3-37

Dribbling—General Coaching Points

Remember that many moves can be used to beat an opponent. As each player gets more comfortable he can combine moves to make more complex, yet very effective, moves. The key is to have players continuously work on their moves and control of the ball.

The following points should be shared with your players, perhaps even distributed as a handout. These tips—which are presented for each skill discussed in this chapter—represent the basics that all soccer players must understand to be successful.

- Stay balanced.
- Keep the ball close to your feet.
- Keep your eyes up.
- Use all surfaces of the foot (instep, inside, outside, bottom, and toe).
- When dribbling to beat an opponent
    - ✓ Dribble at the defender with speed
    - ✓ Use quicker, shorter touches
    - ✓ Generally try to make your move one to one-and-a-half yards from the defender.
    - ✓ Cut your move across the front foot of the defender when possible
    - ✓ Accelerate for two to three touches past the defender
- When dribbling with speed in open space
    - ✓ Keep the toe pointed down as you push the ball ahead
    - ✓ Push the ball further away from your body
- When dribbling for possession/shielding
    - ✓ Make yourself "big" by keeping the ball on the foot furthest away from your opponent, keeping your body between your opponent and the ball
    - ✓ Extend your arm and bend the elbow slightly
    - ✓ Keep your knees bent
    - ✓ Maintain your balance

Dribbling Activities

The keys for the activity diagrams included in this chapter are shown in Figure 3-38.

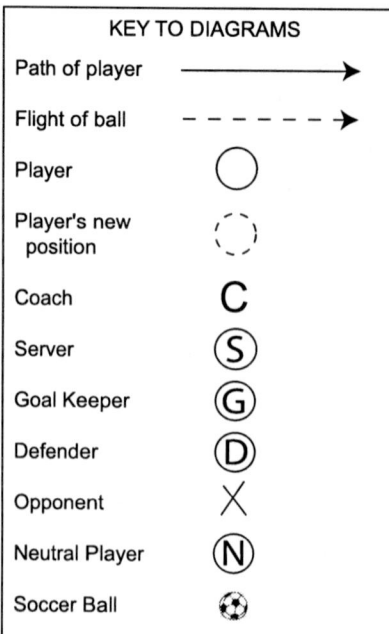

Figure 3-38. Key for activities

Space Invaders (Figure 3-39)

Set-up: 10 to 18 players, each of whom has a ball. Cones are set up as illustrated in Figure 3-39.

Directions: In a 25- x 10-yard grid, every player dribbles around freely. On command, players dribble to a cone and stop the ball so that it touches the cone.

Variations:
- Remove a cone and play again. Everyone getting to a cone gets one point or the player who doesn't get to a cone does crunches, etc.
- Give players one minute and 30 seconds to touch as many cones as possible with their ball. Keep track of touches.
- Make players use a feint or basic move before they touch a cone or every time they come face-to-face with a teammate.

Coaching Points:
- Players should keep their eyes up.
- Remind players to keep their knees bent and the ball close.
- The players should dribble into space.

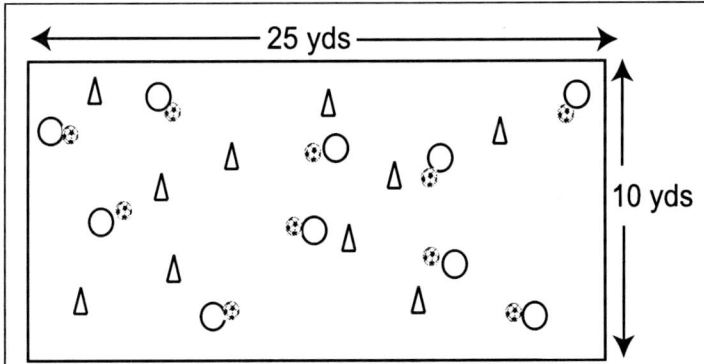

Figure 3-39. Space invaders

Gates (Figure 3-40)

Set-up: Mark out a 20- x 25-yard grid. Place pairs of cones one yard apart throughout the grid that represent 10 to 15 "goals." All players have a ball.

Directions: All players dribble for one to two minutes while keeping count of how many gates they can get through.

Variations:
- Make each player perform a basic move before going through each gate.
- Divide the players into two teams. Have each team compete separately and add up how many gates everyone on the team went through.

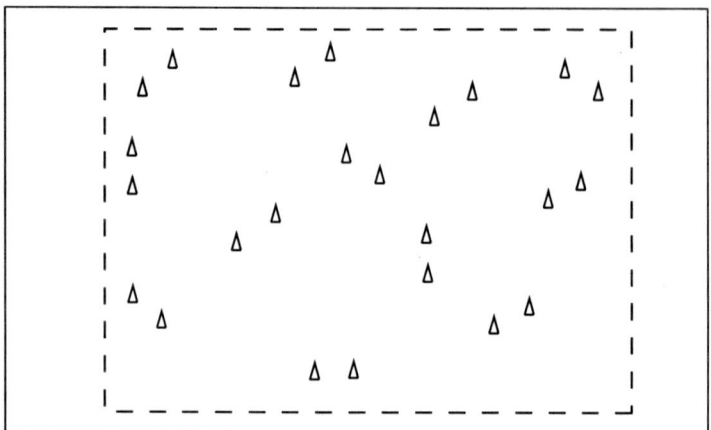

Figure 3-40. Gates

Dribbling With Speed (Figure 3-41)

Set-up: Mark off a 25- x 20-yard grid with additional cones as illustrated in Figure 3-41. All players have a ball and are divided into three teams and given a team color.

Directions: The three teams each dribble in the grid. One team is "it." On the command of "go," all players speed dribble around the nearest outside cone and back as fast as possible without being touched by a player on the team that is "it."

Variation:
- Change the game inside the grid to restrict touches to get around a cone and back to seven or fewer, four or fewer, etc.

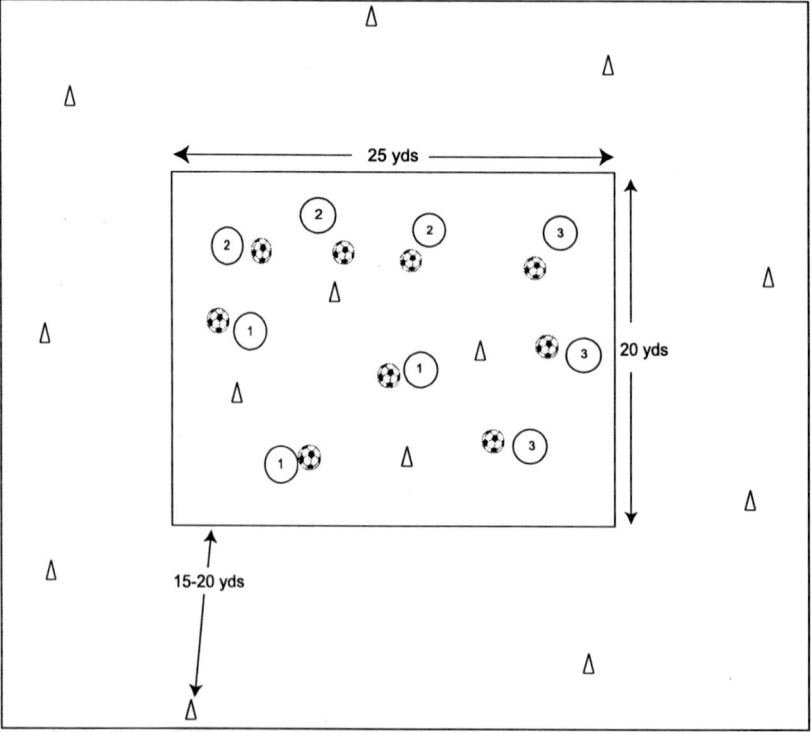

Figure 3-41. Dribbling with speed

74

Coaching Points:
- The first touch should be longer.
- Players should use the top or outside of the foot with the toe down.
- Remind the players to look up.

Knock-Out (Figure 3-42)

Set-up: All players have a ball and are stationed inside a 20- x 25-yard grid as shown in Figure 3-42.

Directions: All players dribble while one or two players are designated as "it" and try to knock the ball away from other players while still maintaining possession of their own ball. When players are knocked out, they run to the coach, who assigns a move to practice 20 times, and then they go back in.

Variations:
- The players who are "it" do not have a ball.
- Players who are knocked out can retrieve their ball and continue to play while the coach keeps track of how many times the player who is "it" knocks someone's ball out of play in a specified amount of time (usually one or two minutes).
- When a player is knocked out, he should go to the coach and demonstrate a basic footwork skill five times and rejoin the game.

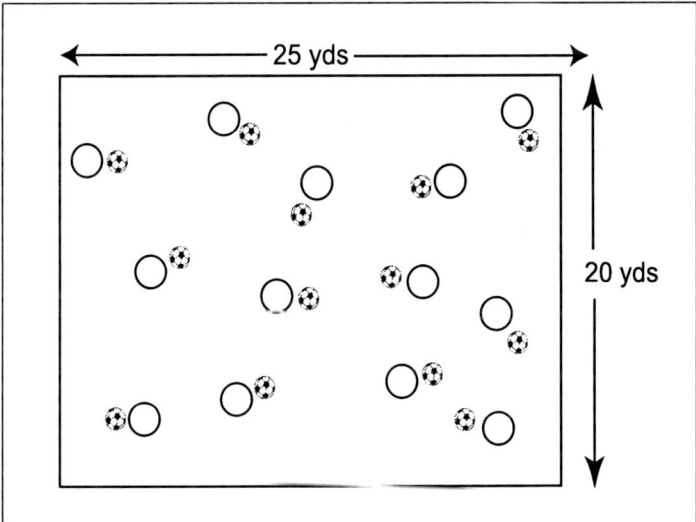

Figure 3-42. Knock-out

Passing/Striking—General Coaching Points

Passing or striking a ball is a skill that requires subtle adjustments. A player can pass a ball with almost any part of his body. This section covers passes with the foot.
- The nonkicking foot should be placed next to the ball.
- The nonkicking foot should be bent at the knee.

- The toe of the nonkicking foot should point in the direction you want the ball to go.
- Keep your head down, and your knee and shoulders over the ball.
- The hips also determine the direction of the pass by opening in the direction you want the ball to go.
- Lock your ankle.
- Follow through the pass or shot by stepping forward.
- When passing with the inside of the foot
    - ✓ The toe should face out and up
    - ✓ The ankle should be locked
- When passing with the instep for a drive or shot
    - ✓ The toe should point down
    - ✓ The plant foot is placed slightly in front of the ball
    - ✓ The knee and shoulders should remain over the ball
    - ✓ The head should be down
    - ✓ Push off your plant foot as if you are jumping a creek when you follow through
- When passing with the outside of the foot
    - ✓ The toe should point inside and down
- When passing to chip a ball
    - ✓ Utilize a short chip under the ball with the laces
- To loft a ball in the air
    - ✓ Plant the foot slightly behind or even with the middle of the ball
    - ✓ Lean back slightly
    - ✓ Contact the ball below the midline
- To keep the ball down
    - ✓ Plant the foot even with, to slightly ahead of, the middle of the ball
    - ✓ Stay over the ball with the knee and shoulders
- When bending a cross
    - ✓ Play the ball with the inside of the foot
    - ✓ Strike the ball a little under and to the outside of the ball
    - ✓ Lean back slightly
- When driving a cross
    - ✓ The ball should be played with the instep of the foot
    - ✓ Stay over the top of the ball with the knee and shoulders

Passing/Striking Activities

Shuttle Drill (Figure 3-43)

Set-up: Groups of three players face each other about 15 to 25 yards apart with one ball as illustrated in Figure 3-43.

Directions: Player #1 passes to Player #2 and runs to the end of the line. Player #2 takes one touch to prepare the ball and one touch to pass it to Player #3, and runs to the end of the line, and so on.

Variations:
- The players must play their first preparation touch to a side.
- The players pass with one touch and no preparation.
- Have a relay race between lines of groups. The first group to get through the lines three times and back to their original starting point wins.
- Change the passing surface to inside, outside, and instep.

Coaching Points:
- Remind the players to lock the ankle.
- Make sure the plant foot (nonkicking foot) of each player is next to ball.
- Remind the players to keep the hips open toward the target.

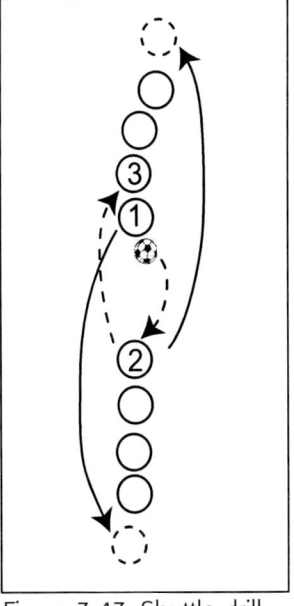

Figure 3-43. Shuttle drill

Box Drill (Figure 3-44)

Set-up: Position six players inside the grid without a ball (the "O's") and position the remaining players on the grid (the "X's") five to eight yards apart as shown in Figure 3-44. All the "X's" have a ball.

Directions: The "O's" check to an "X" on the outside. The "X" (Player #2) passes the ball to Player #1 and he passes it back to Player #2.

Variations:
- Make all passes one-touch.
- Make all passes two-touch.
- Player #1 receives a ball, turns, and looks for another player on the grid who doesn't have a ball.
- Change the surface areas for passing (inside, outside, and instep).

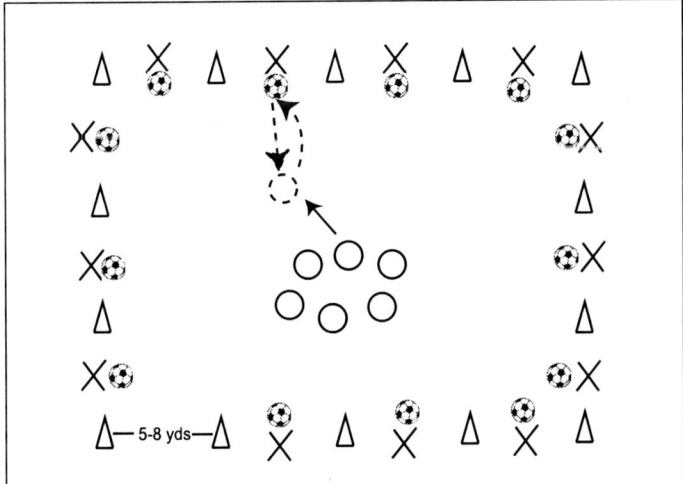

Figure 3-44. Box drill

Corner Game Activity (Figure 3-45)

Set-up: On a 40- x 60-yard grid, play 8v8 to 5v5 with a goalkeeper. Two "X's" and two "O's" stand with a set of balls at the corner flags as illustrated in Figure 3-45.

Directions: The athletes play a normal game except that every time the ball goes out for a throw-in, goal kick, or corner kick, the team awarded the set play plays a corner kick. Throw-ins and goal kicks are eliminated to allow for more opportunities to cross balls. Switch after five minutes. Play for 20 minutes.

Variations:
- Driven balls or balls on the ground may be played.
- Any cross may be played. The person crossing the ball can call his cross, and if his team scores you award them five points.

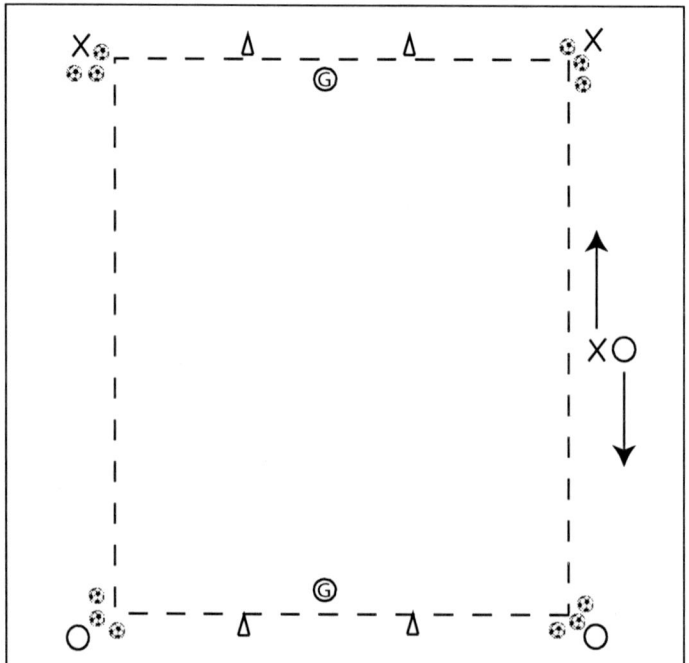

Figure 3-45. Corner game activity

Combination Play Activities

Two-person combination plays are passing sequences used when two attackers can isolate one defender.

Wall Pass (Figure 3-46)

Set-up: This drill requires three players and one ball.

Directions: Player #1 dribbles at the defender and uses the outside of the foot closest to Player #2 (who is considered the "wall") to pass to Player #2. Player #1 sprints past the defender on the opposite side of the pass and receives a one-touch pass from Player #2. Player #2 then aligns himself parallel to the defender, two to five yards away and facing the defender's shoulder.

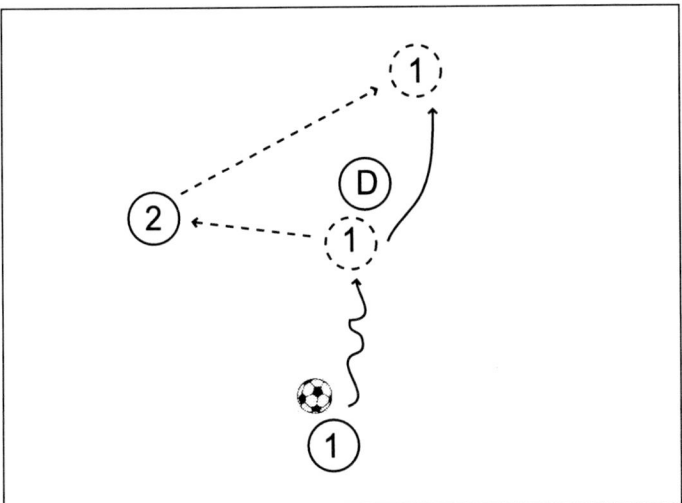

Figure 3-46. Wall pass

Overlap (Figure 3-47)

Set-up: This drill requires three players and one ball.

Directions: Player #1 passes to Player #2 and then runs to the outside into space to receive a return pass. Player #2 should turn and dribble inside to create more space for Player #1.

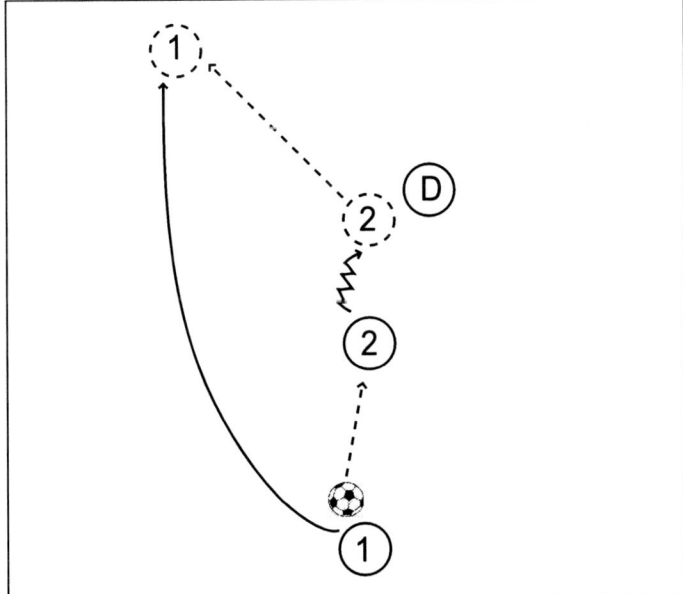

Figure 3-47. Overlap

1-2s (Figure 3-48)

Set-up: This drill requires three players and one ball.

Directions: Player #1 dribbles at the defender and uses the outside of the foot closest to Player #2 and passes to him (similar to the Wall Pass). Player #1 sprints past the defender on the opposite side of the pass while Player #2 dribbles or turns, taking more than one touch before passing back to Player #1.

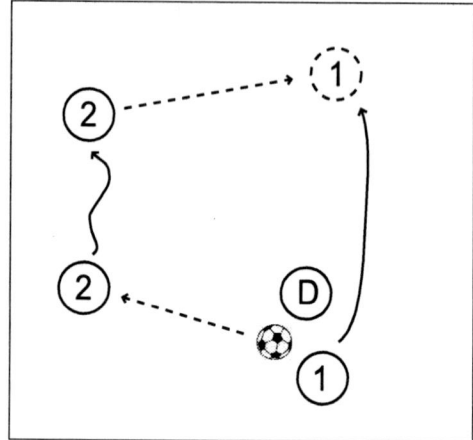

Figure 3-48. 1-2s

Double Pass (Figure 3-49)

Set-up: This drill requires three players and one ball.

Directions: Player #1 passes to Player #2, who then passes back to Player #1 at an angle. Player #2 spins around the defender to receive a pass.

Coaching Point:
- This combination is done when Player #2 is playing with his back to the goal and a defender is marking him from behind.

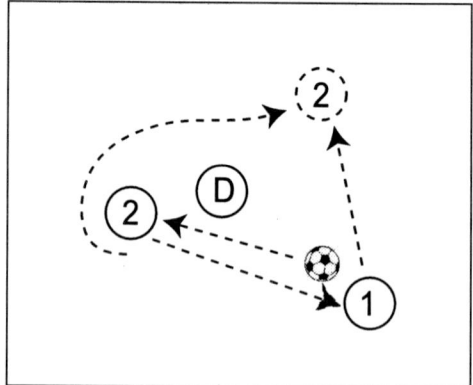

Figure 3-49. Double pass

Takeover (Figure 3-50)

Set-up: This drill requires three players and one ball.

Directions: Player #1 dribbles toward Player #2, right foot to right foot or left foot to left foot, keeping the defender on his outside shoulder and the ball on the opposite side. As Player #2 passes Player #1, Player #1 either passes his foot over the ball for Player #2 to take or continues to dribble.

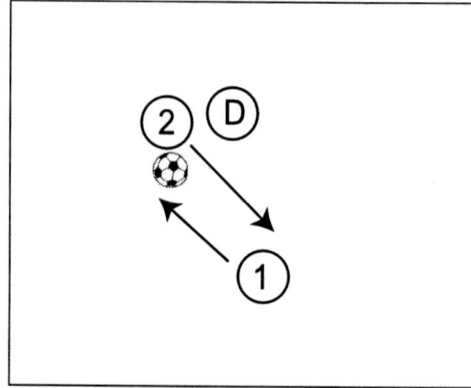

Figure 3-50. Takeover

Coaching Points:
- The player with the ball dictates if the ball is to be taken by his teammate.
- If Player #2 takes the ball, it is important that his first touch is longer and pushed further away to get separation from the defender.

Combination Game (Figure 3-51)

Set-up: Divide players into teams of six to nine. Play is in a grid that is determined by the number of players on each team (eight yards by six yards per player on each team). Put a goal in each of the four corners that measures four yards.

Directions: The players must successfully compete a combination play before scoring.

Variation:
- Play to the goals, with a goal counting for one point and a combination leading to a goal counting for five points.

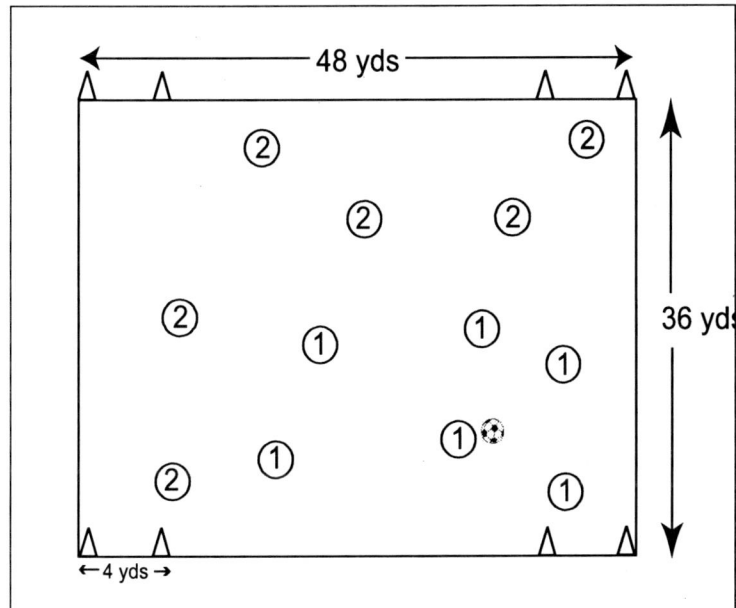

Figure 3-51. Combination game

Receiving—General Coaching Points

Receiving the ball is a vital skill in soccer. To play the game, each player must first learn how to dominate the ball, making the ball go wherever he wants it to.
- Line your body up behind the ball.
- Pick the proper surface to receive the ball.
- Keep your eye on the ball.
- Cushion the ball by withdrawing a little as the ball hits the surface.
- Use the biggest surface of the foot.
- Always receive the ball and direct it into space.
- When using the thigh to receive the ball
    - ✓ Stay balanced
    - ✓ Lift the leg with the knee bent to meet the ball coming down, but drop your leg at contact so the ball falls and does not pop up

- When using the chest to receive the ball
  - ✓ Stay balanced
  - ✓ Bend at the waist and knees and react like a spring that is pushed when the ball hits the chest
  - ✓ Be able to direct the ball to a side as well as in front by flicking your chest to the left or right
- When using the inside of the foot to receive a ball
  - ✓ Keep the knee of the standing leg bent
  - ✓ Angle your foot to the side to direct the ball away from an approaching defender
  - ✓ Pull the foot back slightly to keep the ball in front of you
- When using the instep to receive a ball
  - ✓ Lift the foot to meet the ball
  - ✓ Bring the foot down quickly as the ball touches the foot

Receiving Activity

Head to Toe (Figure 3-52)

Set-up: Divide players in half and arrange them into a circle as illustrated in Figure 3-52. Each player inside the circle has a soccer ball.

Directions: Players on the inside of the circle (the "O's") pass the ball to players on the outside of the circle (the "X's), who pick up the ball with their hands. The "O's" then turn and go to an "X," who tosses the ball to their thigh. The "O's" receive the ball on the thigh, trap, turn, and pass to an "X" that does not have a ball. The "O's" then find and "X" who is ready to serve, receive the ball, and then go again. Set a time limit of one to two minutes and switch players from outside to inside.

Variation:
- Practice receiving with the foot, thigh, chest, and head.

Figure 3-52. Head to toe

Heading—General Coaching Points

Heading can be perfected as a means to receive, pass, or shoot a ball. It can be used defensively to head a cross out of the box by getting under the ball and pushing it high and wide. It can also be used as an offensive weapon when trying to get the ball closer to the goal. It is very important to teach the correct methods to head a ball. If done improperly, neck, head, or spinal injuries could occur.

- Lock your neck.
- Use the forehead (the hair line) to contact the ball.
- Keep your eyes open.
- Move the head forward to contact the ball.
- Keep the chin up.
- Follow through.
- *Never* move your head up or down.

Note: Heading practices should not be conducted over a great length of time for younger players except to teach and demonstrate for safety purposes.

Heading Activities

Heading Progression

Set-up: Have two players sit five yards apart with one ball.

Directions: Player #1 tosses the ball to Player #2, who heads the ball back. Switch after five times.

Progression:
- Five yards apart with the tosser sitting
- Eight to 10 yards apart with the tosser kneeling
- Eight to 10 yards apart with the tosser kneeling and the player heading the ball falling forward on contact
- 10 yards apart with the tosser standing

Clearing a Cross (Figure 3-53)

Set-up: Position two players on the field as illustrated in Figure 3-53.

Directions: A server tosses a ball to each player. Player #1 heads the ball to the ball side. Player #2 heads the ball to the weak side. Rotate players after contact.

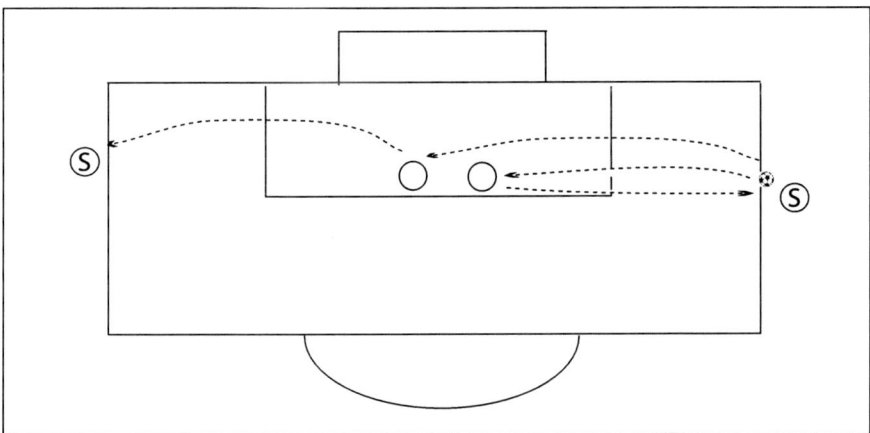

Figure 3-53. Clearing a cross

Head Challenge (Figure 3-54)

Set-up: This drill requires four players and one ball.

Directions: Player #1 serves the ball with his feet to Players #2 and #3. Player #1 tries to flick the ball toward Player #4 while Player #3 tries to head the ball back to Player #1. Points are awarded to each player with a successful "flick" or "head back." Play to five points and rotate.

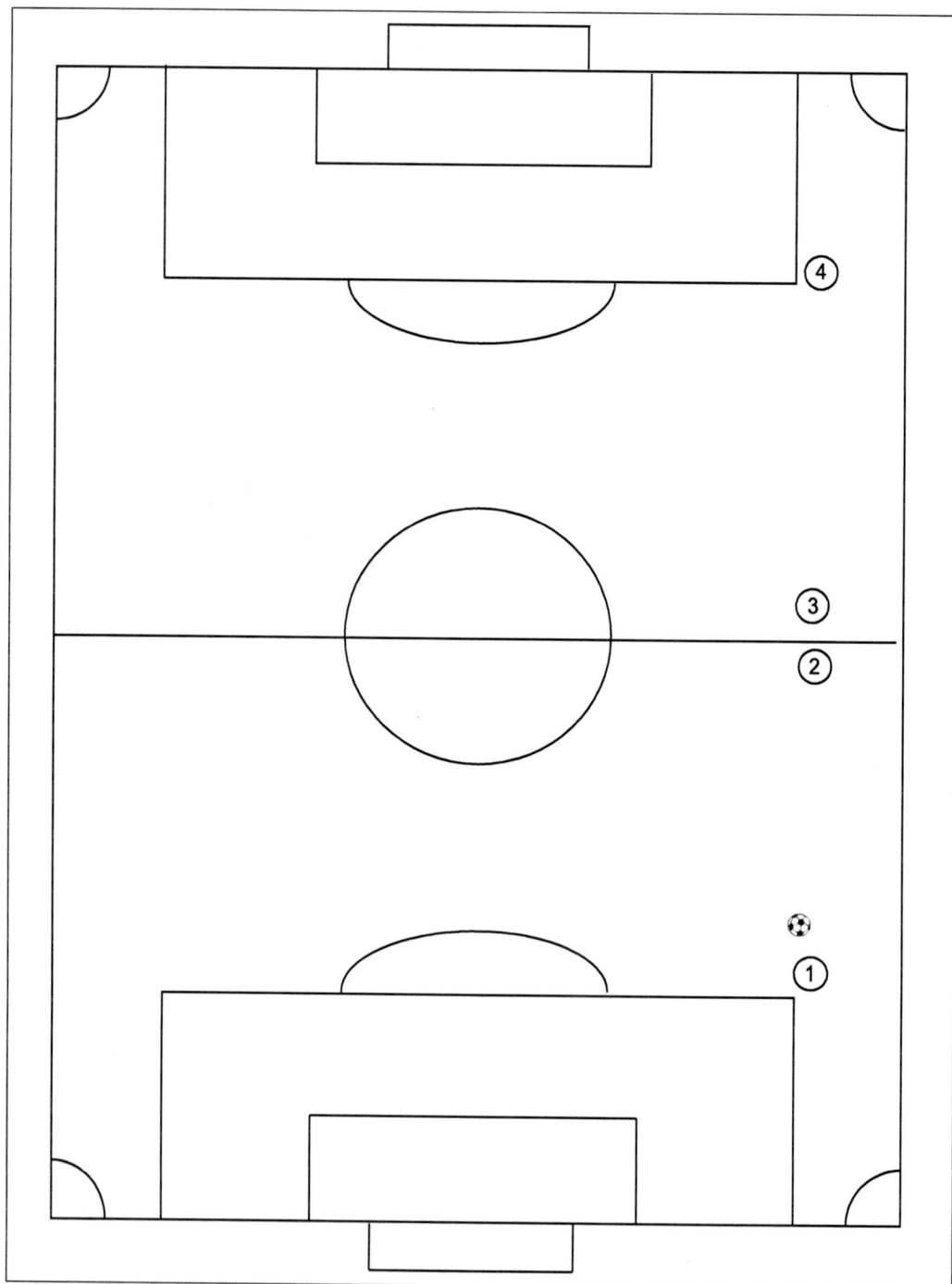

Figure 3-54. Head challenge

Head War (Figure 3-55)

Set-up: Four players perform this drill with two goals positioned 10 yards apart.

Directions: Player #1 tosses the ball to Player #2. Player #2, keeping his feet on the goal line, heads the ball and tries to score against Player #3. The ball is dead when a goal is scored, the ball rolls out of play, or the ball touches the ground with no return. Player #4 then tosses the ball to Player #3, who attempts to score against Player #2.

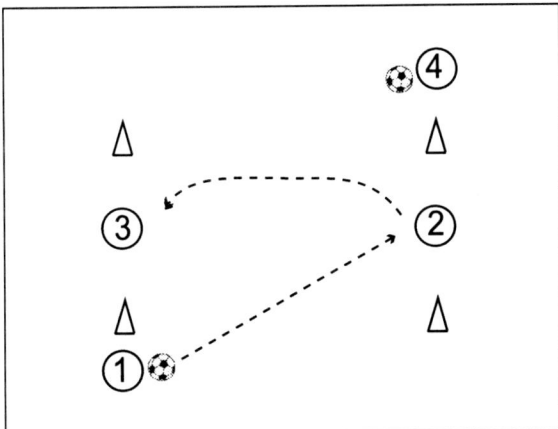

Figure 3-55. Head war

Turning—General Coaching Points

Turning with the ball is one of the skills that is very important and rarely emphasized. It is practiced in conjunction with receiving, but deserves more attention. A number of turns exist, but if your players can master the two listed here, they will be able to handle pressure much better.
- Look over your shoulder.
- Pick the surface to receive the ball.
- "Sell" your move.

Types of Turns While Receiving a Ball

Facing Up

This turn is useful when a player is checking toward a teammate without much pressure on his back. When the ball arrives, he opens his body and lets the ball go across his body and touches it with the inside of the front foot. The idea is to be able to turn 180 degrees as quickly as possible with only that one touch.

Receiving With the Outside of the Foot

With this turn, the player is receiving a pass with his body almost perpendicular to a defender who is putting pressure on his back. This movement is referred to as receiving the ball "side-on." The player must use the outside of his foot to either turn away from the defender if he is playing on the inside shoulder or push the first touch back the way the pass came to give himself space and enable him to turn and face his opponent.

Turning Activities

Turning Activity #1 (Figure 3-56)

Set-up: Put players in groups of four and position them as illustrated in Figure 3-56. Player #1 has a ball.

Directions: Player #1 passes to Player #2. Player #2 turns and passes to Player #3. Player #2 follows the pass and takes Player #3's place. As Player #3 receives the ball, Player #1 runs toward Player #3. Player #3 passes to Player #1. Player #1 turns and passes to Player #4, follows the pass, and play continues.

Variations:
- Work on both turns.
- Have a relay race and the group that completes the circuit three times and returns to their original places wins.

Coaching Points:
- Turns must be fast.
- Remind players to take quick strides after the turn.
- Players should keep the head up.

Figure 3-56. Turning activity #1

Turning Activity #2 (Figure 3-57)

Set-up: Place four to five players inside a grid and five or six players on the grid with balls as illustrated in Figure 3-57.

Directions: The "O's" check to an "X" with a ball. An "X" passes to an "O" who turns, makes two dribble moves, and finds and "X" without a ball and passes. The "O" then finds another "X" with a ball and repeats.

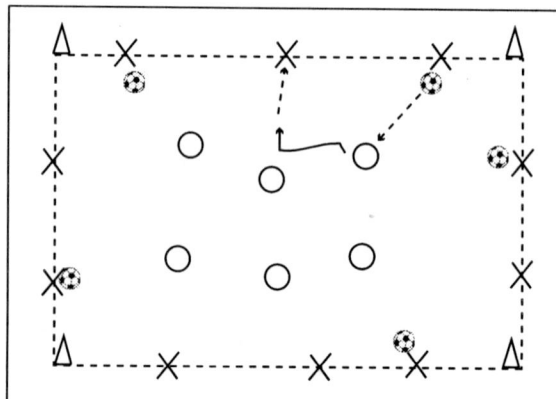

Figure 3-57. Turning activity #2

Tackling—General Coaching Points

Tackling is a very important skill to teach. While so much emphasis seems to be placed on taking the ball away from the opposition, a good defender tackles only when he knows he can win possession of the ball, tip the ball to a teammate or out of bounds, or as a last-resort effort to get the ball. It is important that younger players are taught the correct way to block tackle, poke tackle, and slide tackle to prevent injury.

- Lock your ankle.
- The toe should be pointed up.
- Get the nontackling foot as close to your opponent as possible.
- Tackle the ball across or at an angle.
- If you are not in position to tackle the ball, push a foot out to "poke" the ball away while maintaining a bent and balanced "nonpoking" leg.

Tackling Activities

Number Battle (Figure 3-58)

Set-up: Have two teams of "X's" and two teams of "O's" lined up as illustrated in Figure 3-58. Put two cones to the right and left of the teams positioned four yards apart. One server has the soccer balls and is positioned in the middle of the two sets of teams.

Directions: The server passes the ball into space on the left side and right side as illustrated in Figure 3-58. The first person in line for each team runs to get the ball. Whoever gets to the ball first is on offense. The defender then tries to tackle the ball while the offensive player tries to score by putting the ball through the cones. The next service occurs when the ball is tackled, a goal is scored, or a shot is missed.

Variations:
- Allow only poke tackles.
- Place a time limit on the drill and keep track of successful tackles for both teams.

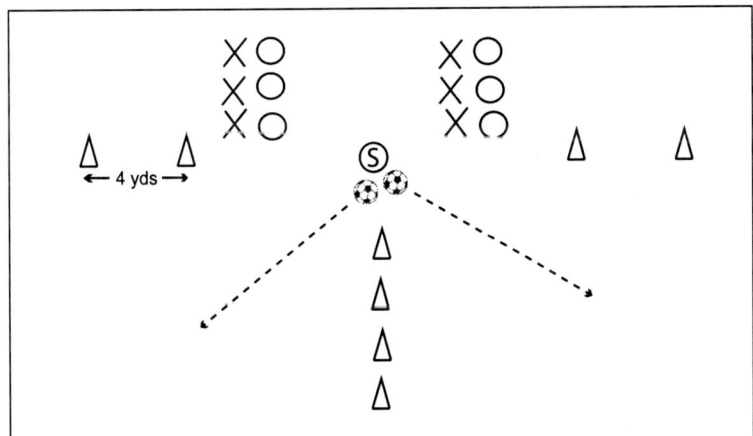

Figure 3-58. Number battle

4v4 to Lines (Figure 3-59)

Set-up: Mark off a 30- x 25-yard grid and position eight players as illustrated in Figure 3-59.

Directions: Play 4v4 on a smaller grid to promote more tackling opportunities. Keep track of successful tackles and missed tackles. Teams get a point for a successful tackle and lose a point for a miss.

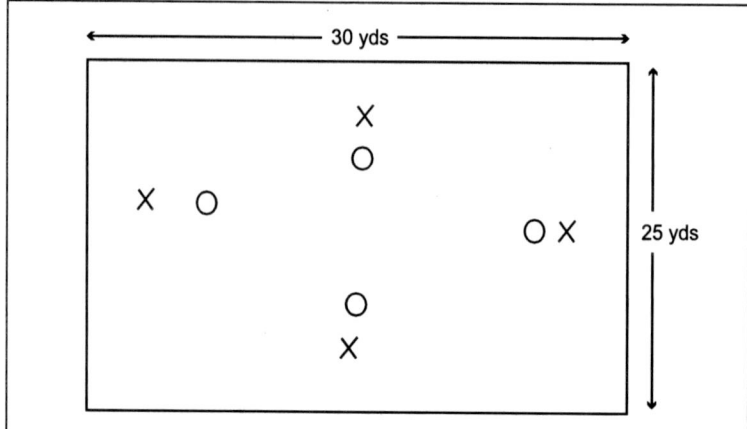

Figure 3-59. 4v4 to lines

Shooting/Finishing—General Coaching Points

The phrase "defense wins championships" is a truthful one, but in soccer, effective shooting and finishing decides the outcome of games. During practices, decide on your shooting and finishing strategy, such as when to shoot, how many players to commit to the attack, and how to organize runs into the box. When teaching the techniques for shooting and finishing, relay the following points to your players.

- The non-kicking foot should be placed next to the ball.
- The non-kicking foot should be bent at the knee.
- The toe of the nonkicking foot should point in the direction you want the ball to go.
- The hips also determine the direction of the pass by opening in the direction you want the ball to go.
- Lock the ankle.
- Follow through the pass or shot by stepping forward.
- When shooting for power, your toe should be pointed down and the ankle should be locked.

Shooting/Finishing Activities

Shooting/Finishing Activity #1 (Figure 3-60)

Set-up: Three players and one ball are positioned as illustrated in Figure 3-60. Place two sets of cones out for the players to use as goals.

Directions: Player #1 takes a touch to the side and then "shoots" to put the ball in between the cones. He then follows the shot and takes Player #2's spot in the middle. Player #2 takes Player #1's spot. Player #3 takes a touch and shoots to Player #2.

Variations:
- Shoot only with the instep.
- Shoot with the inside of the foot.
- Shoot with the outside of the foot.

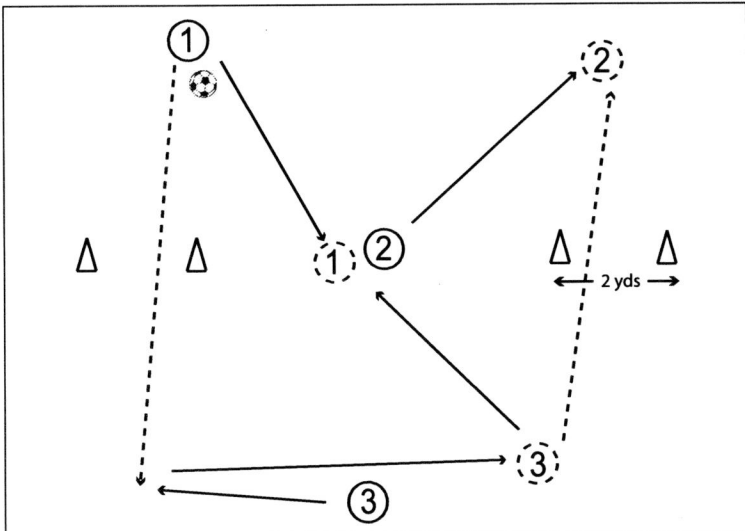

Figure 3-60. Shooting activity #1

Finishing a Cross (Figure 3-61)

Set-up: Divide your players into two lines with two servers as illustrated in Figure 3-61. The two servers should have at least three or four balls each.

Directions: Server #1 dribbles to the end line to cross. Player #1 makes a run toward the near post while Player #2 runs towards the far post. One of the two players must score. Server #2 then dribbles to the end line while Player #3 runs toward the near post and Player #4 runs towards the far post.

Variations:
- Finish with the inside of the foot.
- Serves must be in the air.
- Finish with a volley or a side volley.
- Add a goalie.

Coaching Points:
- When volleying, players should keep the knee and head over the ball, use a short leg swing, and try to hit the ball on the way down.
- When side-volleying, players should turn to face the ball with the shoulder to the goal, move their feet, drop the shoulder away from the ball, bring the leg up, and keep the knee even or over the ball.

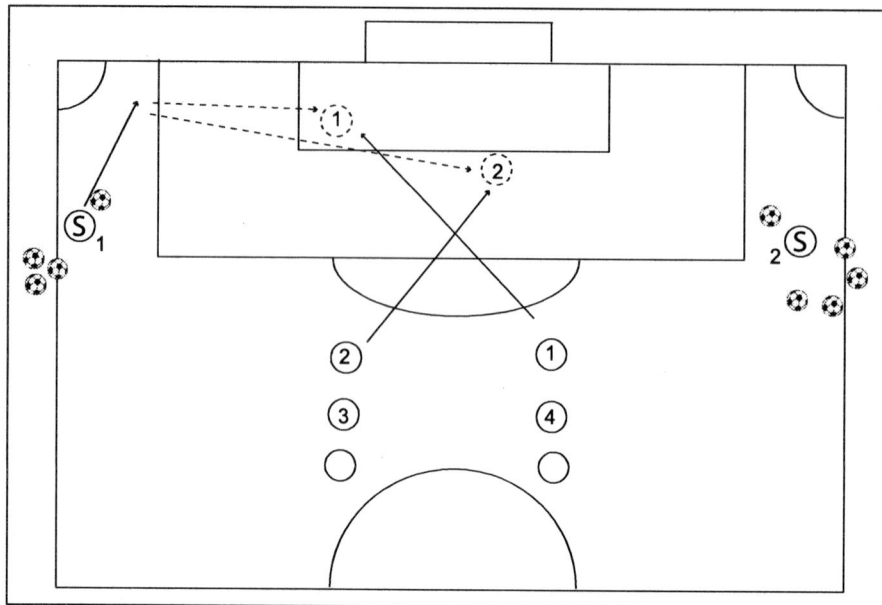

Figure 3-61. Finishing a cross

Throw-Ins—General Coaching Points

Coaches rarely emphasize the technique of the throw-in, but, like any individual skill, it is a detail that is important to your success. Because the ball frequently goes out of play, your team may end up getting as many as 20 throw-ins during a match. Teach proper technique so that a throw-in does not become an automatic turnover.

- Keep both feet on the ground.
- The ball must be thrown in coming from behind the head, then over the head with a follow-through of the arms and hands.

Throw-In Activity

Throw-In Game

Set-up: Have the players play 4v4 to 8v8 with the grid size length set at 10 yards per offensive player (e.g., 40 yards for 4v4, 80 yards for 8v8). The width of the grid shoud be three-quarters of its length.

Directions: Play soccer, but every time the ball goes out, play it back in with a throw-in.

Conditioning

Due to the nature of the game of soccer, anaerobic and aerobic fitness are equally important. Stress to your players that they should work hard to improve their fitness level during the off-season. This will make them better prepared and less prone to injuries. While "conditioning" practices are important, the ability to plan practices that force your players to maintain a high level of intensity while playing is a far better use of your practice time.

Conditioning Activities

Mirror Drill (Figure 3-62)

Set-up: Divide the players into two lines facing each other with cones set 20 yards apart.

Directions: Player #1 and Player #2 jog toward each other. Player #1 makes a cut and tries to run to one cone or the other. Player #2 must react and try to beat Player #1 to the cone. The players then switch lines.

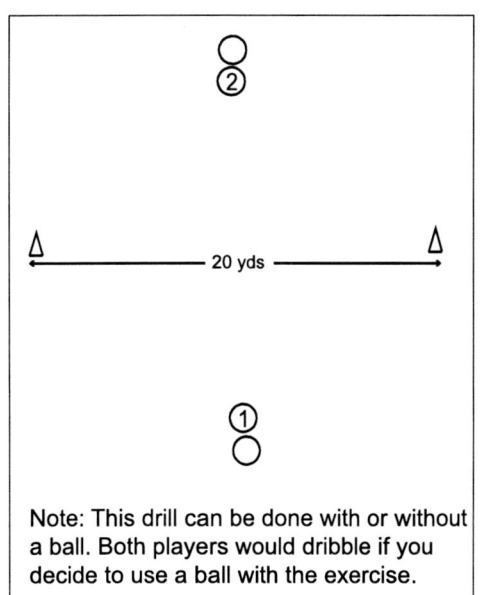

Figure 3-62. Mirror drill

Conditioning Activity #1 (Figure 3-63)

Set-up: Place cones five to eight yards apart on a 20- x 20-yard grid.

Directions: Players sprint and jog between cones, working on acceleration and changing directions.

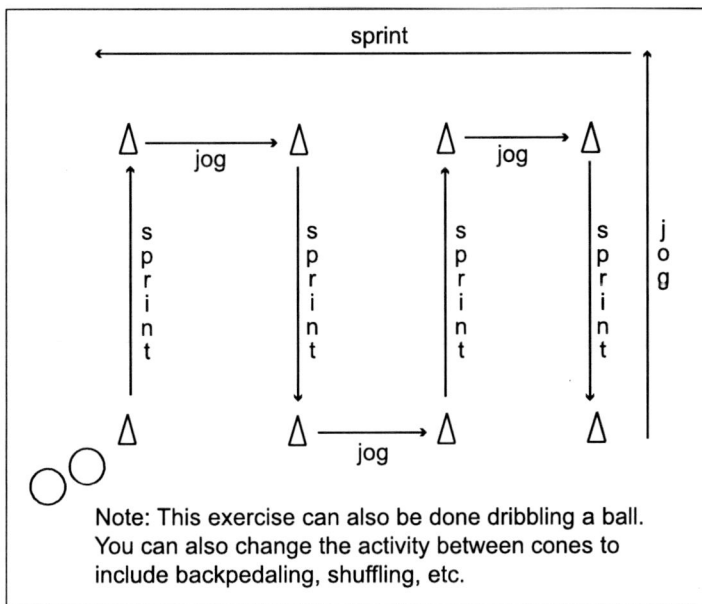

Figure 3-63. Conditioning activity #1

Conditioning Activity #2 (Figure 3-64)

Set-up: Position cones five to eight yards apart as illustrated in Figure 3-64.

Directions: Players sprint around each cone and jog back to the start.

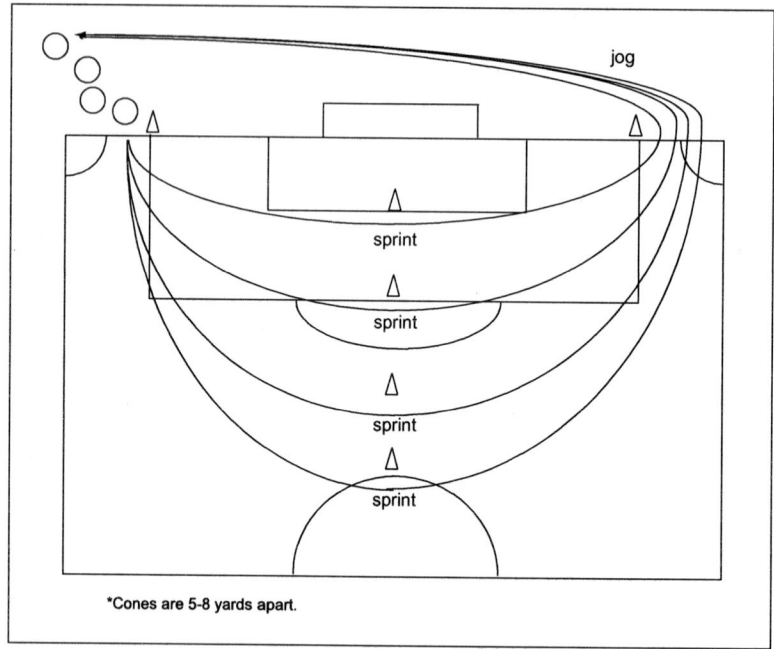

Figure 3-64. Conditioning activity #2

Game Situations—Possession Games

3v3+4 (Figure 3-65)

Set-up: Form teams of three with four neutral players on a 40- x 40-yard grid.

Directions: Play keep-away with four neutral players in the corners. Neutral players play two-touch. Play for two minutes and see how many times the team with the ball loses it to the defending team. When the defending team gains possession, they give the ball back. Switch every two minutes (times can vary).

Variation:
- Each team gets a point every time they play to a neutral player and get the ball passed back to them to retain possession.

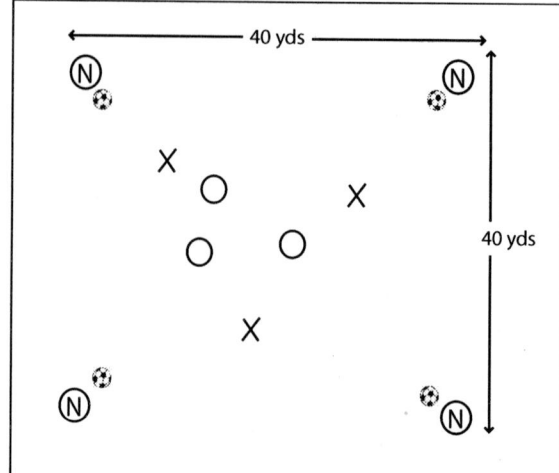

Figure 3-65. 3v3+4

Three-Team Possession

Set-up: Create three teams of six.

Directions: Two teams work together and play keep-away from the third team. The team that loses the ball becomes the defending team.

Danish Drill (Figure 3-66)

Set-up: Position four sets of two players in a grid as illustrated in Figure 3-66. Two defenders are in the center of the grid.

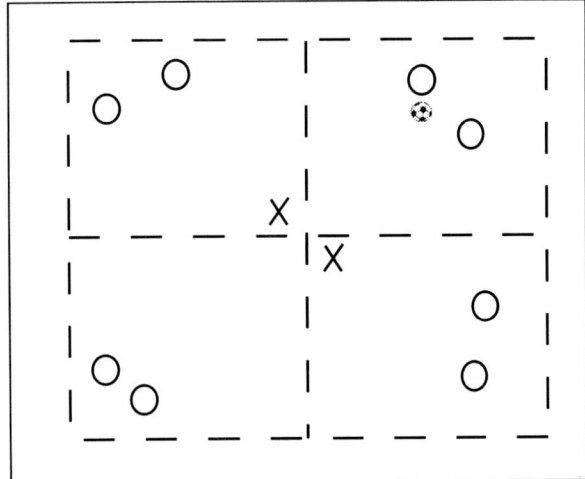

Figure 3-66. Danish drill

Directions: The two defenders must take the ball away from the players. Players in the grids must make two passes before passing to another grid.

Variations:
- The players in the grid must do a combination before passing to another grid.
- The touches can be restricted (e.g., all one-touch, mandatory three-touch)

4v4 to Targets (Figure 3-67)

Set-up: Set up two targets on opposite sides of a grid as illustrated in Figure 3-67.

Directions: Play 4v4 to targets. Teams get points if they can keep possession while playing from one target to the other.

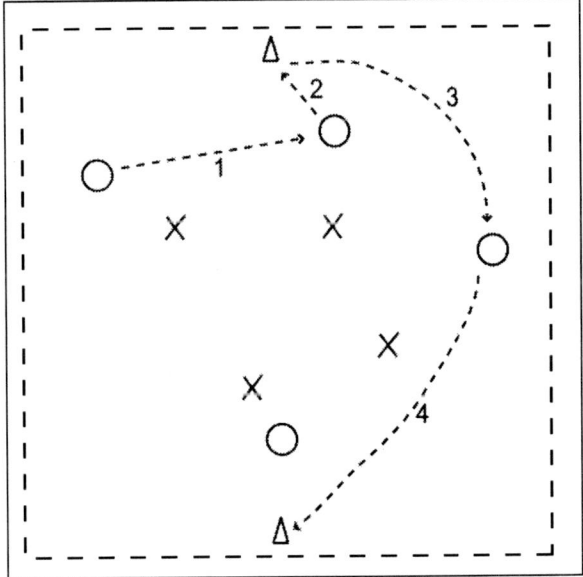

Figure 3-67. 4v4 to targets

4

Planning a Practice

The time you spend practicing with your team is valuable. Don't waste any of it. If you let your players drag themselves out to the field, then you may have lost three minutes that day. Over the course of a school year, those three minutes a day become nine hours of missed practice time. After planning for your season, you have the task of breaking all the planned drills and practices down into individual workouts designed to target the needs of your team. Ensuring that your team's practice is well organized and well spent requires that you address several areas, including general practice guidelines, a general practice outline, a master practice outline, a daily practice schedule, and other practice concerns.

General Practice Guidelines

Adhere to the following general guidelines while planning a practice:
- Practices should develop from simple with low numbers of participants to complex with high numbers of participants.
- Emphasize one theme throughout the practice, from warm-up activities to the final scrimmage.
- Practices should be dynamic with many activities rather than a passive collection of static drills.
- Create a game-like atmosphere during practice as much as possible. Two players passing to one another standing 10 yards apart is not realistic. Soccer is a game of movement.
- If you are teaching basic technical skills, make sure the skill is taught with appropriate movement and that some type of pressure such as a defender, time, size of the grid, or number of players involved is introduced as quickly as possible.
- Practice should be as long as your games. If you are playing 45-minute halves, a practice should not last more than two hours, preferably just one and a half hours.
- Do not lecture. Teach.
- When teaching players, understand the correct methodology and use it to illustrate the desired picture.

General Practice Outline

Each practice should contain some or all of the following components:

- Meetings (optional)
- Warm-up
- Main session
- Game
- Warm-down

Meetings

Meetings are important but should not cut into practice time. Schedule meetings either before or after practice. Use the time set aside for meetings to:
- Address issues brought up in the leadership council meeting.
- Watch and critique film.
- Emphasize a character trait (e.g., courage, loyalty, boldness, decisiveness, dependability). A very helpful resource for emphasizing character is a book called *Coaching to Change Lives* by The Zig Ziglar Corporation.

Warm-Up

The warm-up should use approximately 20% of the practice time and should be focused on the theme of the day. It should be an activity rather than running a lap around the field, which is poor use of practice time.

Main Session

The main session is usually broken up into two to three activities that progress from simple to complex. These activities will consume approximately 50% of the practice time. Consider using a variety of drills in a circuit during the early stages of the season.

Game

This should be an 8v8 or 11v11 game if possible and should consume 25% of your practice. The game is your opportunity to see how well you have taught the theme of the day. Initially, you can facilitate the game by continuing to make corrections, but at least 10% of the time should be spent with you observing the practice and making notes while the players play without interruption.

Warm-Down

The warm-down will take about 5% of the practice time. It can also follow the theme of the day.

Assessing Your Practice Session

For a final practice assessment, ask yourself the following questions:
- Did you plan your session around one theme?
- Did your practice follow a progression from simple to complex?
- Did the players understand the topic as you moved along the progression?

- Were the players challenged both physically and mentally?
- Did you keep your coaching points short and avoid lecturing?
- Did you let the players play and effectively paint the picture of what you wanted during the game?
- Did you coach the game of soccer or did you coach the drill?
- Did the players have fun?

Master Practice Outline

Write down all of your favorite activities on three by five index cards and keep them in a file. Then, write all of your favorite activities for each component of practice and make a master practice outline. If you do this well, you won't have to hunt or browse through books to find what you like, and you can periodically go to your file box for new ideas. Keep your practice sheets in a three-ring binder (Figure 4-1).

Individual Skills	Dribbling	Passing/Striking
1. Touches	1. Dribbling Drill #1	1. Passing/Striking #1
2. Rolls	2. Dribbling w/Speed	2. Passing/Striking #2
3. Turns	3. Knock-Out	3. Wall Pass
4. Fakes	4. Other favorite here	4. Overlap
5. Other favorite here	5. Other favorite here	5. 1-2's
Receiving	Heading	Turning
1. Head to Toe	1. Clearing a Cross	1. Turning Drill #1
2. Other favorite here	2. Head Challenge	2. Turning Drill #2
3. Other favorite here	3. Head War	3. Other favorite here
4. Other favorite here	4. Other favorite here	4. Other favorite here
5. Other favorite here	5. Other favorite here	5. Other favorite here
Tackling	Shooting/Finishing	Conditioning
1. Number Battle	1. Shooting Drill #1	1. Mirror
2. 4v4 to Lines	2. Finishing a Cross	2. Conditioning Drill #1
3. Other favorite here	3. Other favorite here	3. Conditioning Drill #2
4. Other favorite here	4. Other favorite here	4. Other favorite here
5. Other favorite here	5. Other favorite here	5. Other favorite here

Figure 4-1. Master practice outline

Sample Coaching Outline

A sample coaching outline is illustrated in Figure 4-2. Fill one out before each practice and then save them in your notebook for future reference.

```
┌─────────────────────────────────────────────────────────┐
│                    COACHING OUTLINE                     │
├─────────────────────────────────────────────────────────┤
│  Date:                      Topic:                      │
│                                                         │
│  Area:                      Objectives:                 │
│                                                         │
│  Equipment Needed:                                      │
│   Portable Goals: [ ]   Balls: [ ]   Cones: [ ]         │
│   Scrimmage Vests: [ ] - Yellow  [ ] - Red  [ ] - Blue  [ ] - Green │
├──────────┬───────────┬────────────────────┬─────────────┤
│  Phase   │  Activity │ Organization/Diagram│ Coaching Points │
├──────────┴───────────┴────────────────────┴─────────────┤
│  Warm Up:                                               │
│                                                         │
├─────────────────────────────────────────────────────────┤
│  Main Theme:                                            │
│                                                         │
│                                                         │
├─────────────────────────────────────────────────────────┤
│  Game:                                                  │
│                                                         │
├─────────────────────────────────────────────────────────┤
│  Areas still needing improvement:                       │
│                                                         │
├─────────────────────────────────────────────────────────┤
│  Notes for next practice:                               │
│                                                         │
└─────────────────────────────────────────────────────────┘
```

Figure 4-2. Sample coaching outline

Sample Practice Plans

Many drills and useful terminology are fully explained in Chapter 3. The following practice plans are best used as a guide to illustrate how to create a theme for your individual practice sessions and carry that theme over several sessions. Remember that you as the coach are the key to teaching any topic in practice. Setting up these practices will not help your team if you do not understand the coaching points of your topic. More importantly, if you fail to see the proper time to correct any problems or can't illustrate through demonstration how to properly execute a skill or tactical situation, the session you run will not be very effective.

Each practice session includes a warm-up, a main session, and a game that all relate to the theme of the week. Following each practice session, players should participate in a cool-down consisting of some light jogging and stretching. The cool-down is an excellent time for you to talk with the team and give players information about the next practice or next match.

Practice Week #1—Dribbling

Dribbling for Possession

❑ Warm-Up
- Introduce three to four basic moves, depending on the level of your athletes.
- Give half of the players a ball inside the grid while the other half stand without a ball between the cones as illustrated in Figure 4-3. Show the players inside the grid a basic move and let them do the move three times and then pass to a player outside the grid. The new player dribbles in the center and does the move three times and then again passes to someone outside.

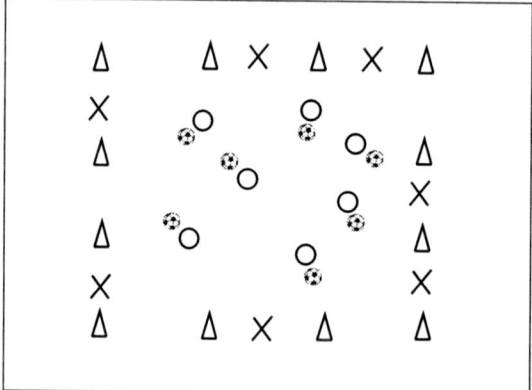

Figure 4-3. Dribbling for possession warm-up drill

❑ Main Session
- Activity 1: Play 1v1 for time. Players should try to keep the ball for 30 seconds, one minute, etc. (Figure 4-4).
- Activity 2: Give players one to two minutes to dribble through as many gates as possible, as illustrated in Figure 4-4.
- Variation 1: When the player dribbles through a gate, he must do one of the basic moves.
- Variation 2: Split the players into two teams. Each member keeps track of how many gates he goes through and the totals for the whole team are added together. Use the basic moves.

- Coaching points
  ✓ Remind the players to keep the head up.
  ✓ Teach the players to keep the body between the ball and the defender.

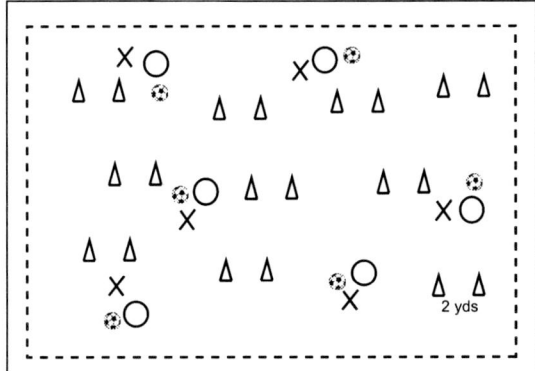

Figure 4-4. 1v1 for time

❑ Game
- Play small-sided games: 4v4 in a 40- x 30-yard grid to 8v8 in an 80- x 50-yard grid, depending on the numbers.
- Play the games to lines or four goals. Score by dribbling through the goal or stopping the ball on the line.
- The emphasis should be on moves.
- For the first five minutes, players must use a basic move before the team can shoot.
- The last 10 to 15 minutes should be free play.

Note: If you want players to understand the idea of possession by using space and changing the point of attack, the four-goal game works well. Playing to touch the ball on the lines is good for encouraging players to take on a defender 1v1 and beating that defender or encouraging penetration.

Dribbling for Penetration

❑ Warm-Up
- Review the three or four moves from the previous practice.
- Introduce three to four more moves that emphasize feints/fakes to get around an opponent (e.g. scissors, hip swivel, step-over, pull chop).
- Place every player in a 15- x 18-yard grid and introduce the first move. Use cones or flags in the center as illustrated in Figure 4-5. Players dribble at their own pace, completing the move every time they get to a cone. When the coach shouts, "Stop" everyone must get to a cone (one player per cone).
  ✓ Variation: Remove one or two cones after each round. Players that don't make it to a cone must practice the move five times before continuing.
- Coaching points
  ✓ Remind the players to keep the head up and always dribble into space.

✓ The knees should be bent. Encourage the players to change speed after each move.

✓ The players should try to complete the move as quickly as possible.

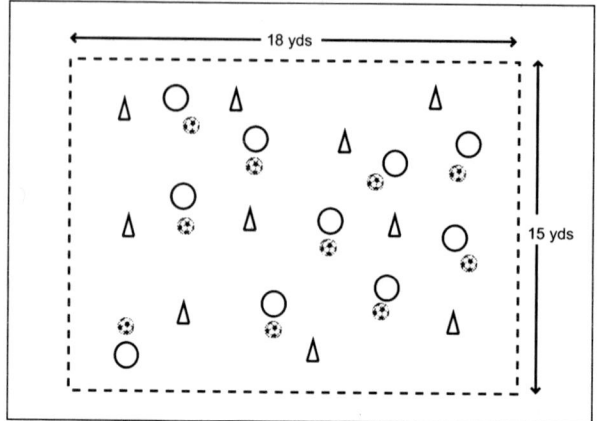

Figure 4-5. Dribbling for penetration warm-up drill

❑ Main Session
- Classic 1v1: Players score by dribbling through the goal as illustrated in Figure 4-6. Games should vary in length and rest should always be included between games.
- 1v1 to goal: Defenders pass to an offensive player as shown in Figure 4-7. The offensive player receives three points if he can beat the defender and score and two points if he can beat the defender but doesn't score. Emphasize beating the defender.
- Coaching points

   ✓ Players should be aggressive with the move. Encourage them to change the pace.

   ✓ Remind players to use both feet and be unpredictable.

   ✓ Remind players to keep the head up, knees bent, and avoid being flat-footed.

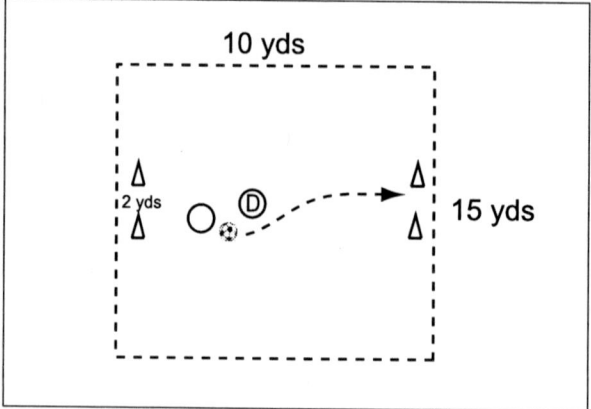

Figure 4-6. Classic 1v1

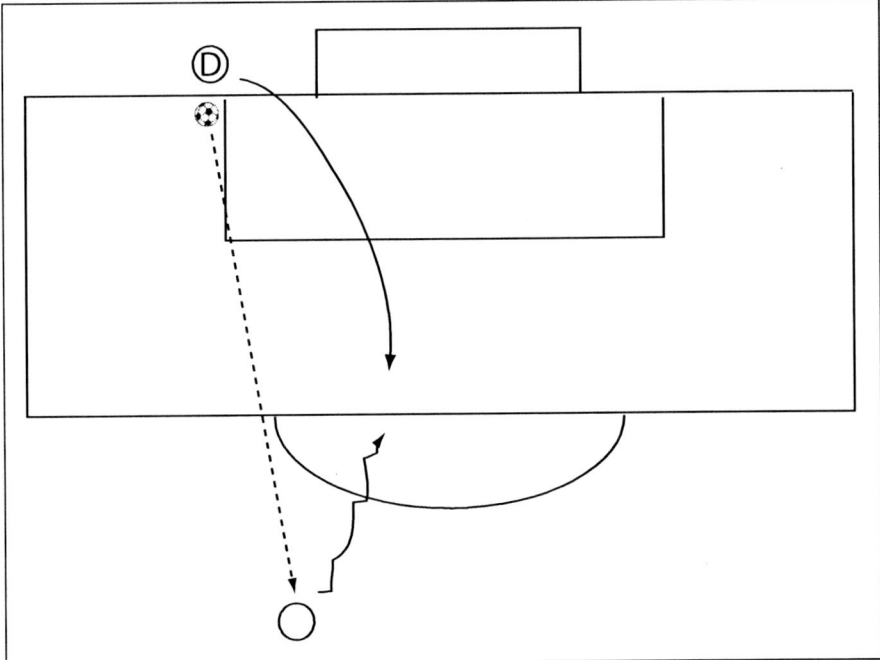

Figure 4-7. 1v1 to goal

❏ Game
- Play small-sided games: 4v4 to 8v8 depending on the numbers.
- For the first five minutes, players must use a basic dribbling move before the team can shoot.
- The last 10 to 15 minutes is free play.

Dribbling—1v1 Tactics

❏ Warm-Up
- Review the three to four moves from the previous practice and introduce three more.
- Introduce a new move and have players play 1v1. A point is scored every time a player gets around his opponent with a new move. Keep track of wins and losses.

❏ Main Session
- 2v2+2: Play a 2v2+2 game designed for a player to receive the ball with his back to the goal. The object is to try to turn or use a teammate to help isolate the defender and pass the ball to the other side of the grid as illustrated in Figure 4-8. A completed pass to the opposite neutral player is one point. The grid size should be 20 x 15 yards or 30 x 20 yards to allow plenty of room to succeed.
- Coaching points
  ✓ Teach players to attack the standing foot (closest).
  ✓ The players should always look for an opportunity to isolate one defender.
  ✓ Encourage your players to be aggressive and pass to a teammate only to isolate defenders.

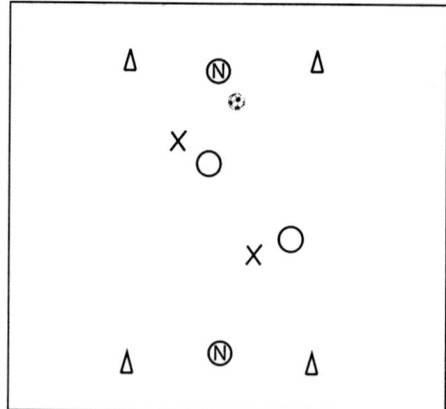

Figure 4-8. 2v2+2

❑ Game
- Play a four goal game for the first 10 minutes and free play for the last 15 to 20 minutes. Focus on the shape of the team as a way to set up defenders to be isolated 1v1. This will allow attackers to recognize when to take on and beat an isolated defender.

Practice Week #2—Passing/Receiving

Passing/Receiving for Possession—Day 1

❑ Warm-Up
- "Windows": Divide the team into two groups, with half of the players in the grid and half of the players outside the grid, each with a ball at his feet. Each player in the center receives a pass and completes the following for two minutes before switching groups.
  ✓ Receive and pass back to server.
  ✓ Teach or review the turns (pull, inside and outside of the foot, Cruyff, and step-over). Add the turns to the windows by receiving, completing one basic turn, and then passing to a different server.
  ✓ Receive, turn, complete one basic turn, pass to a different server, and take that server's place on the outside.
- Coaching points
  ✓ Players should lock their ankles.
  ✓ Remind the players to keep the hips open to the target (with the plant foot toward the target).
  ✓ Players should strike with the inside of the foot and follow through.
  ✓ Communication between players involved in the pass is key.
  ✓ The plant foot must be next to the ball.

❑ Main Session
- Activity 1: Play 4v4 to two goals keeping a diamond shape. Have players pass three consecutive times before scoring or play with everyone having two touches—one touch to trap, one to pass.

- Activity 2: Split players into two teams with a grid size of 8 to 10 yards for every team member. The grid should have several two-yard gates within as shown in Figure 4-9. Teams play possession and earn a point every time they pass to a teammate through the gate. Points are scored for each successful pass through a gate.
- Coaching points
  - ✓ Focus on all technical aspects of passing.
  - ✓ Introduce opening up the body to receive the ball so the entire field becomes an option.
  - ✓ Encourage communication and eye contact.

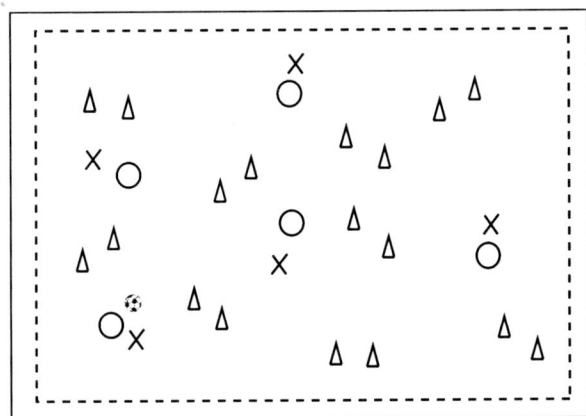

Figure 4-9. Passing/receiving main session drill

❑ Game
- Play a game of 8v8. For the first five minutes, players must pass three to four times before the team can shoot. The last 10 to 15 minutes are free play.
- Emphasis should be on technique, communication, and body positioning.

Passing/Receiving for Possession—Day 2

❑ Warm-Up
- Give each player a ball and have him toss it in the air and receive it with each of the following:
  - ✓ Instep
  - ✓ Inside of foot
  - ✓ Outside of foot
  - ✓ Thigh
  - ✓ Chest
- Coaching points
  - ✓ Teach the players to get in line with the ball.
  - ✓ Have them relax the part of the body they are using.
  - ✓ Remind the players to trap into space.
  - ✓ Remember to have the players use the right and left side.

❑ Main Session
- Team handball: Play 4v4 to 7v7 team handball (Figure 4-10). Players advance the ball by throwing it in the air to a teammate. The teammate must receive the ball with his chest, thigh, or foot, and then pick it up to retain possession before the other team can intercept the pass. A point is scored by receiving a ball within the goal. The ball may be intercepted in the air by catching it, but if the ball is dropped, it goes to the other team. The ball may not be taken once a player begins receiving the ball. The player receiving gets a free opportunity to trap the ball into space and pick it up.
    ✓ Variation 1: You may award the ball to the other team if a trap gets too far away from the body.
    ✓ Variation 2: Goals are only scored directly on a one-touch shot or head.
    ✓ Variation 3: Vary the types of traps to be used.
- Coaching points
    ✓ Have players get in line with the flight of the ball.
    ✓ Remind the players to cushion the ball with the body and knock the ball into space.
    ✓ Tell your players: *Do not trap* the ball dead. They must always play the ball into space and away from pressure.

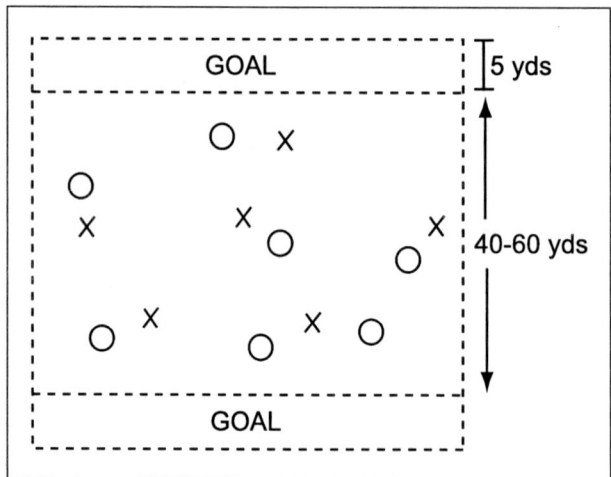

Figure 4-10. Team handball

❑ Game
- Play a small-sided game of 6v6 to 8v8 to two goals.
- For the first five to eight minutes, narrow the field to force throw-ins and give players more opportunities to receive the ball in the air.
- The last 10 to 20 minutes should be free play.
- Coaching points
    ✓ When receiving the ball, the players should keep themselves in line with the flight of the ball and cushion the ball.
    ✓ When passing the ball, the players must keep the ankle locked, point the plant foot and hips toward your target, place the plant foot next to the ball, strike the ball, and follow through.
    ✓ When in possession of the ball, players should always try to open the body to the field, keep shape, give support, and always communicate.

Passing/Receiving for Possession—Day 3: Circuit Training

❑ Warm-Up
- Work on basic moves in a grid or circle using "Dutch windows."
- Introduce or emphasize turns.
- Introduce two feints.
- Coaching points
  ✓ Players should keep the head up.
  ✓ Remind them to change pace as the move is made.
  ✓ Players should shield with turns and use both feet.

❑ Main Session
- Organize your players in groups of six or seven. Players will stay at each station for five to eight minutes. Each player needs a ball.
- Set up the field as illustrated in Figure 4-11 with the following stations:
  ✓ 4v2 possession: Four players keep possession and get a point every time they can pass through one of the three goals to a teammate. If defense wins the ball, they join the offense and two new defenders jump in. Start the count again.
  ✓ 4v2 possession: This is a plain possession game emphasizing shape.
  ✓ 3v3 to goal: Play 3v3 from the top of the circle through the width of the 18 yard box. If defense wins the ball, they must take it back outside the 18 before turning and attacking the goal.
  ✓ 6v6 gate possession: The ball must pass through a gate to a teammate for the team to get a point.
  ✓ Two-touch soccer tennis: Players rotate in and out after each touch across the "net." The ball must be served in the air like a lob. The player receiving gets one touch to set it up and one to lob the ball back.

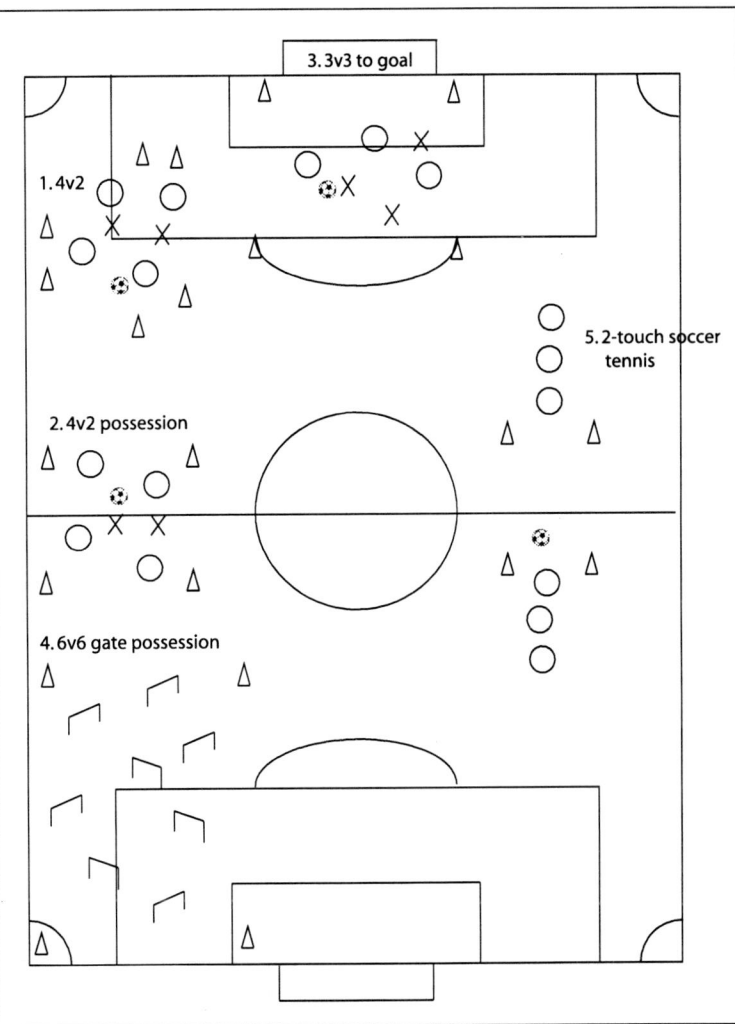

Figure 4-11. Passing/receiving circuit

❑ Game
- Play a full-sided scrimmage.
- Emphasize possession, shape, an open body to receive the ball, support, and the furthest, safest pass.

Practice Week #3—Passing Combinations

Wall pass, 1-2s, and Overlap

❑ Warm-Up
- The defender passes to Offensive Player #1 and approaches to defend. The offensive player sets up for a wall pass and the offense completes the combo. The defender allows the pass to happen and then the players rotate (Figure 4-12).

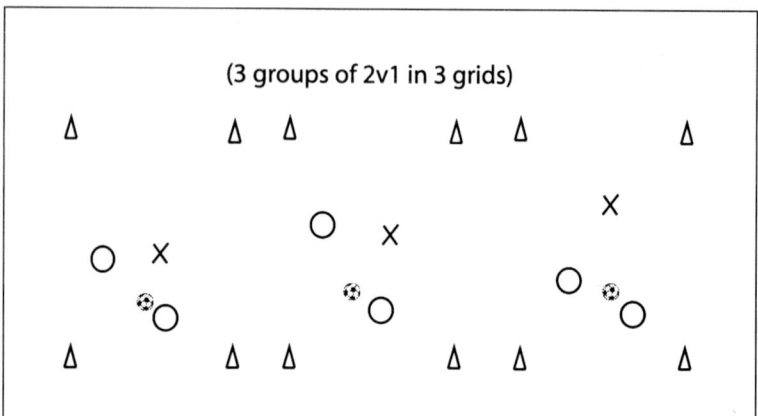

Figure 4-12. Passing combinations warm-up drill

❑ Main Session
- Possession in 4v4 or 6v6: The team gets one point for every successful combination.
- Advance to a four-goal game, but each team must complete a combination before passing through the goal (the ball must go through on the ground).
- Coaching points
  ✓ Focus on technique.

❑ Game
- Play 6v6 to 8v8. For the first 10 minutes the players must perform combinations.
- Allow free play for the last 15 minutes.

Double Pass and Takeover

❑ Warm-Up
- Double pass: Start with players in the middle holding the ball and passing out to the players on the outside to start the double pass. The windows grid should be 10 yards per player in the middle (e.g., the grid is 60 x 60 yards if you have six players in the middle.) The pass must be delivered to the target player with good pace and be flat. Players should pass to the target, spin out to the right, and cut left (or spin out to the left and cut right).
- Takeover: Start with players in the center with a ball. They dribble, do a basic move, and then dribble to a player on the outside and execute a takeover.

- Coaching points
  ✓ Encourage eye contact and have the player dribbling toward a teammate initiate the move.
  ✓ The approach should be right foot to right foot or left to left.
  ✓ If a player dribbling wants to give the ball, he should step over it.
  ✓ The player taking the ball *must* give a heavy/long first touch.

❏ Main Session
- 4v4 to lines: Players must do one of the five combinations before scoring.
- Three-grid game: Four red players have the ball and must complete one combination before sending the ball over to the other side (Figure 4-13).

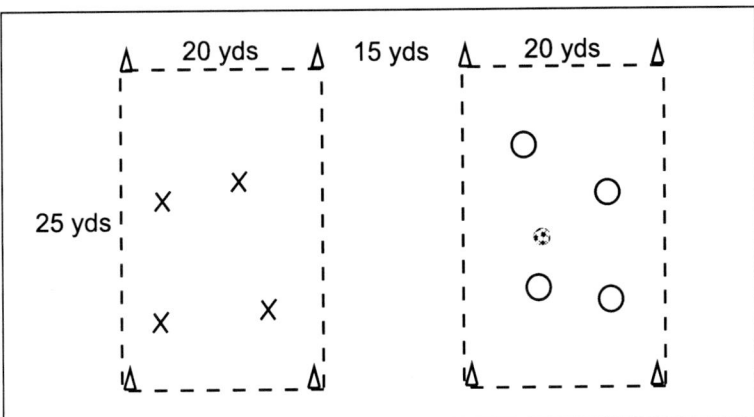

Figure 4-13. Three-grid game

❏ Game
- Play 6v6 to 8v8 to lines for the first 10 minutes. Players must complete one combination before attacking.
- Allow for free play to one goal for the last 10 to 15 minutes.

Shape (4v4) and Roles

❏ Warm-Up
- Play 2v2 to lines, concentrating on using space to make it difficult for the defense to cover.
- Games should be three to four minutes in length and played on a 20- x 20-yard grid.

❏ Main Session
- 4v4 to two goals: Maintain the diamond shape (Figure 4-14).
  ✓ The target must be able to check into space and needs to stretch the defense by getting high
  ✓ The wings stay wide and look to cover back, check high, or check in.
  ✓ The sweep gives support and looks to overlap wide.

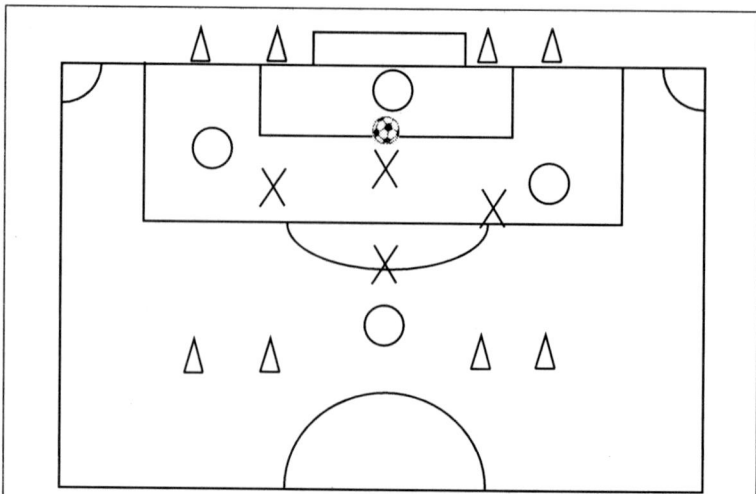
Figure 4-14. 4v4 to two goals

- 6v6 to goal: Reinforce roles from the 4v4 game. Play to forward and let them play wide. Continue to emphasize maintaining a shape and balancing out the shape as players move.

❑ Game
- Play 8v8 to 11v11.
- For the first 15 minutes, continue to correct the shape.

Practice Week # 4—Defense

1v1 Technical

❑ Warm-Up
- In a 10- x 10-yard grid, play 1v1 with the player with the ball passing to another player to start the game. An offensive player tries to dribble to the end line and the defensive player plays defense. Continue until each player gets five chances to play defense and then switch partners.
- Coaching points
  ✓ Players should try to close space as quickly as possible (speed of approach).
  ✓ Players should make a bent run to force to one side (angle of approach).
  ✓ Focus on containment.
  ✓ Remind players to be patient until they get an opportunity to tackle.

❑ Main Session
- Play four or five games of 4v4 at eight minutes each.
- Stop and correct the individual defensive techniques.

❑ Game
- Play 6v6 to 8v8. Stop and correct as needed for the first five to eight minutes.
- Allow free play for the last 10 to 15 minutes.

Defense in Pairs

❑ Warm-Up
- Numbers game: Divide the players into two teams. Give each player on each team a number. The two teams stand on either touchline of a 20- x 20-yard grid. Throw a ball into the grid and call two numbers. The corresponding players race into the grid and play 2v2 to pre-set sides. Play for five to eight minutes.
- Coaching points
    - ✓ The first defender should get pressure on the ball and try to make the player with the ball put his head down. He should then push the player with the ball to the line and focus on speed and angle of approach.
    - ✓ The second defender should give support at a 45-degree angle inside, cut off the passing angles, and verbally support the first defender.

❑ Main Session
- 2v2 progression
    - ✓ Play 2v2 to two small goals with neutral players on the side. The neutral players have one touch. They can move along the line and pass to the team that passes to them (Figure 4-15).

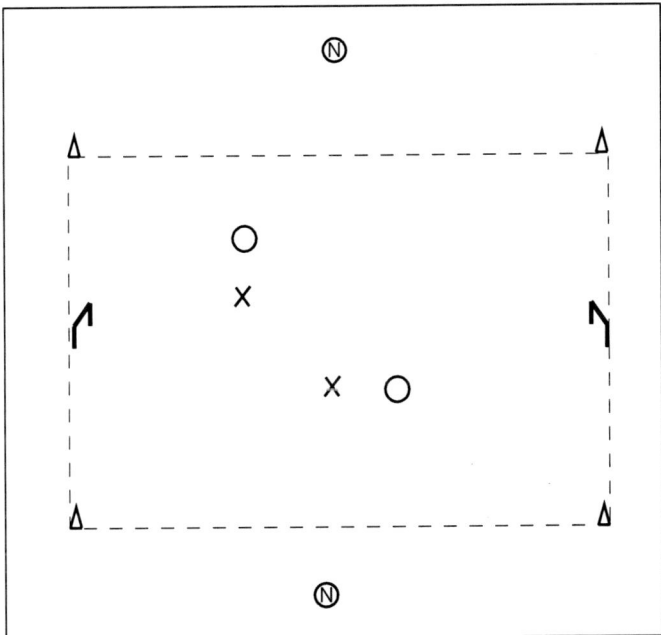

Figure 4-15. 2v2 progression #1

   - ✓ Play 2v2 with two neutral players on each end line as a target (Figure 4-16).
   - ✓ Play 2v2 with one neutral player in the goal who can be used for support only when his team has possession (Figure 4-17).

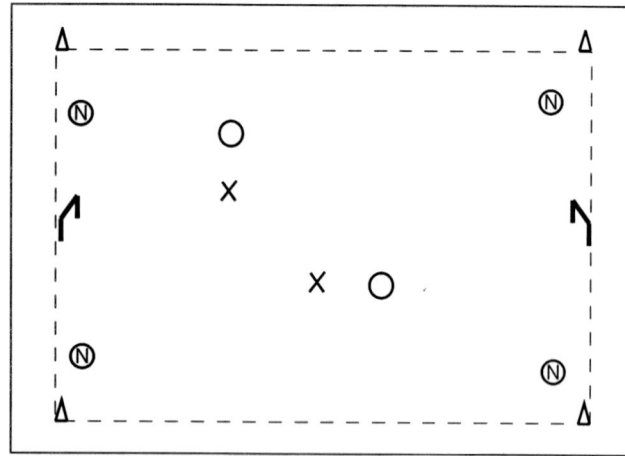

Figure 4-16. 2v2 progression #2   Figure 4-17. 2v2 progression #3

❏ Game
- Play 4v4 to 8v8 to goal.
- For the first 15 minutes, continue to teach the idea of first defender. second defender.

Pressure, Cover, Balance

❏ Warm-Up
- 5v3 possession to lines: Work on recognizing teachable moments. Play for six to eight minutes, stretch, and repeat.
- Coaching points
  ✓The first defender should pressure the ball, deny penetration, and channel where directed.
  ✓The second defender should provide cover and support while playing 45 degrees off the inside shoulder of the first defender.
  ✓The third defender should provide balance and squeeze space centrally.

❏ Main Session
- Two box possession: Start with 5v3 in one square. The five players try to keep the ball as long as possible. Keep time with a stopwatch. When the three defenders win possession, they pass into the next grid where two players are waiting and the previous group of five must send three players in to defend the new group (Figure 4-18). For a variation, add two goals on each end line giving players a sense of direction.

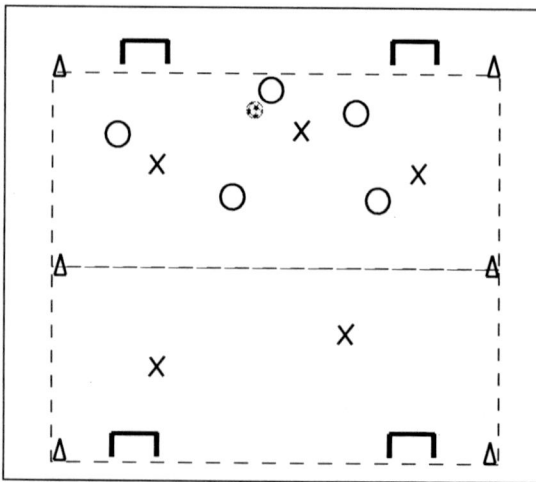

Figure 4-18. Two box possession

❑ Game
- Play 6v6 to 8v8 and for the first eight to 10 minutes continue to correct.
- Allow free play for the last 10 minutes or go to a controlled scrimmage for 20 minutes.

Practice Week #5—Striking/Finishing

Finishing with the Feet

❑ Warm-Up
- Striking progression: Players should be in groups of three. The player with the ball starts by playing it with the inside of the foot to the other side. After playing to the other side, the player takes the place of the goalie. The player receiving the ball takes one touch to prepare and then puts the ball back through (Figure 4-19).
  ✓ Play with the inside of the foot and pick a corner.
  ✓ Play with the inside of the foot and try to bend the ball.
  ✓ Play with the outside of foot.
  ✓ Play with the instep and drive with accuracy.

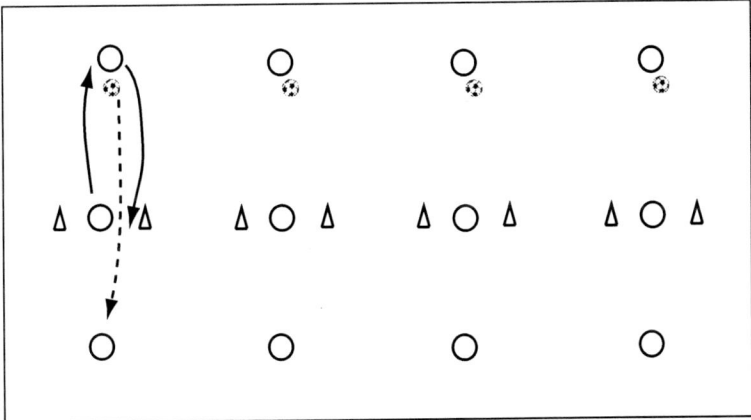

Figure 4-19. Finishing with the feet—warm-up

❑ Main Session
- 1v1v1: This game is played within the box and runs for two minutes. The idea is to take half chances. In other words, players shouldn't wait until they have a "perfect" opening for a shot. They should take shots when they have any opportunity—even if they only have a "half chance" of making one. Players should utilize the various parts of the foot to get a shot off. Play four to five games.
- 3v3 in the box: This is a high-intensity game that should last four minutes. The team of three must play to the neutral player or coach on the flank for a serve into the box. Play three to four games.
- 4v2–4v2: Each team must have four players in their attacking half and two players in the defending half. Each grid is 30 x 40 yards. The idea is to force players to look for good shots first and then pass. Play for 10 minutes.

- ❑ Game
  - Play 8v8 to 11v11.
  - All out-of-bounds plays call for a quick restart from a corner kick.

Sample Week for High School

Monday—Technical Day

- Emphasize individual techniques.
- Have players perform 120s or sprint recovery runs at end of practice.

Tuesday

- Develop small-sided games to build offense.
- Review Monday's technical topic.
- Add in tactical implications of Monday's technical topic.
- Make sure practice is taught in the part of the field that the technique is used most often. For example, don't teach 1v1 attacking in front of your own goal using defenders.

Wednesday

- Continue the topic by adding more numbers and addressing each third of the field in terms of how you will play your next game.

Thursday—Shadow Play

- Run through any game series you have developed.
- Shadow play should give you a framework for:
  - ✓ Playing out of the back down the same/one side
  - ✓ Playing down the middle of the field
  - ✓ Playing out of the back starting on one side and switching your point of attack

Friday—Set Pieces

- Go over any set pieces (e.g., corner kick plays, free kick plays)
- Review shadow play.
- Perform a walk-through.
- Perform fun drills that emphasize finishing.

Saturday

- Saturday is game day.

Other Practice Concerns

First Game Preparation

As you prepare for your first game, explain to your less experienced players the substitution procedures and other rules. Practice these things during an intrasquad scrimmage with officials and a clock. This step will help eliminate confusion on game day.

Communication

Ongoing, clear communication must be present during the game. Emphasize it in practice so it becomes second nature in a game situation. Lack of communication is unacceptable.

5

Offensive Strategy

Basic Offensive Principles

The best attacking teams do a great job of spreading their opponent to create seams or gaps through which they can attack or penetrate. This can be done by maintaining a good attacking shape, methodically moving the ball to isolate and outnumber a defender or a group of defenders, or by attacking quickly to find gaps during transition from defense to offense.

The best way to think about the attacking side of the ball is to understand that you must attack and penetrate the gaps between defenders when you are presented with the opportunity. The ability of your team to create width and height on the field to pull apart the defense is dictated partly by the system of play you choose (Chapter 8), the type of style you adopt (direct or indirect), the ability to recognize quick passing combinations (Chapter 4), and most importantly the speed with which your team recognizes the gaps to penetrate. It's essential that you begin to teach shape and space—to maximize your team's ability to pull apart the defending team—as well as the two styles of play and the offensive principles within in each third of the field.

Individual Offensive Roles

First Person Offense—The Person with the Ball

The role of the person with the ball is to first look to penetrate or attack a gap in the defense.

- Shooting—If the team is in the attacking third of the field, the player with the ball should look to see if he has a shot.
- Passing—If no shot is available, he should look for a pass that will lead to a shot (in the attacking third) or a better opportunity to penetrate.
- Dribbling—If no pass is available, he should check for space to dribble into to create a shooting or passing opportunity (in the attacking third). In your defensive end of the field, dribbling is risky because of the chance of losing the ball.
- Passing/dribbling to maintain possession—If no opportunities to penetrate exist, the player with the ball should dribble or complete a safe pass to allow your team to maintain possession.

Second Person Offense—Support

The second person offense consists of players who are fairly close to the player with the ball (10 to 15 yards).
- They must make themselves available to receive a pass, complete a passing combination, or look to make a penetrating run.
- They should also be available as a possession alternative and to support in front of or behind the player with the ball.
- They can help create space for the third person to run into.

Third Person Offense—Penetrate and Pull Apart

The third person offense consists of the players located further away from the player with the ball.
- The primary role of these players is to make forward penetrating runs into space.
- Their goal is to create space by pulling defenders away from the player with the ball by their movements (runs forward or balancing shape by getting out to the touchlines and providing width).

Once your athletes understand these three roles, shape and space become easier to teach.

Shape and Space

Basic 4v4

The game of 4v4 is ideal for teaching basic shape and space because four is the smallest number that allows a team to provide width, height, and depth. The basic shape adopted in 4v4 should be a diamond to allow for all three directions to be available as shown in Figure 5-1.

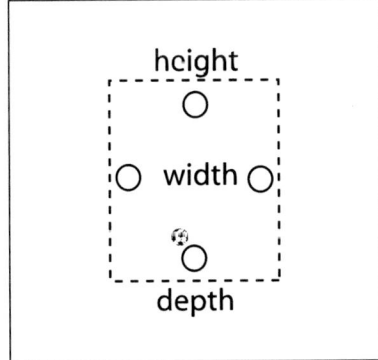

Figure 5-1. Basic shape of 4v4

❏ Roles in 4v4
- The bottom of the diamond gives support in the direction of the ball.
- The players on the side are responsible for
    ✓ Getting wide and creating width on the side of the ball

    ✓ Looking for penetrating runs
    ✓ Looking to balance shape
- The player at the top is creating space by staying high/far up the field.

After teaching the basic roles in a diamond shape, you can then extrapolate these into you system of play in regular game-play, pointing out the diamond shapes created as the ball is passed from player to player in the system.

Direct Play vs. Indirect Play

Direct Play

Direct play is characterized by playing a safe ball as far up the field as possible while still maintaining possession. This is most evident in teams who like to counterattack quickly when they win the ball.

Indirect Play

Indirect play is characterized by teams that use short passes and that look to push forward but will go anywhere to maintain possession. You will see this in teams who like to start their offensive possession with their defensive backs and build from the back forward into the midfield and then into the attacking third as they look for gaps to attack in the defense.

Offensive Principles Within Each Third of the Field

Defensive Third

First Attacker

- Looks to pass to maintain possession
- Does not dribble if under pressure
- Plays a long ball over pressure if no other options exist

Second Attacker

- Supports behind the ball in a conservative position, which allows for:
    ✓ Receiving a ball to maintain possession
    ✓ Being in good defensive position if the first attacker loses possession
    ✓ Supports in front of the ball within gaps between defenders

Third Attacker

- When on the side with the ball
    ✓ Creates width if possible
    ✓ Stays high, then checks toward the first attacker for a ball passed to his feet
    ✓ Looks for a long ball over the top of the pressure

- When on the side without the ball (weakside)
  - ✓ Balances back to be ready to create width if the point of attack switches from one side to the other
  - ✓ Looks for penetrating runs on a switch from one side to the other

Middle Third

First Attacker

- Looks to penetrate with the pass
  - ✓ Looks to dribble to create a chance to pass if space is available, taking some risks if necessary
  - ✓ Dribbles to penetrate
  - ✓ Passes to maintain possession
  - ✓ Dribbles to maintain possession

Second Attacker

- Supports behind the ball in a conservative position. which allows him to:
  - ✓ Receive a ball to maintain possession
  - ✓ Be in good defensive position if the first attacker loses possession
- Supports in front of the ball
  - ✓ To create opportunities to attack a defender with a combination pass
  - ✓ To receive a ball in a gap between two defenders

Third Attacker

- When on the side with the ball
  - ✓ Looks for diagonal or bent penetrating run
  - ✓ Creates width if possible
- When on the side without the ball (weakside)
  - ✓ Looks for penetrating runs on a switch from one side to the other
  - ✓ Balances back to be ready to create width if the point of attack switches from one side to the other

Attacking Third

First Attacker

- Looks to shoot
- Looks to penetrate with the pass
- Looks to dribble to create a chance to shoot if space is available, taking risks if necessary
- Dribbles to penetrate and pass for an opportunity to shoot
- Passes to maintain possession
- Dribbles to maintain possession

Second Attacker

- Supports behind the ball in a position that allows for
  - ✓ Receiving a ball to shoot
  - ✓ Receiving the ball to maintain possession
- Supports in front of the ball
  - ✓ To receive a pass for a first touch shot
  - ✓ To create opportunities to attack a defender with a combination pass
  - ✓ To maintain possession

Third Attacker

- When on the side with the ball
  - ✓ Looks for diagonal or bent penetrating run leading to a shot
  - ✓ Creates width if possible
  - ✓ Makes a run to open space by pulling a defender with him
- When on the side without the ball (weakside)
  - ✓ Looks for penetrating runs on a switch from one side to the other for the creation of a shot
  - ✓ Balances back to be ready to create width if the point of attack switches from one side to the other or if possession is lost

6

Set Pieces

Set pieces include direct and indirect free kicks, corner kicks and throw-ins. In a sport in which goals are traditionally hard to come by, set pieces offer a wonderful opportunity for your team to dictate scoring opportunities within designed plays.

- Corner kicks (Figures 6-1 through 6-3)
- Throw-in play from anywhere on the field (Figure 6-4)
- Throw-in play from the attacking third (Figure 6-5)
- Goal kick playing out of the back (Figure 6-6)
- Kickoff (Figure 6-7)
- Indirect free kicks (Figures 6-8 and 6-9)

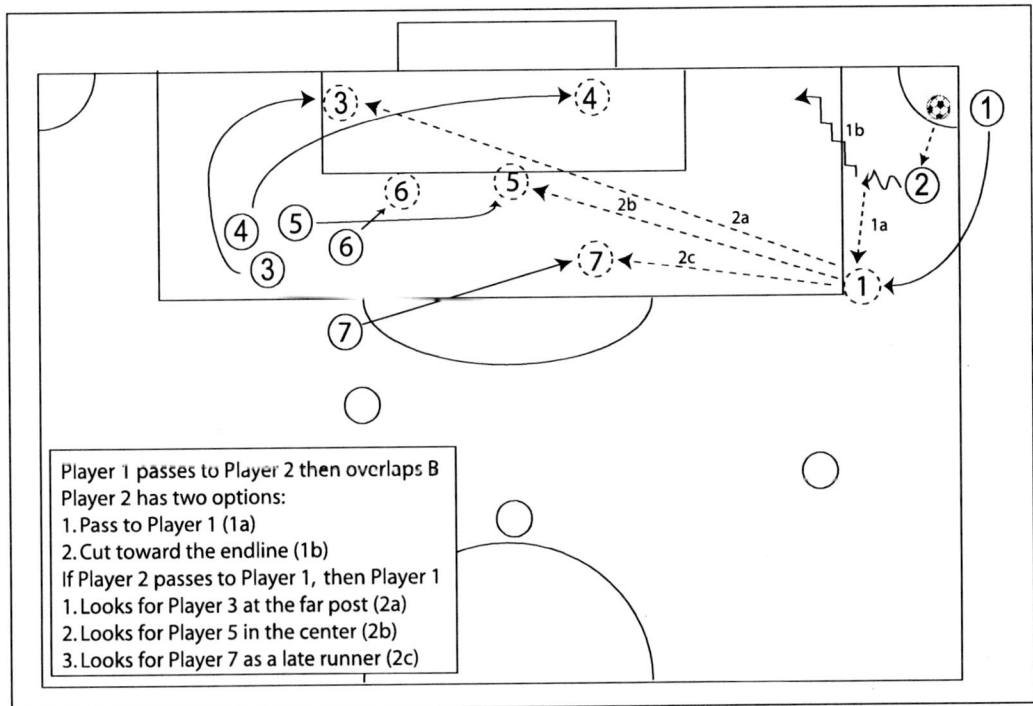

Figure 6-1. Corner kick #1

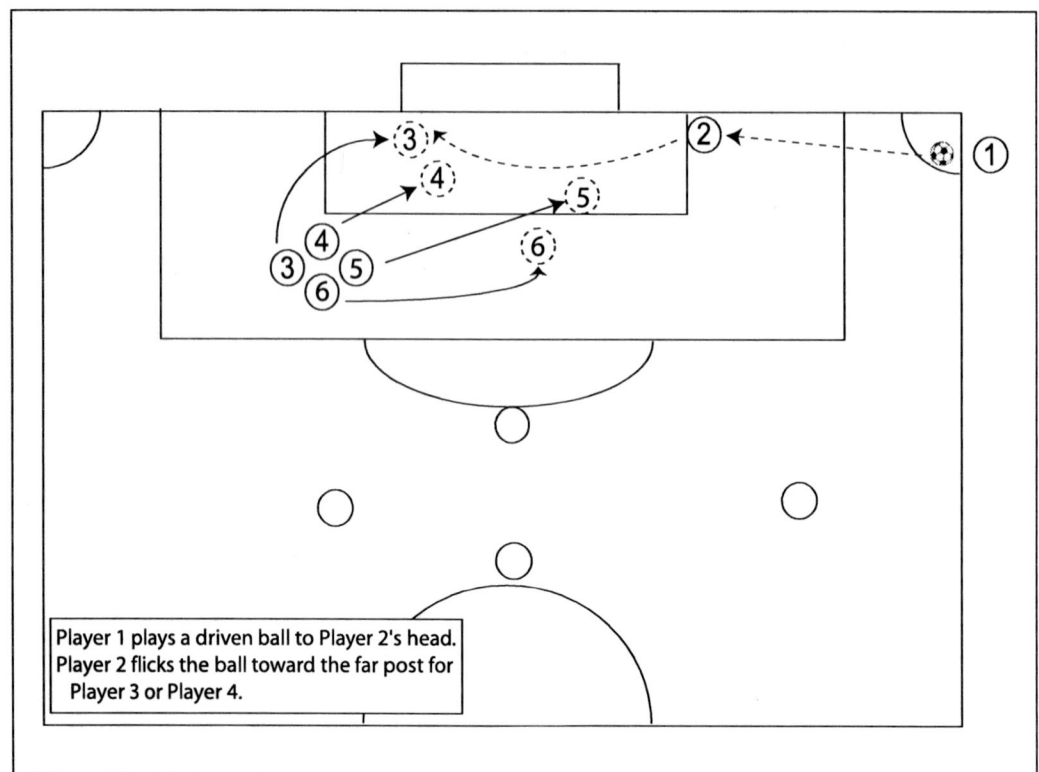

Figure 6-2. Corner kick #2

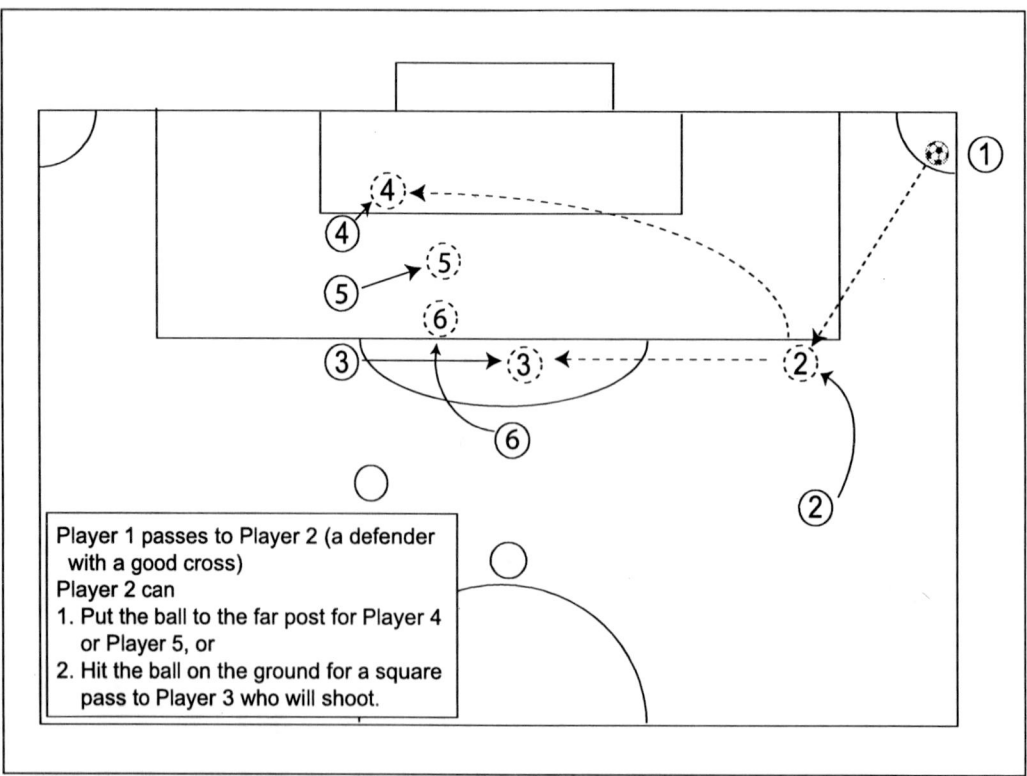

Figure 6-3. Corner kick #3

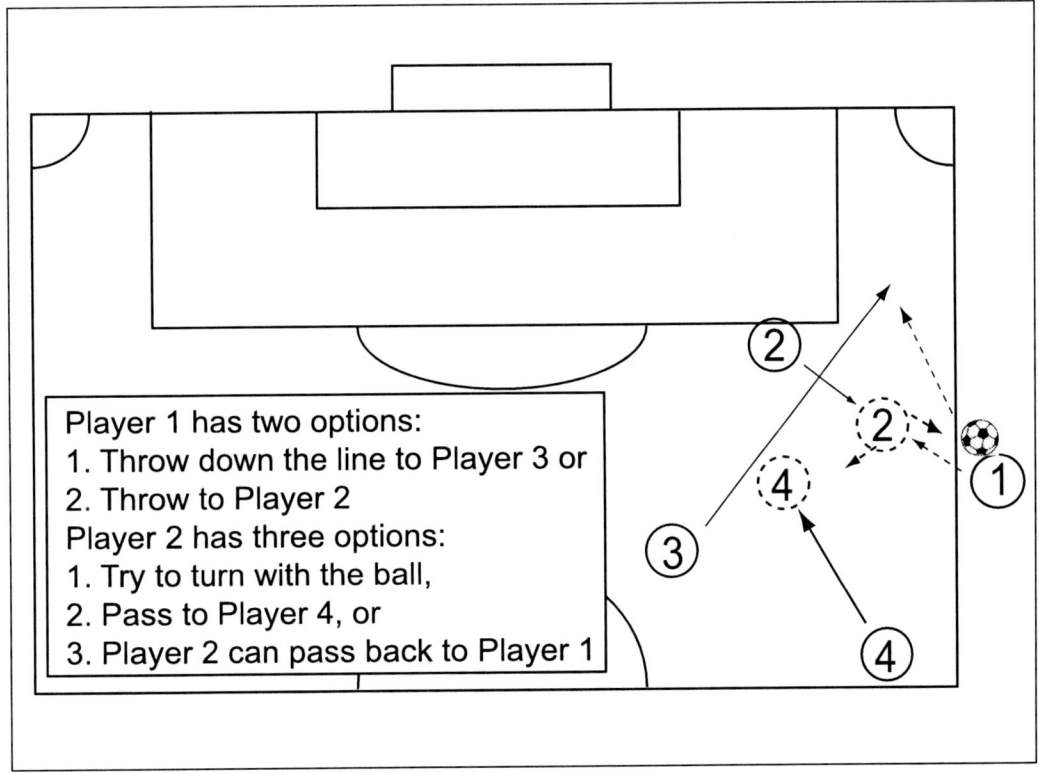

Figure 6-4. Throw-in from anywhere on the field

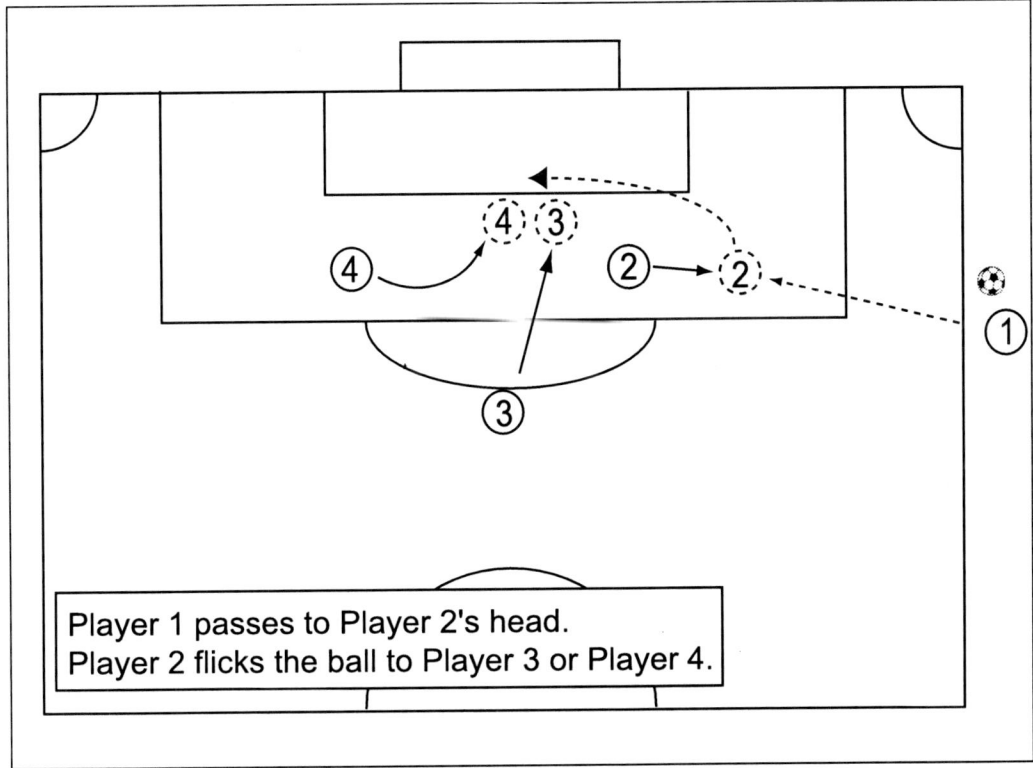

Figure 6-5. Throw-in from the attacking third

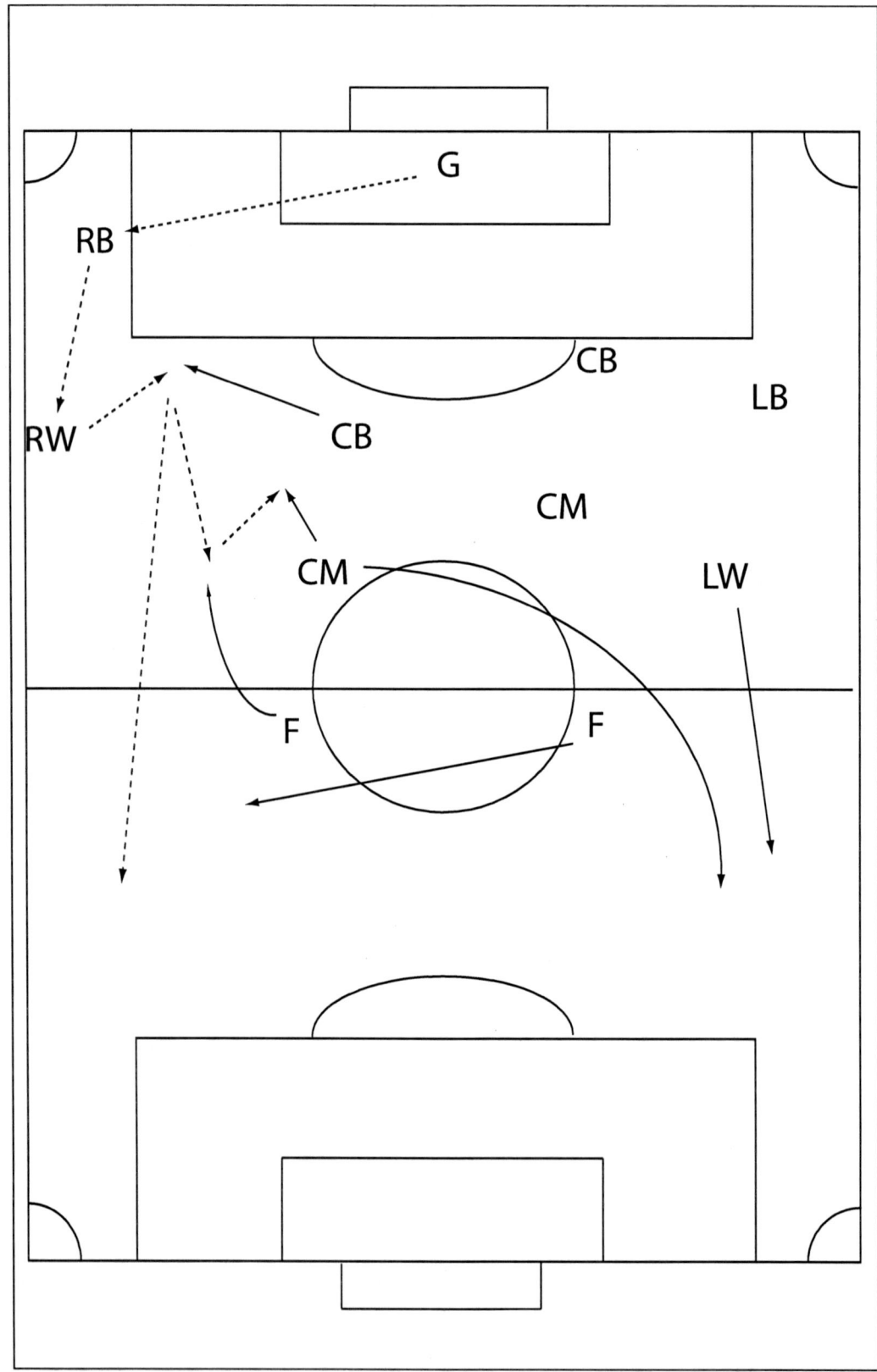

Figure 6-6. Goal kick

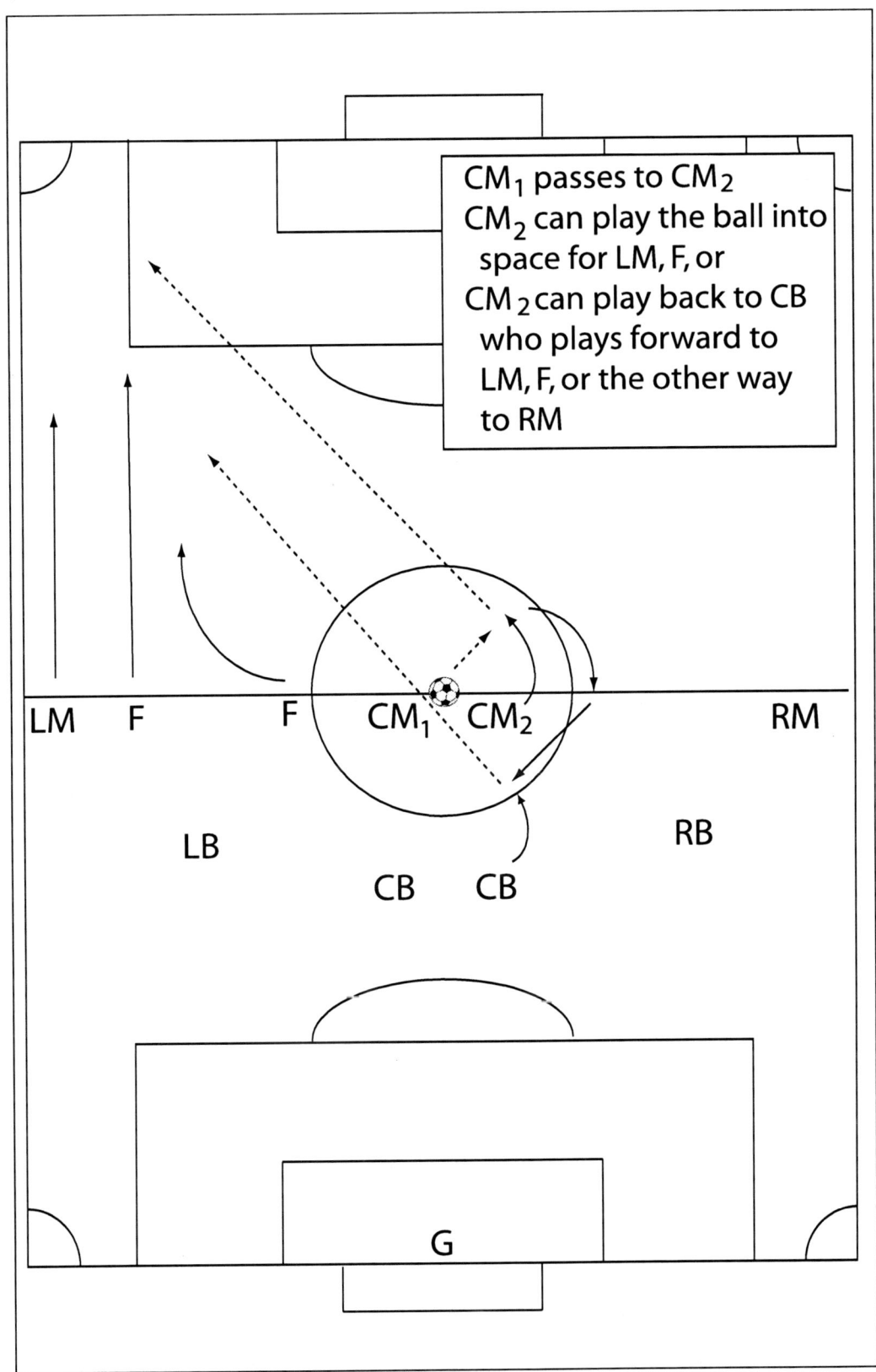

Figure 6-7. Kickoff

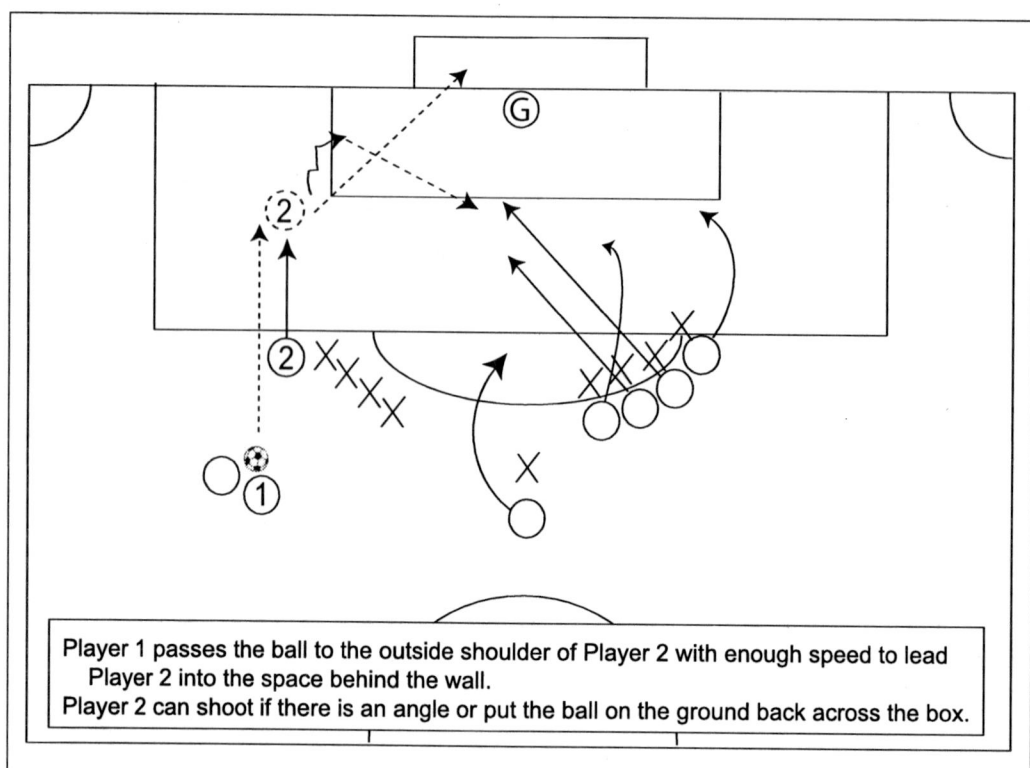

Figure 6-8. Indirect free kick #1

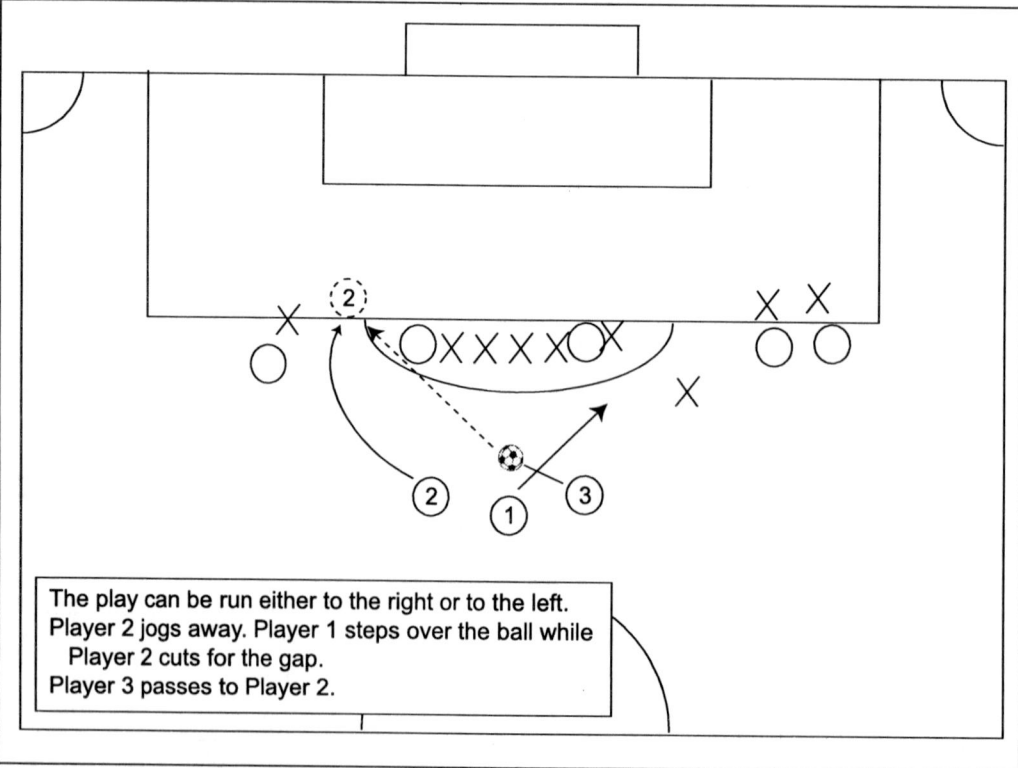

Figure 6-9. Indirect free kick #2

7

Defensive Strategy

Basic Principles of Defense

The basic principles of defense are pressure, cover, and balance. The idea of any defense is to limit the amount of space your opposition has to work in and the amount of time they have to make good decisions with the ball at their feet.

First Person Defense—Pressure

Pressure on the ball is the responsibility of the closest defender to the ball. The player applying pressure on the ball has the following responsibilities:
- Delaying—Forcing the player with the ball to slow down and/or turn back
- Making the play predictable by trying to force the player with the ball to go one way
- Denying any penetrating pass
- Tackling and winning possession when able to do so successfully

Second Person Defense—Cover

This player is positioned eight to 15 yards off the inside shoulder of the defender who is applying pressure. His responsibilities include:
- Helping make the play predictable by taking a good support angle to deny penetrating passes
- Maintaining the gap between the supporting position and the player applying pressure. The closer the offensive team is to your goal, the smaller that gap should be. This condensing of space is called compactness
- Balance out the defensive shape by denying passing lanes

Third Person Defense—Balance

This player's main responsibility is to maintain depth and balance by reading if the player with the ball is about to play a long ball behind the defense. Other responsibilities include:
- Reading if the point of attack is going to be changed
- Tracking players who run forward
- Trying to take away space by anticipating and stepping into passing lanes

Defensive Principles Within Each Third of the Field

Defensive Third

First Defender

- Approaches cautiously
- Channels or forces the offensive player to become predictable by pushing them outside toward the touchline or inside toward a support defender
- If tackling, always wins the ball

Second Defender

- Maintains very compact support. This means that the closer the offensive player is to the goal, the less space should be present between the first defender and the second defender.
- Maintains an angle of support that is flatter (less than 45 degrees)
- Utilizes verbal communication, which is extremely important so the first defender knows where the support is

Third Defender

- Balances back to eliminate weakside space or passing lanes
- Marks any runners going forward, especially in the box

Middle Third

First Defender

- Denies and force the offense into predictable spaces (toward the touchline or into a double-team)
- Approaches faster
- Tackles when an offensive player makes a mistake

Second Defender

- Provides support that is deeper (45 degrees)
- Provides support on both sides
- Communicates to the first defender about which direction he should force the attacker

Third Defender

- Balances shape by taking away longer passes
- Plays in space to eliminate passing lanes
- Is a little more aggressive in trying to intercept passes

Offensive Third

First Defender

- Takes a fast approach to pressure
- Takes risks in tackling

Second Defender

- Provides flatter support
- Looks to intercept passes even if he must take risks
- Communicates with first defender

Third Defender

- Reads passes
- Risks stepping up to intercept longer passes

The defensive principles within each third of the field are illustrated in Figure 7-1.

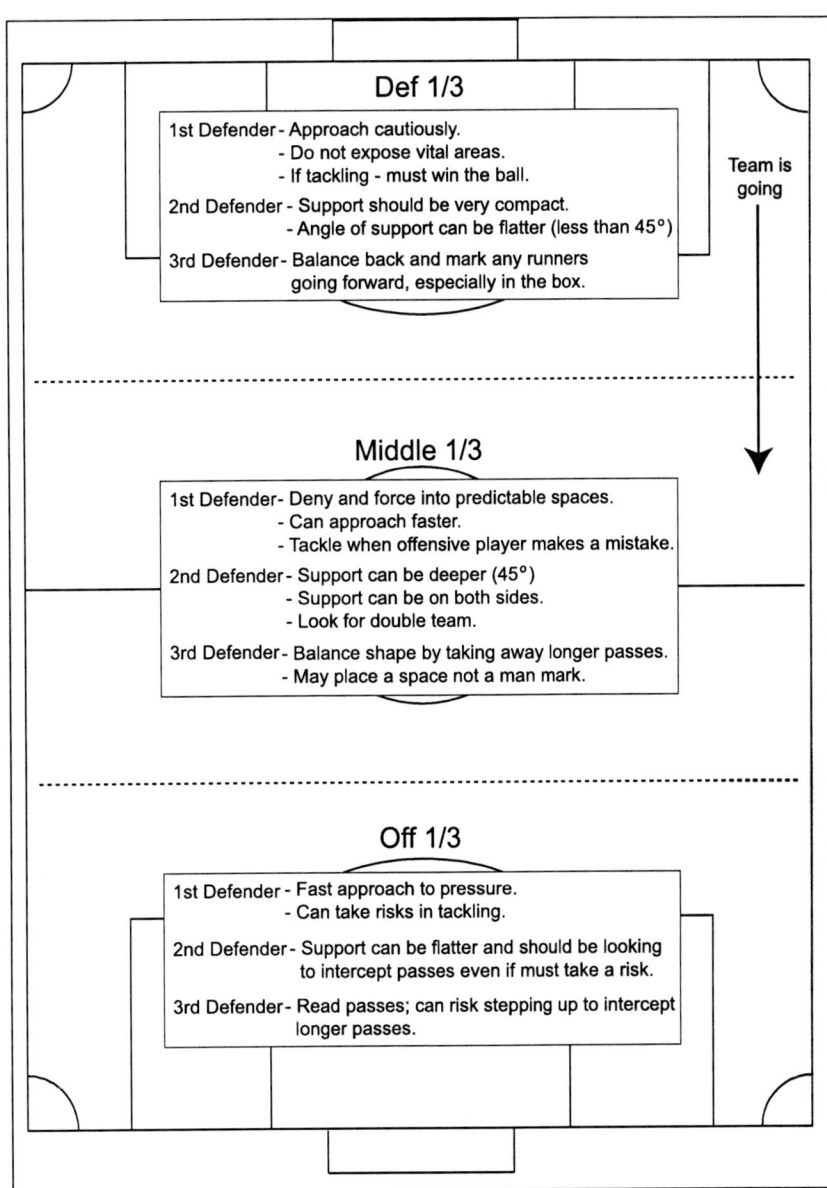

Figure 7-1. Defensive principles within thirds

8

Systems of Play

Regardless of the system of play you choose, it will only be successful if you have athletes who can remember what to do and have mastered the basic fundamentals, including dribbling, passing, creating space, keeping shape, finishing, and applying pressure.

When determining which system to choose, ask yourself the following questions:
- What are your team's strengths and weaknesses?
- What system does your opponent use?
- What are the weather conditions?

While not an exhaustive list of potential issues, these questions should give you an idea of where to start. The truth is that players win games—not systems of play—and it's hard to use a particular system if you don't have the right mix of players. This chapter will give you the advantages and disadvantages of each system.

1-3-5-2

Description

This popular system is used by a number of professional and national teams (Figure 8-1). It efficiently utilizes increased numbers in the midfield, thereby allowing your team to control the middle of the park.

Advantages

- Two players remain up top for attacking combinations.
- Five players in the midfield will give you a numerical advantage over opponents in other systems such as the 1-4-4-2 and the 1-4-3-3. Possession is often won or lost in the middle, so an advantage in this area often will dictate the flow of the game.

Disadvantage

- Having only three players in the back leaves a large amount of space to cover defensively, which can be a problem against teams that play more direct down the flanks or look for long, driven diagonal passes.

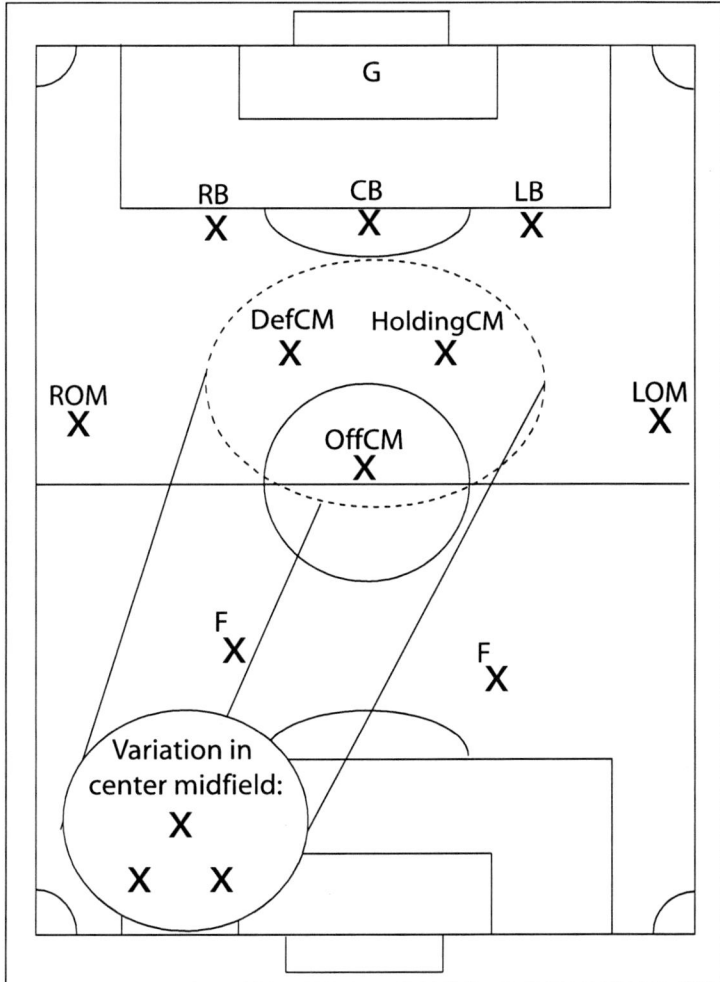

Figure 8-1. 1-3-5-2

Attacking

When you play out of the back, the outside midfielders give your team width. This system lends itself to playing balls through the midfield in a short-pass, indirect style of play.

Defending

Usually a flat three zone is employed, or you can utilize two man markers and a sweeper balanced by the outside midfielder on the weak side.

1-4-4-2

Description

This very popular and versatile formation is easy to teach because each side is a mirror image of the other (Figure 8-2). Therefore, the roles of a left back are the same as those for a right back. This system is good for balancing numbers, which can easily attack or defend.

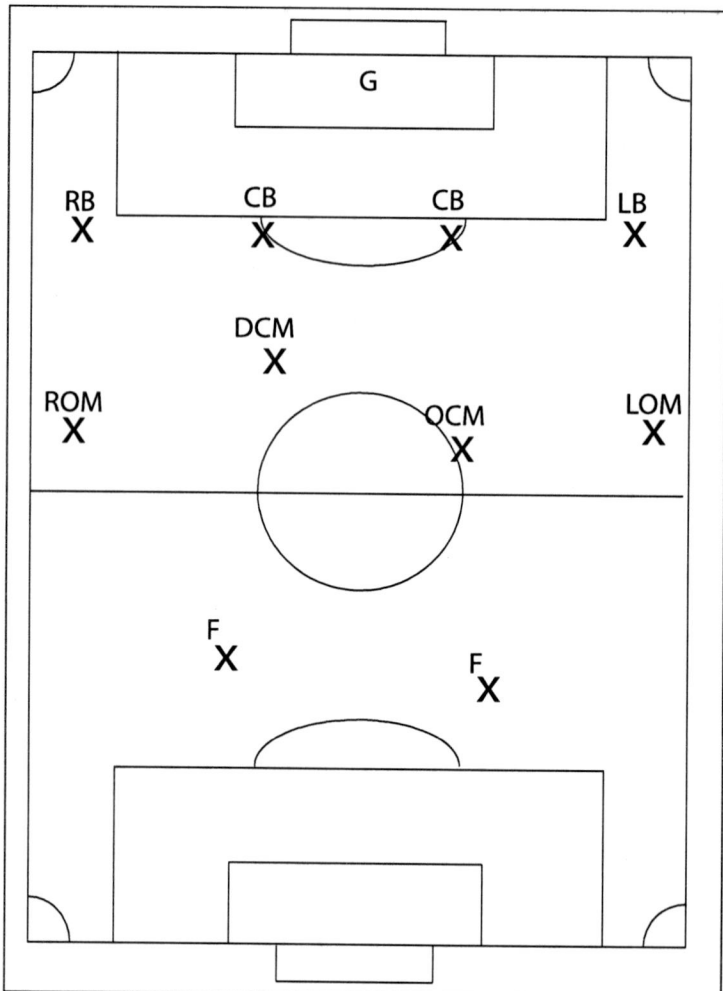

Figure 8-2. 1-4-4-2

Advantages

- This mirror-image system makes it easy for players to switch positions from one side to the other and still be effective.
- This system is balanced defensively.
- A team using this system will always have adequate numbers in defense.

Disadvantages

- It can sometimes be hard to get enough players forward into the penalty box if the forward consistently receives the ball down in the corners.
- This system may allow other 1-4-4-2 teams to push a defender into the attack to gain a numerical advantage in midfield and leave the remaining three defenders to mark (guard) your two forwards.

Attacking

When attacking, the outside midfielder creates the width in the attacking half and outside backs create width in the defending half. This system takes advantage of the four backs, as the outside backs can step into the attack by receiving balls on overlaps or start the attack by receiving a ball from the other side in a quick switch.

Defending

A zonal flat four or a stopper/sweeper is usually used, which gives a numerical superiority in the back over systems that have two to three forwards. Midfielders must follow any mark running toward the goal and pass off any runners going across the field.

1-4-3-3

Description

This system of play is easy to teach because the basic 4v4 shape is prevalent throughout (Figure 8-3). It permits the use of a sweeper and a designated striker. The two outside attackers can be withdrawn back to the position of wingers, thus packing in defensively. They also can remain up higher on the field to create more attacking opportunities.

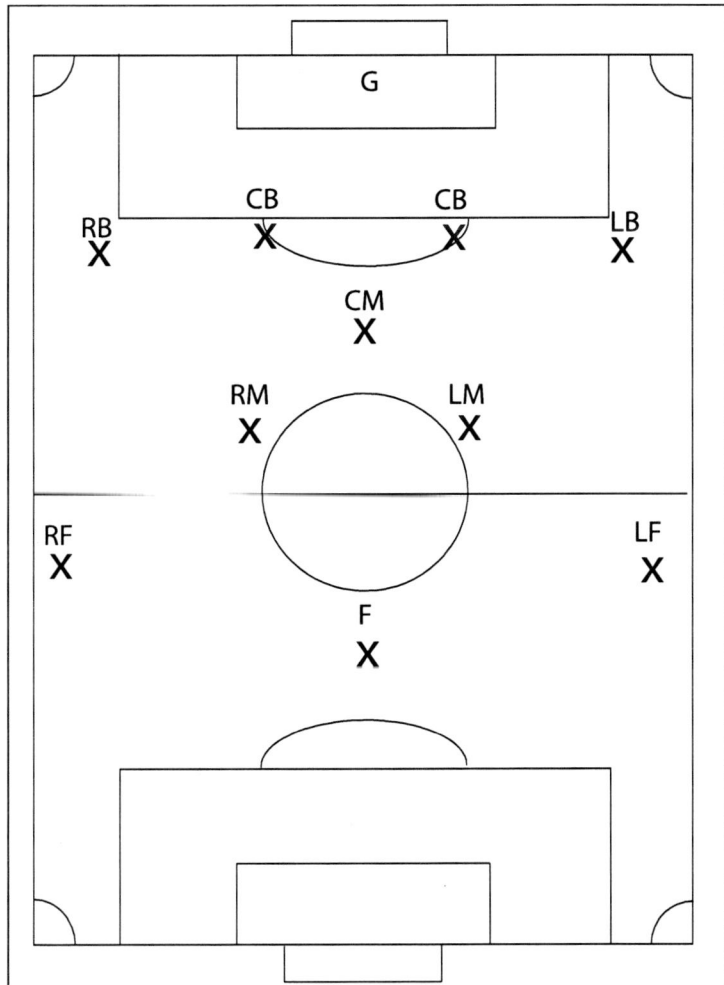

Figure 8-3. 1-4-3-3

Advantages

- This system allows for increased numbers in attack.
- The team can still maintain four in the back to organize defensively.
- This system allows for high pressure on other teams' defense by pushing three forwards up on their four defenders, as opposed to systems with only two forwards.

Disadvantages

- Your team will be outnumbered in the midfield against most systems.
- If the front three do not pressure the defensive backs and allow easy services, then your team will be exposed more easily in the midfield and may experience more stress in the defensive third.
- One good serve from the backs to the midfielders by the opposing team will bypass your three attackers and could leave you defending with inferior numbers.

Attacking

This system offers the ability to set your width higher, as the outside/wing forwards create the width. Balls may be played forward in a more direct method. Midfielders are the supporting links between forwards and defenders.

Defending

In this system, your team will still have superiority in numbers in the back. Midfielders must support on the inside toward the goal while staying pinched in. Forwards must put pressure on other teams' defenders and not allow them to serve long balls. Forwards must also pressure back and look for double-team opportunities along the touchline.

1-3-4-3

Description

This classic formation balances all players evenly across the field (Figure 8-4). A typical center striker must be utilized with this formation. In defense, the three fullbacks have to be supported by the midfield with at least one defensive midfielder helping in the center and an outside midfielder covering the weakside.

Advantages

- This system allows you to attack with three players and still maintain numerical superiority in the back against a team with two forwards.
- Your team is able to match teams in midfield if they play a traditional system.
- This system gives you the ability to get more players forward.

Disadvantages

- Three forwards must pressure the defender up top or you are very vulnerable to quick counters and long diagonal balls.

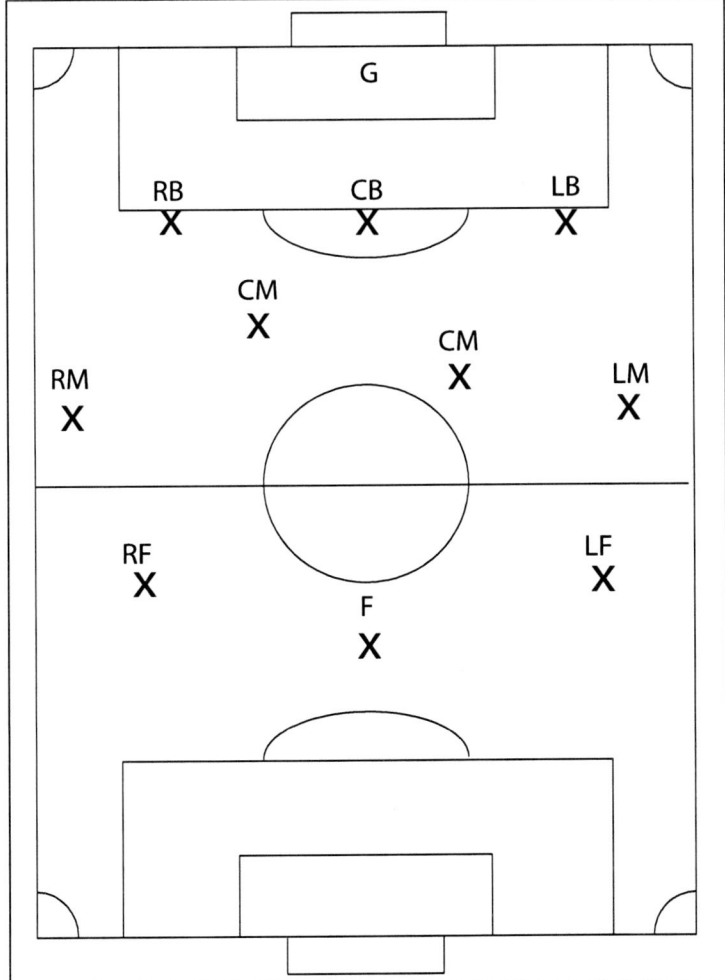

Figure 8-4. 1-3-4-3

- Your team can get caught with numbers down in the defending third or be forced to mark players 1v1 if you are playing a team in a 4-3-3 with their three forwards playing against your three defenders.

Attacking

This system offers the ability to attack with seven players and defend with seven players. The midfielders provide width in the defending half, with your forwards reforming that width in the attacking third. Your team can play through the midfield or be more direct.

Defending

Defending in this system starts with pressure from the forwards. Everyone must track back to maintain numbers, with the outside midfielders balancing the shape on the weak side, similar to the 1-3-5-2 system.

1-4-5-1

Description

This formation crowds nearly all parts of midfield, thereby slowing down enemy attacks (Figure 8-5). From an offensive point of view, the system relies on wing attacks supported by the midfield. The downside is that the lone striker is left on his own up front and may become isolated.

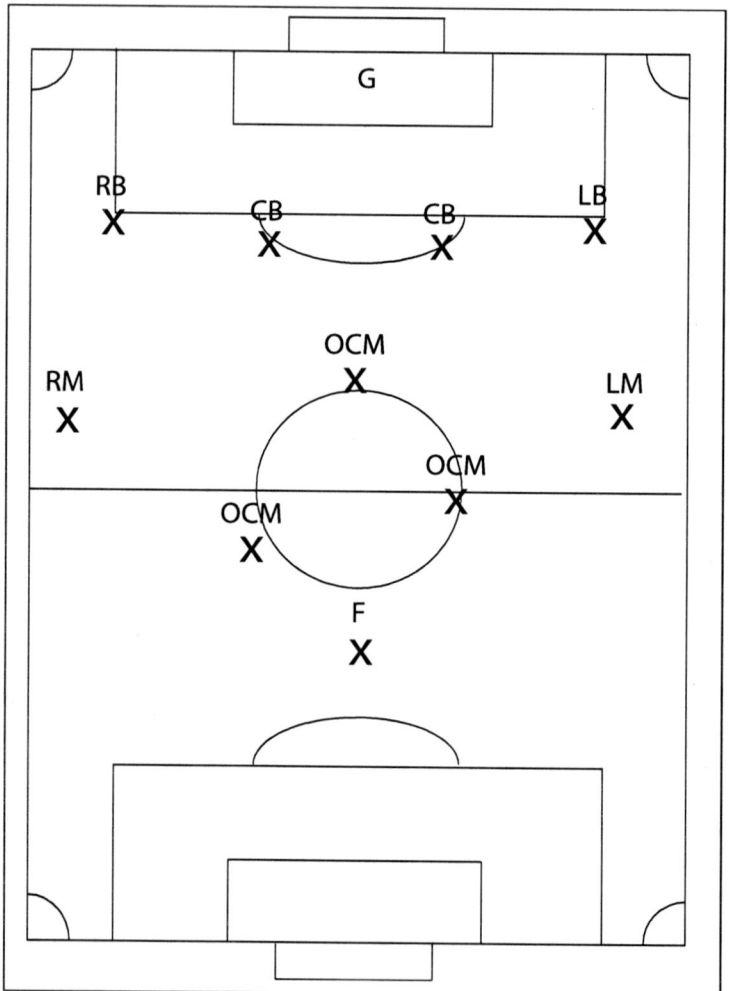

Figure 8-5. 1-4-5-1

Advantages

- This systems allows you to outnumber your opponent in midfield.
- Center midfield penetrating runs are hard for defenders to mark.
- This system allows for many supporting options for the lone striker if the midfield stays connected.
- This system provides numbers behind the ball.

Disadvantages

- The lone striker may be isolated.
- It may be hard to stretch the defense if the lone striker can't provide height.
- It may be hard to attack with numbers.
- This system can become predictable offensively and static defensively.

Attacking

This system enables the team to push center midfield players forward in penetrating runs and utilizes width effectively with five in the midfield. Multiple options can be created for building out of the back.

Defending

The outside midfielders force play into the middle to limit the space used by the opposition. This system is very effective in a low-pressure situation against better teams.

Goalkeeping

Tamara Hageage

Every player and coach who has been involved in soccer for any length of time can recall a game or two when one team dominated the other in terms of possession and out-shot the other team 30 to two but lost the game 1-0. That is soccer, but it is also why a good goalkeeper is a must. A good goalkeeper makes the saves he should make, leads his team defensively with his voice and presence, and doesn't let in too many "soft" goals. A *great* keeper does all of that, but also makes those tough saves that keep your team in the game.

Coaches often overlook the position of goalkeeper because they don't have either the time or expertise to train a goalkeeper correctly, or both. This chapter provides insight into making an average goalkeeper good and a good goalkeeper great, but it is important that you review videos and books dedicated solely to this skill.

Characteristics of the Goalkeeper

A goalkeeper must not only exhibit excellent physical characteristics, but also mental toughness. The characteristics of a quality goalkeeper may include:
- "Good hands," or the ability to catch a ball at all heights and angles
- Quick feet
- Strength
- Great vision and awareness
- Fearlessness
- Leadership skills
- An understanding of defensive shape

Goalkeeping Techniques

Footwork

Start every goalkeeping session with footwork. Not only does it warm up the body, but it also helps to develop coordination, balance, and timing.

Coaching Points

Remind your goalkeeper to:
- Focus on balance and coordination
- Get the body behind the ball
- Move toward the ball

Common Mistakes

- Staying back on the heels
- Not keeping the hands in the "ready" position
- Not keeping the head and eyes forward

Angle Play

You can best describe angle play by telling your goalkeeper to visualize lines connecting the posts to the ball. The closer he gets to the ball, the closer those lines get to him.

Coaching Points

Remind your goalkeeper to:
- Know how far he can come out of the goal and still cover the ground behind him
- Know the location of the goalposts

Common Mistakes

- Standing inside the near post on sharp, angled shots
- Standing on the goal line

Catching

Having soft hands is the key to success. If the keeper has rigid hands, he will push the ball away and not be able to hold on to it. The following four techniques should be taught.

The "Scoop"

The goalkeeper should have his fingers spread with the pinkie fingers almost touching. He should come from behind the ball. If it is an easy ball to handle, he can bend at the waist. His legs only need to be close enough together so that the ball cannot fit through. If his legs are tight together, balance and mobility will greatly suffer. If it is a difficult ball or weather conditions are bad, he should kneel flat so that the knee of the leg furthest from the ball almost touches the heel of the foot closest to the ball. By doing this, all gaps between the legs will be covered. In both techniques, he should always step through, come forward, and safely tuck the ball away in his arms.

The "Tuck"

When using this technique, the goalkeeper needs to keep his legs apart for balance. He should receive the ball with outstretched arms and cushion it by bending over. His head should be over the ball and his elbows should be as close together as possible.

Catching the Ball at Chest Height

Make sure the keeper meets, cushions, and tucks the ball.

Catching the Ball Above the Head

The keeper should catch the ball at the highest point and keep it in front of him so that he can always see it. His wrists should be slightly bent, so that the ball will fall in front of him if he cannot hold onto it, which gives him a second chance to gain possession.

Common Mistakes

- Waiting on the ball rather than getting the hands out to it first
- Trying to snatch at the ball instead of receiving it
- Using poor hand placement or technique

Diving

The keeper should land on his side and be sure the top hand is on top of the ball and the bottom hand is behind the ball. Stress the importance of letting the ball hit the ground first to cushion the fall and using the ground as a third hand.

Coaching Points

Remind your goalkeeper to:
- Get into position using good footwork
- Stay square to the shooter
- Catch the ball with the hands
- Land on the side
- Use the ball to cushion the fall

Common Mistakes

- Landing on the elbows
- Landing on the stomach
- Landing on the back

Throw Distribution

For all throws, the goalkeeper should step in the direction that he is throwing and bring his back leg forward as his arm comes around and he releases the ball. By doing this, he will maintain better balance and his throws will be more accurate. Make sure he gets her whole body behind the ball and does not throw just with his arm.

Coaching Points

Make sure your goalkeeper understands the characteristics and techniques of each type of throw:
- Roll: most accurate, but provides the least distance
- Javelin throw: medium accuracy and distance
- Sidearm throw: medium accuracy and distance
- Overhand throw: least accurate, most provides the most distance
- Javelin throw: starts from beside the head
- Overhand throw: must keep the hand on top and the elbow locked
- Javelin and overhand throws: roll the fingers under the ball at the end of the throw to provide backspin

Common Mistakes

- The ball drops from the hand to the ground on a roll
- High, arcing throws that are difficult to receive
- On an overhand throw, the elbow is not locked or bends halfway though the throw
- Poor release point on overhand throws
- Poor follow-through

Kick Distribution

Punting, drop-kicking, and goal kicks can be the first point of attack. Thus, they should be trained often. Repetition is the key. Have the goalkeepers practice six to 10 of each kick after practice.

Coaching Points

Remind your goalkeeper to:
- Step into the kick at a slight angle
- Point the plant foot toward the target
- Release the ball without spin when punting or drop-kicking
- Follow through

Common Mistakes

- Tossing the ball in the air when trying to punt or drop-kick
- Allowing the kicking foot to swing around the body instead of straight
- Following through poorly
- Not striking the center of the ball

Basic Communication Skills Required for the Goalkeeper

The secrets to good goalkeeper communication are simplicity and specificity. For example, "Doug, pick up eight on left." The action in a game moves quickly and leaves little time for complete sentences. Have your goalkeeper work out his choice of words with the defense to make sure they understand exactly what he means. For example, the command "contain" could be given to the defender covering the opposing player with the ball, and would tell him to hold the player and not to dive in because his covering defender is not there yet.

A goalkeeper's ability to communicate effectively is the most important skill he can possess. If your keeper can verbally direct the defense to deny all scoring opportunities, he will not have to make any heart-stopping saves. A goalkeeper needs to communicate with his defense because he has the best view of the field. One of the goalkeeper's most important responsibilities is to give helpful information and direction. The goalkeeper's voice should provide a sense of confidence and comfort to the players in the defensive third. The ability to be a strong leader and communicator to stop goal-scoring opportunities before they are a serious threat on goal *is* great goalkeeping.

Training Focal Points for Goalkeepers

Several focal points require emphasis at different levels of play. These training focal points can be broken down into three categories: beginner, intermediate, and advanced. Once a goalkeeper can perform the techniques in one category, he can advance to the next level.

Beginner

Fitness

- Flexibility
- Upper- and lower-body strength
- Midsection strength
- Coordination (balance, orientation, reactions, rhythm, and footwork)

Technique

- Competent field skills training
- Catching/receiving balls high and low
- Basic positions and angle play
- Diving for low balls
- Distribution: punting, throwing, and bowling
- Safely dealing with a one vs. one

Training Tactics

When working with a goalkeeper at the beginner level, you should:
- Build confidence through safe technique
- Correct only major mistakes
- Avoid dwelling on details
- Train basic communication such as "keeper," "away," and "man-on"
- Help develop a love for the position

Intermediate

Fitness

- Continued focus on beginner-level fitness
- Jumping power and speed
- Aerobic endurance

Technique

- Continued focus on beginner-level skills
- Tipping over the crossbar
- Boxing and catching crosses
- Distribution: goal kick and dropkick
- Dealing with the back pass
- Power diving and diving forward

Training Tactics

When working with a goalkeeper at the intermediate level, you should:
- Help him improve on all skills listed in beginner section
- Teach better communication for leadership and better understanding of defensive shape
- Train him to become the first line of attack and make better distribution decisions
- Prepare him to maintain mental focus for the entire 90 minutes
- Encourage him to accept the responsibility of the position

Advanced

Fitness

- Continued focus on beginner- and intermediate-level fitness.
- Maximum aerobic fitness

Technique

- Continued focus on beginner- and intermediate-level skills
- Realistic practices—continue perfecting all techniques

Training Tactics

When working with a goalkeeper at the advanced level, you should:
- Help him improve on the skills listed in the beginner and intermediate sections, but at a more intense level (when age-appropriate)
- Stress the importance of details
- Train technical and tactical situations together

Drills

Jumping

Set-up: Place eight to 10 cones about one yard apart in a line

Directions: Have the goalkeeper hop over each cone with his legs together, using his arms to propel the body into the air. He should land softly on the balls of his feet, which will enable him to quickly jump again without taking any extra small jumps between cones. Emphasize the height of his vertical jump, not how quickly he gets through the cones. He must work through the 10 cones three times consecutively.

Variations:
- Have the goalkeeper hop forward over two cones and then backward over one.
- Have the goalkeeper hop over each cone on one leg, making sure he is using not only the arms, but also the nonjumping leg to propel his body in the air.

Pattern

Set-up: Place two cones on the six-yard box, one yard wide of each goal post (Figure 9-1).

Directions: The goalkeeper starts at the right post, square to the field (facing the pitch). On command, he quickly shuffles to the left post, then runs to the right cone, shuffles to the left cone, then backpedals to the right cone. Set a target time to complete the circuit (e.g., 30 seconds). Depending on the keeper's fitness level, he can rest for 30, 60, or 90 seconds between each circuit.

Variations:
- Have the goalkeeper start at the right post, square to the field, but sprint to the left cone, shuffle to the right cone, and then backpedal to the left post.
- Have the goalkeeper start the drill at the left post.

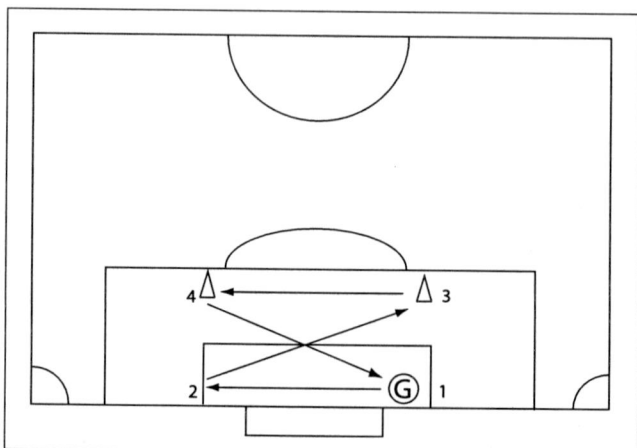

Figure 9-1. Pattern drill

Catching

Set-up: The goalkeeper stands between two servers who are about three yards away. Each server has two balls.

Directions: Using a dropkick or striking the ball from the ground, the servers alternate serves to the goalkeeper. After the goalkeeper saves a shot, he tosses the ball back to the server, and then quickly turns to the other server for the next ball. Each goalkeeper should do four sets of 12 (scoop, tuck, chest height, above the head). Change goalkeepers after each set.

Catching and Footwork

Set-up: Make a small goal with two cones approximately three to five yards wide. A goalkeeper stands in the middle of the small goal just behind the cones while a server stands in front of him with a supply of balls (Figure 9-2).

Directions: The server serves a ball to one side. The goalkeeper quickly shuffles from behind the cone and then around to meet the shot. After a save is made, the keeper should quickly shuffle back to the starting position. As soon as he reaches the middle again, the server can serve the next ball to the other side. All four catching techniques can be used in this exercise (scoop, tuck, chest height, and above the head).

Variation: Have the goalkeeper quickly collect the ball inside the cone (Figure 9-3).

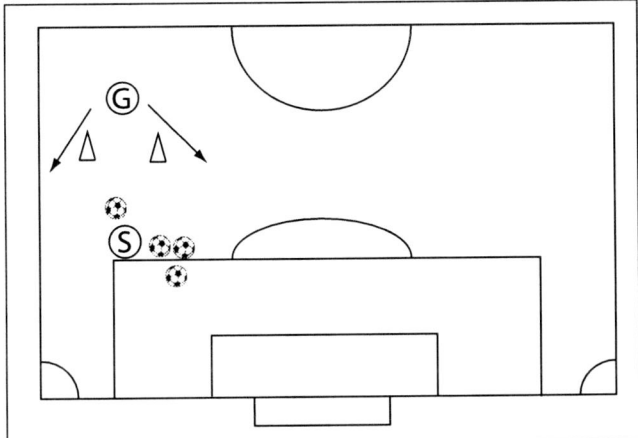
Figure 9-2. Catching and footwork drill

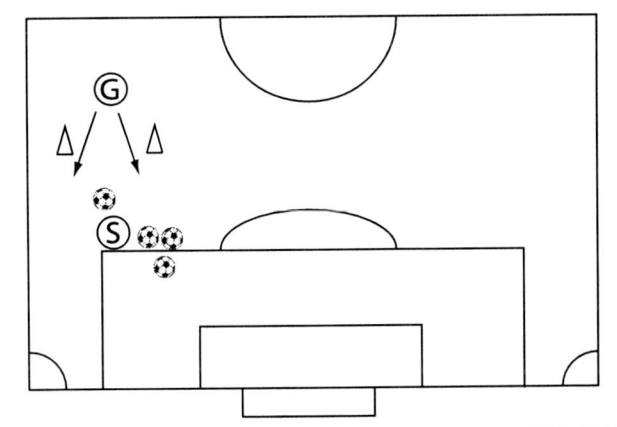
Figure 9-3. Catching and footwork variation

Diving Exercises

Set-up: Place a cone three yards from the near post and three to six yards out from the goal line with a server stationed as illustrated in Figure 9-4.

Directions: The goalkeeper approaches the cone. As soon as he is in front of the cone, the server directs the ball between the near post and the cone. Both low and high diving can be used and goalkeepers should always train from both sides. Use sets of eight to 12 repetitions.

Variations:

- Place the cone three-quarters of the way in from the near post on the goal line. Have the goalkeeper stand facing the corner flag with his shoulder next to the near goal post. On the server's command, have him turn quickly, face the field, and shuffle over to save the shot (Figure 9-5).
- Have the goalkeeper start the drill flat on her stomach with her arms outstretched.

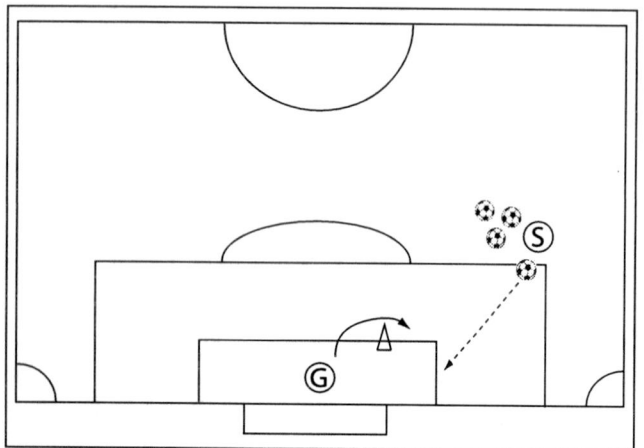

Figure 9-4. Diving exercise

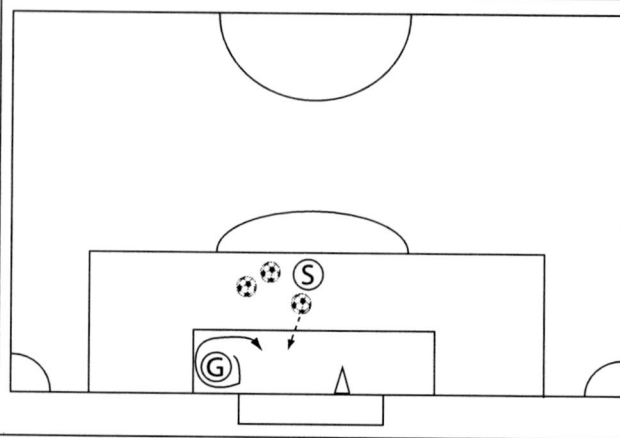

Figure 9-5. Diving exercise variation

Fun Games for Two Goalkeepers

Hot Pepper

Set-up: Have two goalkeepers stand six yards apart with a supply of balls.

Directions: The goalkeepers take turns drop-kicking a ball to each other. The goalkeeper cannot move out of the way of the kick. If the ball touches the goalkeeper and he fails to catch it, the other goalkeeper gets a point. Either play for a predetermined number of drops or for a set amount of time.

Variation: If the goalkeepers have not mastered the dropkick, have them throw the ball to each other instead.

Goalkeeper Wars

Set-up: Place two goals (or four cones) about 18 yards apart with each goalkeeper standing in a goal. Though both goalkeepers should have a supply of balls in their goal, only one goalkeeper starts with a ball in his hands. Divide the grid in half with two cones for the midfield markers.

Directions: Each goalkeeper must stay on his half of the field and can throw, drop-kick, volley, or shoot the ball to score on the other goalkeeper. If a goalkeeper makes a save and the ball is deflected into the other half, he loses possession of the ball and the same goalkeeper gets a second shot. Once a goalkeeper has control of the ball, he must shoot from where he made the save. Play to a predetermined number of goals or for a set amount of time.

Goalkeeper Golf

Set-up: Randomly place nine to 18 cones on the field at different angles and distances. Each goalkeeper has a ball.

Directions: Have each goalkeeper take turns trying to knock down a cone with a throw. Keep track of how many throws it takes to knock down a cone. After the first goalkeeper knocks down the cone, he sets it up for the other goalkeeper. The starting position for each new cone (or "hole") is the previous cone. The goalkeeper with the fewest throws (or "strokes") is the winner.

Sample Training Sessions

Session One (Beginner)

Focus: Catching at chest height

Equipment Needed: Three cones and 12 balls

Key Coaching Points:
- Watch for proper hand placement behind the ball with the fingers spread.
- Make sure the goalkeepers catch the ball away from the body with a slight bend in the elbows to help cushion the ball.

Warm-Up Activities

❏ Footwork

Place three cones in a row with eight yards between each. The goalkeepers should perform each of the following exercises three times and stretch and rest as needed between exercises.

- The goalkeepers start at cone #1, jog to cone #3, and then jog back to cone #1.
- The goalkeepers face each other on opposite sides of cone #2, and on "go" shuffle to cone #1, then to cone #3, and then back to cone #2 (Figure 9-6).
- The goalkeepers face each other on opposite sides of cone #2. On "go" they shuffle to cone #1, quickly turn to sprint to cone #3, then shuffle back to cone #2.
- The goalkeepers stand facing cone #3 on opposite sides of cone #2. On "go" they backpedal to cone #1, quickly sprint to cone #3, then backpedal to cone #2.

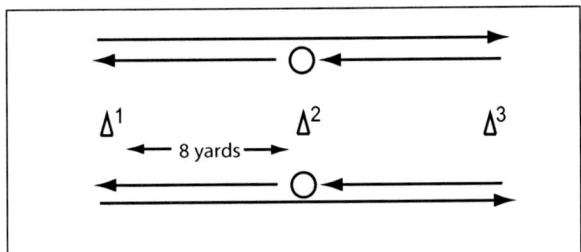

Figure 9-6. Footwork drill

❑ Ball Gymnastics

Goalkeepers should perform two sets of each of the following exercises at 30-second intervals, resting and stretching as needed between each exercise. Each goalkeeper has a ball.

- The goalkeepers bounce the ball on the ground with both hands and then catch it with both hands. Keeping their feet planted, they continue to bounce the ball while twisting as far as they can to one side, and then continue by twisting to the other side.
- With their legs spread slightly more than shoulder-width apart, they bounce the ball between their legs and then quickly turn around to catch the ball.

Main Session

❑ Safe Hands

Set-up: The working goalkeeper stands in the goal, bouncing on the balls of his feet and ready to catch the ball. The nonworking goalkeeper stands in front of the goalkeeper, facing him, and is also bouncing on the balls of his feet. The server is approximately eight to 12 yards away with a supply of balls.

Directions: On the server's command, the nonworking goalkeeper steps out of the way while the server strikes the ball chest-high at the goalkeeper. If the goalkeeper bobbles the ball and loses possession, the nonworking goalkeeper shoots the ball at the goalkeeper again (Figure 9-7). Each goalkeeper should perform one set of 10 repetitions.

Variations:

- Use the same set-up as above, except the goalkeeper begins each repetition with his back to the nonworking goalkeeper and the server.
- Have the goalkeeper start each repetition in a push-up position with his head pointing toward the nonworking goalkeeper and server.
- Have the goalkeeper start each repetition on his back with his feet pointing toward the nonworking goalkeeper and server.

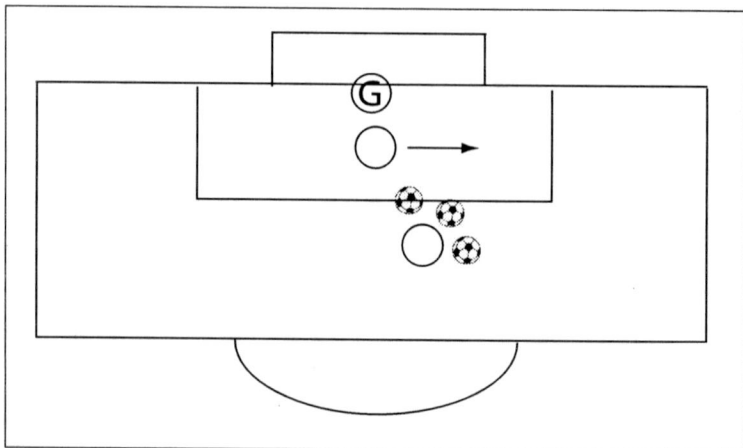

Figure 9-7. Safe hands

❑ Catching With Footwork

Set-up: Place three cones in the mouth of the goal approximately three yards from the goal line. The server stands around the top right corner of the six-yard box and the nonworking goalkeeper stands on the other corner. Each has four to six balls.

Directions: The goalkeeper starts on the side of the server as illustrated in Figure 9-8. The server volleys or throws a hard, chest-high shot at the goalkeeper. The goalkeeper makes the save and tosses the ball back to the server, then quickly shuffles in and out of the three cones. As soon as the goalkeeper is in a "set" position and ready to receive another shot, the nonworking goalkeeper strikes another hard, chest-high shot at the goalkeeper. Have each goalkeeper perform two sets of 10 repetitions.

Variation: After the goalkeeper tosses the ball back the server, have him laterally jump over each cone with his feet together.

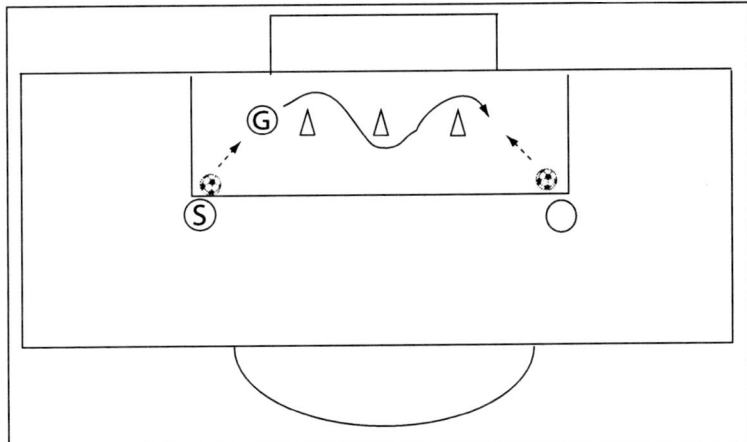

Figure 9-8. Catching with footwork

Session Two (Intermediate)

Focus: Low diving—far post save

Equipment Needed: eight to 10 balls

Key Coaching Points:
- The goalkeeper should land on his side, making sure the top hand is on top of the ball and the bottom hand is behind the ball.
- Stress the importance of letting the ball hit the ground first to cushion the fall and using the ground as his third hand.
- His bottom arm should come out and away from the body.
- After the ball, his shoulder—not his elbow—should hit the ground first.
- He should keep his neck steady and straight.
- He should dive toward the ball at a forward angle. After landing, he should keep the bottom leg slightly bent and on the ground to maintain his balance on his side.

- When diving low, the bottom hand will have the best reach.
- The goalkeepers should always use two hands when possible.
- If he cannot save the shot with two hands, insist that he use a flat palm to redirect the ball out of bounds.
- Remind the goalkeepers to *only dive when necessary*.

Warm-Up Activities

❑ Footwork

Randomly place four soccer balls in the 18-yard box. The goalkeepers jog around in all directions in the 18-yard box. On the coach's signal, they perform the following exercises. They should do each exercise twice, stretching for one minute between each exercise.
- The goalkeepers sprint and touch each ball once before returning to a jog.
- They quickly do three lateral jumps over each ball before returning to a jog.
- The goalkeepers quickly lay flat on their backs next to each ball before returning to a jog.
- They perform a low dive on each ball before returning to a jog.

❑ Ball Gymnastics

The goalkeepers should stretch and rest as needed between the following exercises.
- Reverse Diving: One goalkeeper stands with a ball in his hands while the other goalkeeper is lying on the ground on his side. The keeper with the ball tosses it up in the air so that the keeper on the ground can quickly get up and catch the ball before it hits the ground. As soon as the keeper with the ball tosses the ball in the air, he quickly dives on the ground, staying on his side as if low diving to a ball. Make sure they alternate sides and continue this exercise until each keeper has gone 10 times.
- Hike: Each goalkeeper has a ball. Standing with his legs shoulder-width apart, the goalkeeper bends over, puts the ball between his legs, tosses it up and over his back, and then catches it over his shoulder as he stands up. Make sure he alternates the shoulder the ball goes over. Each goalkeeper should perform one set of 12 repetitions.

Main Session

❑ Near-Far

Set-up: Place a ball three yards out from the goal line and just inside the near post with a goalkeeper and server positioned as illustrated in Figure 9-9.

Directions: The goalkeeper begins performing a low dive on the stationary ball. Once he quickly gains his feet, the server, who is approximately 12 yards away, sends a firm ball just inside the far post. The goalkeeper should perform two sets of eight on each side of the goal.

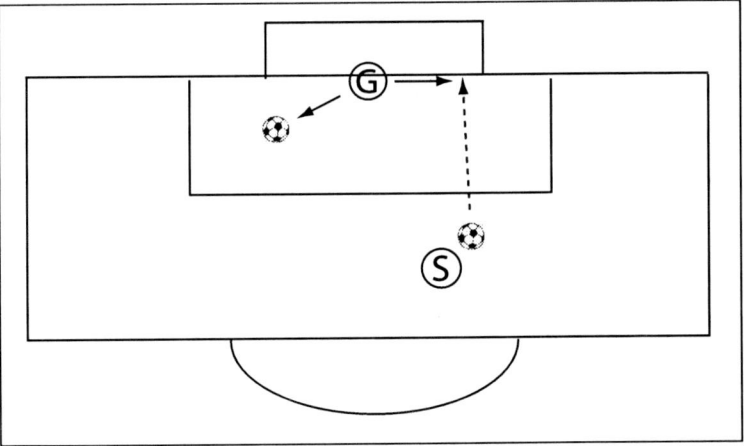
Figure 9-9. Near-far

❑ High Five

Set-up: Goalkeeper #1 stands just inside the goalpost facing Goalkeeper #2. The server is 12 yards away (Figure 9-10).

Directions: Goalkeeper #1 begins the exercise by doing a forward roll toward Goalkeeper #2. Once he is on his feet, he gives Goalkeeper #2 a high five. He then quickly turns to face the server. The server gives a firm ball just inside the far post. Goalkeeper #1 goes back to the starting position and Goalkeeper #2 begins the exercise. Each goalkeeper should perform one set of 10 before switching sides.

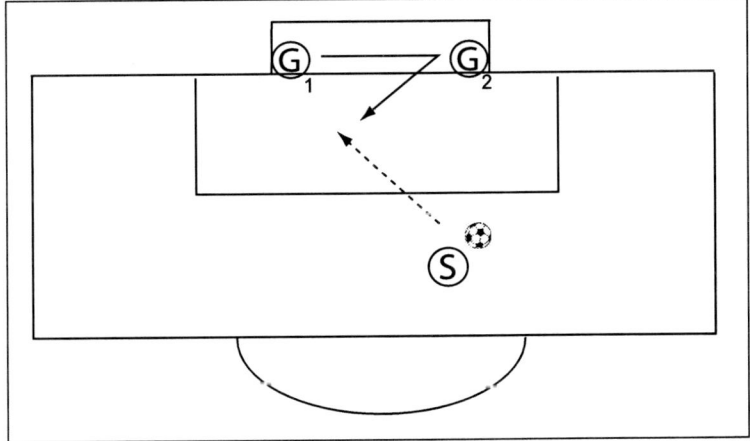
Figure 9-10. High five

Session Three (Advanced)

Focus: Power diving—training the top of the hand (also referred to as high diving or extension diving)

Equipment Needed: Eight cones and 10 balls

Key Coaching Points:
- The keeper should land on his side and be sure the top hand is on top of the ball and the bottom hand is behind the ball.
- Stress the importance of letting the ball hit the ground first to cushion the fall and using the ground as a third hand.
- The bottom arm should come out and away from the body.
- After the ball, the shoulder—not the elbow—should hit the ground first.
- The neck should be kept steady and straight.
- The goalkeeper should dive toward the ball at a forward angle. After landing, he should keep the bottom leg slightly bent and on the ground to maintain his balance on his side.
- The goalkeeper's *top hand* will have the best reach when power diving.
- The goalkeeper should always use two hands whenever possible.
- If he cannot save the shot with two hands, insist that he use a flat palm to redirect the ball out of bounds.
- Remind your goalkeepers to *only dive when necessary*.

Warm-Up Activities

❑ Footwork

Place eight cones or balls two to three feet apart. Each goalkeeper should perform three repetitions of each of the following exercises, stretching as needed between exercises.
- In and Out: The starting position is to the side of the cones. With a slight bend in the knees and while balancing on the balls of the feet, the goalkeeper should weave in and out of the cones, always keeping her hips square, head up, eyes forward, and hands ready.
- Up and Over: The starting position is to the side of the cones. The leg nearest to the cone goes over first and then the second leg follows. With his knees coming up high, the goalkeeper should go up and over each cone while keeping his hips square, head up, eyes forward, and hands ready. The feet should not touch or cross.
- Power Step: The starting position is directly facing the line of cones, one step to the side. The leg nearest the cone power steps forward on a slight angle through the cones. The trail leg should follow but never touch the other leg. After each power step through the cones, the goalkeeper should freeze in the "set" position, demonstrating that he is ready to react to a shot. Throughout the exercise he should stay on the balls of his feet for balance with the head up, eyes forward, knees slightly bent, and hands ready.
- V-Sits: The goalkeeper sits on the ground with his legs out in front of him. The server delivers an underhand toss to one side. The goalkeeper dives at a forward angle, trying to save the ball up toward his feet, thus creating a "V" when he saves the ball. The goalkeepers should perform two sets of 10 repetitions of this exercise.

❏ Ball Gymnastics

Each goalkeeper should perform one set of 10 repetitions of each of the following exercises.
- The goalkeeper starts in a standing position, tosses the ball up in the air, performs a forward roll, and then catches the ball above his head at the highest point possible.
- The goalkeeper begins in a sitting position, tosses the ball up in the air, and then quickly stands up to catch the ball above his head at the highest point. For a greater challenge, have him stand up without using his hands.

Main Session

❏ Top Hand

Set-up: Place two cones 15 yards apart with the working goalkeeper on his knees. The server stands in front of the goalkeeper about a yard away.

Directions: Using an underhand toss, the server delivers the ball just to the left side of the goalkeeper. The goalkeeper can only use his top hand opposite from the ball to pin the ball to the ground. Have the goalkeeper switch hands for a toss to the right side. Perform two sets of 10 reps.

❏ Touch and Go

Set-up: Have a goalkeeper start in the middle of the goal with a server positioned in front of him as illustrated in Figure 9-11.

Directions: On the server's command, the goalkeeper shuffles to the right post, touches it, and then moves back to the middle of the goal. Once the goalkeeper is about in the middle of the goal, the server tosses an underhand shot shoulder-high to the goalkeeper's left side. The goalkeeper performs a power dive. The goalkeeper should

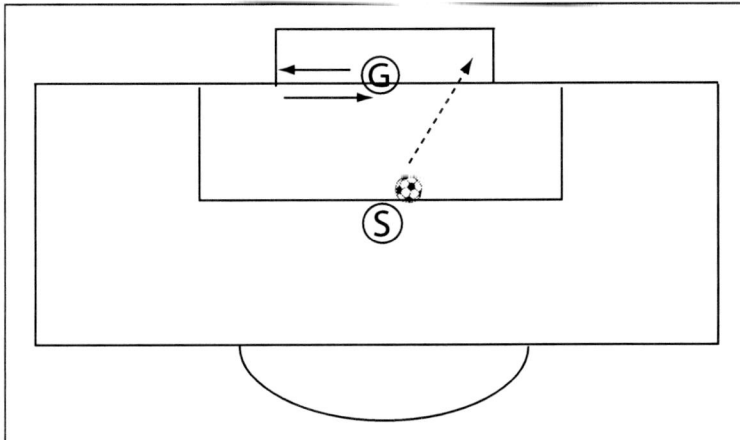

Figure 9-11. Touch and go

10

Scouting

Scouting opponents will give you the specific information needed to carefully prepare your team. Scouting requires careful observation and the ability to focus on the big picture as well as the details. When watching a game, use the following checklists to help keep your focus.

General Checklist

Use the form shown in Figure 10-1 as an example of a scouting report.
- Record the starting lineup, including names and numbers.
- Next to each starter, indicate strengths and weaknesses, position played, which foot he likes to use, and how fast he is.
- Watch for substitutions and note who goes in for each player.
- Indicate the weaknesses of substitutes.
- Who is not afraid to go into 50-50 battles?
- Note where the players generally play defense.
- Find the weak link (e.g., a player who folds under pressure or doesn't handle the ball well).
- Note key players and their strengths.

Offensive Checklist

- Do they play a 1-4-4-2, 1-3-5-2, 1-4-3-3, etc.?
- What is the style of play?
  - ✓ Direct: they play long balls behind the defense
  - ✓ Indirect: they look to build out of the back with a series of passes
  - ✓ High-pressure
  - ✓ Low-pressure
- Does the team use short passes?
- Do they bypass the midfield?
- Do they use long, vertical balls?

```
                          MATCH ANALYSIS

Opponent: _____  Date: _____  Site: _____

| System of Play:                        Style of Play:              |

| DEFENDERS: Flat or Sweep                      Set Plays            |
| 1.                                                                  |
| 2.                                                                  |
| 3.                                                                  |
| 4.                                                                  |
| 5.                                                                  |
| Zonal marking or man-to-man      Gaps big or small                 |

| MIDFIELD: Flat or Diamond                     Set Plays            |
| 1.                                                                  |
| 2.                                                                  |
| 3.                                                                  |
| 4.                                                                  |
| 5.                                                                  |
| Play central or through the wings     Playmaker?                   |

| FORWARDS: Staggered or Flat                   Set Plays            |
| 1.                                                                  |
| 2.                                                                  |
| 3.                                                                  |
| Penetrating runs       Checking runs       Take-on or lay off      |

| GENERAL NOTES:                                                      |
```

Figure 10-1. Scouting report

- Do they like to attack certain sides?
- Do they play through one to two players?
- What are their tendencies?

Set Pieces

- How are the set pieces arranged?
- Who takes the free kicks?
- Where do their goal kicks usually go?
- What plays do they run for a corner kick or throw-ins?

Defensive Checklist

- Identify the team's shape.
- How many do they play in the back?
- Do they play with a flat back or a sweeper?
- What do players do with the ball once they win it?
- Do they play zonal marking or man?
- Do midfielders like to receive the ball with their feet or do they like to run on to it in space?

Goalkeeper Checklist

- Does the goalkeeper usually throw or punt?
- Where does he set up on free kicks or corner kicks?
- When does he come up off the line?

Developing a Practice Plan

Once you have a sense of the opponent, Wednesday's practice should involve putting your players in situations that they will encounter when playing. For example, if your opponent will be playing a high-pressure style, then your practice should be a series building from small numbers to full 11s. Your players should be put in situations where they are constantly under pressure. As a coach you then must correctly identify pressure situations as they occur in your activities and help your players recognize how to get out of the situations or "solve" the pressure.

The walk-through should focus on your attack and how you can exploit defensive weaknesses. Remember to practice set plays briefly and end with an intense activity that will focus your players.

11

Game-Day Considerations

Away-Game Preparation

Uniform Management

Develop a system for handing out and collecting uniforms for an away game. Set them out about 30 minutes before departure time. After the game, the players should put their own uniform—turned inside out—into the laundry bag. The managers should be responsible for getting the uniforms on the bus and then laundered when back at school. For club coaches, make sure you have a couple of extra uniforms that can be used in case a player forgets his or a player gets blood on it and a referee will not let him return until it is removed.

Trip Items

- Your managers should have a travel checklist that includes these items:
- Scorebook
- Rosters
- Statistic sheets
- Balls
- Water bottles
- Towels
- Extra uniforms and socks for goalies
- Extra shin guards and cleats for players
- Cones for the warm-up
- Pinnies for the warm-up
- Medicine kit
- Video camera equipment/tapes

Home-Game Procedures

- Meet the visiting team (you or assistant).
- Get the score clock ready.

- Set up the scorer's table.
- Put out the benches.
- Set the flags out.
- Make sure the nets are on the goals.
- Clean the opponent's dressing room and make sure the lockers are locked.
- Secure a place for officials to dress before and after the game. Have a bottle of water for each official for halftime.
- Have someone available to greet the visitors and show them to their locker room.
- Put together a pregame CD.
- Prepare a national anthem, either live or on CD.
- Check the scoreboard to make sure all lights are working properly.

Pregame Routine

Coach's Responsibilities

Keep your warm-up structured with an emphasis on dynamic, game-realistic movements as opposed to static, unrealistic activities. Key ideas to remember include the following:

- Allow your players to take the first five to 10 minutes for themselves. This time can be used for dribbling, juggling, and jogging. Everyone has a different way to gear up mentally and this time should be used to enable every player to get to the point where he is mentally ready to go.
- Develop a routine. This could involve running across the field, passing and movement activities, possession games, etc. Choose what you will do and do it before every game.
- Include more position- or role-related activities, such as defenders hitting long balls, midfielders playing one- or two-touch 4v4 games to two goals on the wings, and strikers dribbling at each other. Incorporate crosses and finishing with little pressure, then add the defense and play. Nothing gets a player's head into the game more than playing the game.
- Let your players express their ideas for warm-up if your warm-up does not seem to get them ready.
- Practice your warm-up.

Sample Pregame Timeline

Your routine should be intense enough to get the players warmed up and stretched so they feel comfortable and are ready to play. The following illustrates one possible pregame routine:

- Six minutes: Two-line passing (Figure 11-1)
- 10 minutes: Four square game (Figure 11-2)
- 10 minutes: Partner stretching
- 15 minutes: 6v4 (offense and defense specific to the system you will be playing and players are in spots that are specific to their positions)

- Six minutes: Defenders hit long balls to each other 25 to 40 yards apart; midfielders and forwards are shooting and working give-and-go; captains take care of coin toss
- Five minutes: Gather your team and give them three points to focus on during the game (e.g., field conditions, free kick plays, playing on turf)

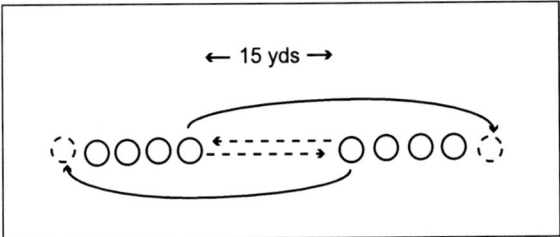

Figure 11-1. Two-line passing

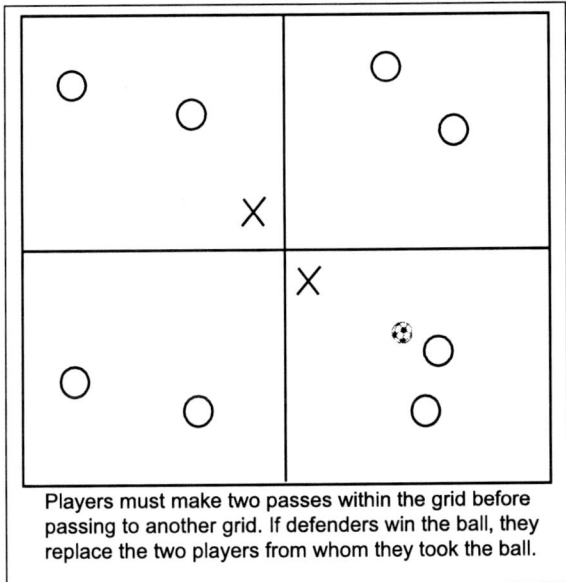

Figure 11-2. Four square game

Keeping Stats During the Game

Use your assistant coaches, managers, knowledgeable parents, or boosters to keep stats for you. Use a pass chart to keep track of passes from one position to another in an attempt to analyze the flow of the attack and the touches each position is getting. Draw an arrow for the direction of a pass and add tally marks for each successful pass in that direction. Keep these stats in 15-minute increments or for an entire half.

Statistical Analysis for Individual Skills

Keep track of the following individual statistics to evaluate game performance:
- Number of touches
- Passes completed
- Passes missed

- 50-50 balls won and lost
- Unforced turnovers

During the Game

Coaching Points

As you watch the game, make an analysis so that during halftime you can make adjustments, if necessary. Don't just watch the movement of the ball, but be aware of the entire field. Remember, you are not a spectator. Try to analyze play by considering the following:

- Your defense: Are they maintaining their defensive shape (pressure, cover, balance)? Are players marking (guarding) their players goalside? Are your players communicating? Are the defenders making good decisions after a take-away?
- Your offense: Are the forwards making the correct runs? Is the timing of the runs correct? Are your midfielders switching the point of attack? Are your players creating shots? Are they creating opportunities for breakaways? Are they finishing? Are they penetrating? Are they holding possession of the ball?
- Opponent's defense: Is there a match-up you can exploit? How big are the gaps between defenders in a zone?
- Opponent's offense: Who is their main "go-to" player? What patterns are developing? How are they scoring? What are their set pieces?

Keep these questions in mind during the entire course of the game so you can make adjustments during halftime or address them during an upcoming practice.

Additional Game-Related Notes

- If you have a lead, remind your players to be conservative in picking their runs.
- Keep most of your players behind the ball playing defense.
- Keep a good pace to the game, but don't hurry.
- Maintain possession if you can.

Halftime

Halftime is a time for your players to recharge physically, emotionally, and mentally. Allow your players to do so before you begin your "talk." You are responsible for making sure the following are completed by the end of halftime:

- Ensure that all injuries, bumps, and bruises are taken care of.
- Allow the players a chance to drink water and relax, even if it is for just a couple of minutes.
- Talk to your players about adjustments they can make or problems they are facing.
- Keep it simple. Pick two or three things that your team did or did not do during the first half and highlight those things. For example:
  ✓ "The defense is too flat. Sweeper, give us some depth."

- ✓ "Outside midfielders are doing a great job of giving us width. Let's continue to use them this half."
- ✓ "Their fast forward only looks for through balls. Let's help Tim mark that player by turning and dropping to give depth as soon as their midfielder has time to serve a long ball."

After the Game

Get the scorebook and all balls immediately after the game. The players should have a warm-down procedure in place that involves light jogging and a stretching routine. Give them feedback and be positive, whether you won or lost. Get players who need treatment into the training room.

When you call in your scores to the local paper, have the following information ready. If you don't have a local sportswriter who covers the games, write a short newspaper article yourself and submit it the day after the game.

- Your opponent and the final score
- All stats
- Your current team record
- Who you play next and where

Have managers start washing the uniforms, rinsing out water bottles, and putting equipment away. Be sure a coach stays until all players are gone. Turn out all the lights, lock up, and go home.

The Next Day

It is important that players begin to "self-analyze." Encouraging this process is key to getting your players to solve problems or situations in the game on their own. Soccer is a game of movement. The dynamic nature of the game demands that players become self-sufficient and develop an ability to not only read the movements of the game but also read the flow of the game and what space the other team is utilizing or shutting down. Discuss evaluation forms with players and have some suggestions for what each player can do better and what they excelled at during the game. Compare your ratings with the players' own ratings

12

End-of-Season Responsibilities

- Distribute an evaluation sheet
- Have individual meetings
- Collect equipment
- Check the fund balance
- Clean up
- Submit inventory
- Update the record board
- Order senior plaques
- Make ballots
- Prepare for the banquet
- Mail all-state nominations
- Prepare the end-of-season slide show
- Prepare the end-of-season report
- Develop a summer workout plan
- Update locker room pictures and quotes
- Work with colleges on recruiting
- Make all-district/all-conference/all-league selections
- Organize a summer league

Distributing an Evaluation Sheet

Give each member of the team an end-of-season evaluation sheet and grade each athlete in four major skill areas: psychological, tactical, technical, and physical fitness. Figure 12-1 is an example of an evaluation sheet that was adopted from one Tom Turner used with the Ohio-North Olympic Development Program.

Having Individual Meetings

Meet with each athlete to discuss the evaluation sheet. This will give you an opportunity to give each athlete some personal attention and feedback.

End-of-Season Evaluation

Name: _____ Date: _____

1=major strength
2=helps performance
3=hurts performance

Physical speed: _____	Aggression: _____
Strength: _____	Vertical Jump: _____
Communication: _____	Enthusiasm: _____
Agility: _____	Toughness: _____
Balance: _____	Leadership: _____

TOTAL: _____

1=major playing strength
2=well-developed skill or concept
3=can perform this skill or concept if given time and space
4=still developing this skill or concept

PSYCHOLOGICAL/MENTAL
Willingness to attack behind defense _____
Creativity _____
Work ethic _____

TACTICAL
Timing of runs _____
Shape of runs _____
Ability to create space for self _____
Ability to create space for others _____
Understanding tactical cues in combination play _____

TECHNICAL
Technical speed _____
Finishing skills _____
Heading skills _____
Defending skills _____

TOTAL . . . . _____

OVERALL SCORE: _____
COMMENTS:

Figure 12-1. Evaluation sheet

Collecting Equipment

Collect all equipment and check for damaged items to repair or replace. Compile a list of needs for the next season, along with a cost analysis. Order equipment as soon as you can (if budgets allow) to eliminate the hassle at the beginning of the next season.

Checking the Fund Balance

After compiling a list of basic needs, check the fund balance and begin considering your needs and wants list to present to the athletic director for the following season.

Cleaning Up

Clean out the storage area with the help of assistant coaches and managers. Inventory the equipment and note the condition of each item. Compile a list of needs for the next season to be used for ordering.

Submitting Inventory

Give the athletic director a copy of your inventory sheet for his file.

Updating the Record Board

Construct a record board and update it at the end of each season. Records to post could include most goals scored, most assists, most improved, etc.

Ordering Plaques

Order plaques well in advance, even if the award winners have not yet been determined. Once the votes have been tallied you can have the plaques engraved.

Making Ballots

Give each team member an opportunity to vote for each award. A sample ballot is shown in Figure 12-2.

Figure 12-2. Sample award ballot

Preparing for the Banquet

The Program

Put the finishing touches on the banquet program and have it printed and bound.

The Awards

Double-check to make sure your senior plaques and special awards plaques have come in and that each one is error-free. Doing this in advance will give you an opportunity to make changes if necessary.

The Speech

Keep one thing in mind: *Be brief*. Figure 12-3 illustrates a relatively brief banquet speech.

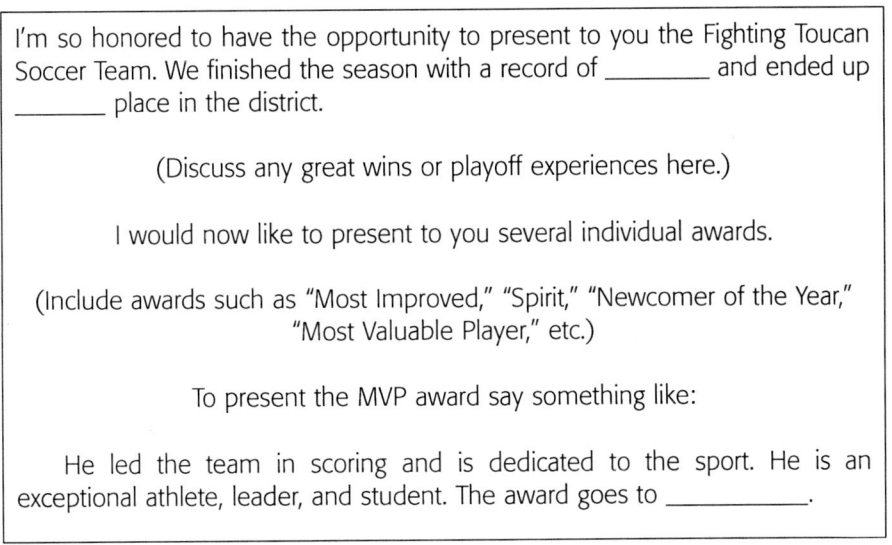

Figure 12-3. Sample banquet speech

Mailing All-State Nominations

If you are a member of a coach's organization, contact them and find out how to nominate and vote for All-State, Academic All-American, and/or All-American recognition. Fill out a National Soccer Coaches Association of America (NSCAA) team academic award nomination form.

Preparing an End-of-Year Slide Show

Solicit help from parents and your team photographer to compile pictures of each player. Find someone who is proficient with PowerPoint to assemble a slide-show presentation with transitions and music. Have a screen and projector ready to use at the banquet.

Preparing the End-of-Season Report

After assembling the banquet program, the work required for an end-of-season report will be minimal. Check with your athletic director for the required form, or he may accept a copy of the banquet program as a substitute.

Developing a Summer Workout Plan

Chapter 13 outlines a complete summer workout plan you can give to your athletes.

Updating Locker Room Pictures and Quotes

Spend one day after the season to clean off the bulletin boards and lockers. With the help of your captains, post new pictures and quotes in preparation for the next school year.

Working with Colleges on Recruiting

Playing the Role of an Agent

At the end of the season, have any sophomores, juniors, and seniors interested in pursuing a soccer scholarship compile a list of schools they are interested in attending, the person to contact at each school, and the phone number or e-mail where he can be reached. Then, make calls to assist these players. Players should fill out a bio form with information that can be sent to college coaches as well. This is a very important step. Understand that college coaches are limited in their ability to contact you.

Playing Club Ball

Most college coaches recruit from club teams, so encourage your players to participate. When choosing a club team, players should be sure it is one that goes to major tournaments in the state.

Recruiting Rules

As a coach, you should know the rules of recruiting and pass these along to your players. Two important rules are as follows:
- College coaches cannot call players more than once a week.
- Coaches cannot start calling until July 1—as players are entering their senior year.

Recruiting Video

If you are adept at video production, help your players put a highlight tape together. This video should feature several quick clips—be sure to include some time before the play so a coach can see how the play developed—and at least one lengthy clip of game play.

Student-Athlete Resume

Have each of your players type up a student-athlete resume to include with the video. This should include information such as position played, other sports played, height, weight, number, awards won, etc.

Making All-District/All-Conference/All-League Selections

When meeting with your colleagues to decide on All-District selections, you might encounter the following "traditional" meeting format. Major awards should be voted on first (e.g., most valuable player, newcomer of the year, defensive player of the year, offensive player of the year). Players who receive one of the major awards are then eliminated from the rest of the voting to give other athletes an opportunity to be nominated. Coaches are not allowed to vote for their own players.

After the major awards have been decided upon, the coaches should decide how many athletes should be on the first-team list (for example, one goalie, four defenders, four midfielders, and two or three forwards). Your own nominations should be written down in the order in which you believe they are deserved. If you are allowed to nominate your own players, having statistics available is a priority. One person at the meeting should write down all the nominations from each coach, along with the following information: name, school, position, and classification.

When all the nominations have been made, each coach votes for one player at each position. Again, coaches may not vote for their own athletes. These votes can be made on any type of note paper, including scraps of paper. The results are then tallied on the board. The top vote-getters are the first-team selections. In the event of a tie, you may revote to break the tie, or coaches may mutually agree to add the extra player.

The names left on the board that were not selected for first team may be left on the board to be considered for second-team selection. Any additional spots can be filled by new nominations and a vote. You can also choose to erase the board and start the nominating process again. Once the voting is complete, coaches may then add players as honorable mention selections without a group vote.

Organizing a Summer League

Starting a summer league program will give your players valuable game experience, especially if your school is in a rural area and club ball is not an option. Use the following guidelines to get started:
- Get approval from the administration to use the facilities for games and practices.
- Find some responsible adult volunteers to coach your team.
- Have your high school players sign up and pay a fee that should cover insurance, uniforms, and officials.

- Talk with surrounding schools to set up a league schedule.
- Schedule several tournaments during the summer. These events will be an additional cost for the players, so let them know about them ahead of time. Entry fees usually run from $100 to $250 per team.
- Consider including younger grades if you have plenty of volunteer coaches.
- Meet with your volunteers to schedule practices. This will help avoid conflicts when using the facilities.
- Make sure you are adhering to all rules regarding summer involvement with your players as set by your state high school athletic association.

13

Off-Season Training

Reflect on the season, look over your practice sheets, watch game film, study your team's season statistics, and then decide what your team's weaknesses were and how you can improve in those areas. The off-season is a good time to reinforce basic fundamentals, but specific emphasis should be placed on fitness during this time. Players should use the season—not the off-season—to improve in the game of soccer.

Off-Season Activities

Your players can make tremendous strides toward improving their fitness, ball skills, strength, agility, and speed during the off-season. Divide your off-season into three phases: strength training, agility and fitness, and ball skills.

Phase I: Strength Training

Strength training should be emphasized during the time of year when no games are being played. If your season is in the fall and your players also play in the spring, then winter is the best time for them to put on muscle and improve core strength. As with everything else in sports, strength training must be conducted all year long to increase and maintain solid muscle mass. With increased muscle strength comes fewer injuries and faster recovery from those injuries that do occur.

During the season, strength training should be done with low weight and high repetitions to maintain muscle as the season wears on. Because soccer involves such high-intensity aerobic and anaerobic movements, muscle mass is typically lost during the season, so it is important to maintain some type of strength training to keep your team strong at the end of the year.

A weight-lifting program should never be implemented unless a strength and conditioning coach shows the proper techniques. This book is not intended to be used as a guide to weight lifting. The following exercises are examples of the types of exercises that benefit soccer athletes and help accentuate the explosive movements performed on the soccer field.

Weight-Lifting Activities

- Day one—Bench press, military press, biceps curls, upright row, push-ups, and crunches
- Day two—Squats, hang clean, hamstring curls, leg extensions, calf raises, step-ups, and lunges
- Day three—Rest
- Day four—Incline press, military press, biceps curls, upright rows, push-ups, and crunches.
- Day five—Squats, snatches, hamstring curls, leg extension, calf raises, step-ups, and lunges
- Days six and seven—Rest

Abdominal Exercises

- V-sits—The player lies on his back with his hands overhead and his legs straight. He then simultaneously brings the arms and legs up and tries to touch his feet with his fingertips. He then lowers his arms and legs slowly. The players should begin with three sets of 10 repetitions.
- Crunches—The player lies on his back with his knees bent and his hands over his chest. He then raises his shoulders off the ground and then lowers them back down. The player should begin with three sets of 20 repetitions.
- Obliques—The player lies on his back with his arms above his head and holding a partner's ankles. He brings his legs straight up, and then lowers his legs to the right and then to the left. The player should begin with three sets of 10 repetitions.

Phase II: Agility and Fitness

The consistent movement and high aerobic and anaerobic demands placed on a player are what separates soccer from other major sports. Improving agility and speed as well as building a strong aerobic and anaerobic fitness base are essential to the serious soccer player.

Fitness should be emphasized throughout the year. In soccer, fitness becomes a lifestyle, not a hobby. It should be noted that jogging a long distance is not the major emphasis in training for soccer. Soccer is filled with start-and-stop movements. One second a player could be jogging forward, and in an instant may need to accelerate for a 20-yard sprint, turn, backpedal, or shuffle before striding forward again. It is the changes of pace and the intervals between sprinting and walking that make training for aerobic and anaerobic fitness for the game of soccer so important.

Activities for Field Players and Goalkeepers

- 40-20 runs
  - ✓ Mark off 40 yards with a cone at the 20-yard mark.
  - ✓ The players sprint 40 yards, then back, and then up again (18 seconds is the standard).

- ✓ Rest should start at a 1-to-3 work to rest ratio (e.g., 18-second run/54-second rest). As a player's fitness level improves, he can move to a 1-to-2 ratio.
- ✓ At the end of the rest period, each player runs 20 yards up, then back, and up again.
- ✓ To rest, the player should walk to the starting line and get ready for the 40-yard sprint again.
- ✓ Repeat this drill eight to 12 times.

- 120s
  - ✓ Mark off 120 yards.
  - ✓ The players sprint 120 yards with a one-minute walk back before the next run.
  - ✓ Repeat this drill eight to 10 times and allow the players to rest for two days before doing this workout again.

- Sprints
  - ✓ Mark off 20, 40, 60, 80, and 100 yards.
  - ✓ Players must run all sprints at 100% effort, with full recovery between reps and the designated time between sets.
  - ✓ Players sprint 6 x 20 yards with 30 seconds of rest after each rep.
  - ✓ Players sprint 5 x 40 yards with 50 seconds of rest.
  - ✓ Players sprint 4 x 60 yards with 60 seconds of rest.
  - ✓ Players sprint 3 x 80 yards with 80 seconds of rest.
  - ✓ Players sprint 1 x 100 yards with 90 seconds of rest.

As players continue to build their anaerobic base, increase the number of reps for each distance and begin to decrease the rest period. Players should not sprint again for 48 hours after completing this workout.

- The race—Mark out a two- or three-mile course. Players should run that distance as fast as possible. Keep track of players' time and have them work to beat that time the next time they run.

- Fartlek training (speed play)
  - ✓ Two-minute jog
  - ✓ One-minute stride
  - ✓ 25-second sprint
  - ✓ 35-second walk
  - ✓ Two-minute jog
  - ✓ One-and-half-minute stride
  - ✓ 40-second sprint
  - ✓ 50-second walk
  - ✓ One-minute jog
  - ✓ Total running time = 10 minutes

A minimum of 20 minutes of Fartlek training should be completed. This drill may be run every day if varied.

- The "W"—To complete this drill, players do the following:
  - ✓ Place cones in the shape of a "W"
  - ✓ Shuffle from cone to cone
  - ✓ Shuffle back while facing the same direction
  - ✓ Rest for 10 to 15 seconds and then repeat
  - ✓ Complete five repetitions in each direction
  - ✓ Sprint to the center cone
  - ✓ Shuffle back to bottom point of the "W"
  - ✓ Backpedal to the start
  - ✓ Sprint to the farthest bottom point of the "W"
  - ✓ Shuffle to the center cone
  - ✓ Turn and backpedal to the point of the "W" opposite the starting point
  - ✓ Rest for 20 to 25 seconds and repeat
  - ✓ Complete five to eight repetitions

- Stairs—To complete this drill, players do the following:
  - ✓ Step up on the stair with the left foot
  - ✓ Power up with the right foot
  - ✓ Step down with the left foot
  - ✓ Step down with the right foot
  - ✓ Continue this pattern as quickly as possible for one to three minutes
  - ✓ Switch and continue with the right foot stepping up first
  - ✓ Continue for one to three minutes
  - ✓ Rest for two minutes and repeat with both legs

- Jump rope—To complete this drill, players do the following:
  - ✓ Perform single jumps with both feet
  - ✓ Perform single jumps with the right foot
  - ✓ Perform single jumps with the left foot
  - ✓ Jump with both feet, side-to-side over a line
  - ✓ Jump with both feet front-and-back over a line
  - ✓ Perform two single jumps with the left foot and two single jumps with the right foot
  - ✓ Jump with the right foot, side-to-side over a line
  - ✓ Jump with the left foot, side-to-side over a line
  - ✓ Jump with the right foot, front-and-back over a line
  - ✓ Jump with the left foot, front-and-back over a line
  - ✓ Perform three single jumps and one double jump with both feet
  - ✓ Perform consecutive double jumps with both feet

- Box drill—To complete this drill, players do the following:
  - ✓ Mark out a 10-yard by 15-yard box
  - ✓ Shuffle 15 yards
  - ✓ Backpedal 10 yards
  - ✓ Sprint 15 yards
  - ✓ Carioca 10 yards

- Cones—To complete this drill, players do the following:
  - ✓ Set six markers 10 yards apart, for a total of 60 yards
  - ✓ Sprint 10 yards and back, 20 yards and back, 30 yards and back, etc.
  - ✓ The standard time is one minute of running and one minute of rest
  - ✓ Repeat four to eight times

Phase III: Ball Skills

As the old saying goes, "speed kills," but in soccer if a player does not have some skill with the ball at his feet, speed does not help. Ball skills and technique should be trained throughout the year. While some coaches set aside specific time during each practice to work on dribbling or receiving, remember that every time you put your players on the field and have them play any game or activity with the ball at their feet, they are developing their skills.

Activities for Field Players

- Quick touch
  - ✓ Have the players jog while dribbling the ball.
  - ✓ Instruct them to alternate feet, with each foot touching the ball with each step.

- Juggle circuit—This circuit is done from the end line to the top of the 18-yard (penalty box) and back.
  - ✓ The players juggle with their feet while walking toward the top of the 18-yard box and back. Every time the ball hits the ground, the players must do two to five push-ups or 10 crunches and start again at the point where the ball hit the ground.
  - ✓ Variations on this drill including having the players juggle with their thighs or their head.

- Basic foot skills
  - ✓ Refer to Chapter 3 for drills.

- Wall circuit—Each player should find a wall—or use a teammate—against which to perform these activities. To complete these drills, players do the following:
  - ✓ Stand two yards from the wall. Pass the ball with the inside of the right foot to the inside of the left foot and then back to the right. The player then increases speed

to the point where he passes on every step. He should work the drill for two minutes, rest for one minute, and then repeat for two minutes.

- ✓ Stand one yard from the wall. Strike the ball with the toe pointed so the ball is being passed with the laces of the shoe. After striking the ball against the wall continuously with the same foot for one minute, the player then switches feet and repeats the drill.
- ✓ Stand six to eight yards from the wall and shoot the ball with the laces in a quick snapping motion at the knee. As the ball comes off the wall, he repeats the action with the same foot. This activity is designed to improve technique, so players don't need to shoot the ball hard. The knee should be over the ball and the ball should have no spin upon contact. The player should continue the drill for two minutes and then switch feet.
- ✓ Stand five to 10 yards from the wall. With the ball in his hand, he throws the ball so it bounces off the floor, hits the wall, and kicks up in the air. He then jumps and heads the ball, catches the rebound, and repeats. He should continue to perform this drill for two to three minutes.
- ✓ Stand 20 yards from the wall. The player shoots the ball as hard as possible, trying to keep the knee over the ball and the head down. He then receives the ball as it comes off the wall with one touch and shoots again with the next touch. He should continue for four to six minutes. To increase the difficulty, the player can get closer to the wall.

Competition-Day Activities for All Players

Another off-season activity that can be used to develop your players involves having your athletes compete against each other in a series of games and drills. To make competition days more interesting, have the assistant coaches pick teams. Drafting players is recommended to ensure a fair distribution of talent. Have coaches draw for first, second, third pick, etc., and then pick according to the number of teams and coaches you have. Figure 13-1 illustrates the drafting order for four teams.

	Rd 1	Rd 2	Rd 3	Rd 4	Rd 5
Team #1	1st pick	4th pick	3rd pick	2nd pick	(start over)
Team #2	2nd pick	1st pick	4th pick	3rd pick	
Team #3	3rd pick	2nd pick	1st pick	4th pick	
Team #4	4th pick	3rd pick	2nd pick	1st pick	

Figure 13-1. Drafting order example

Keep a running total of scores until the end of the year to crown a winning team. Assign point totals for first, second, third, and fourth place (10, eight, five, and three points). Choose games (e.g., kick ball) and relays that are not only competitive, but athletically challenging as well. The following relays and games are for teams of eight players.

Relays

❑ Relay #1

Set-up: Run this relay on a track. Athletes are stationed at locations on the track, as illustrated in Figure 13-2.

Directions: Team members can decide who will run the following distances: 400 m (one player), 200 m (one player), and 100 m (two players). Use a relay baton (or something more cumbersome to add a measure of fun and entertainment to the relay).

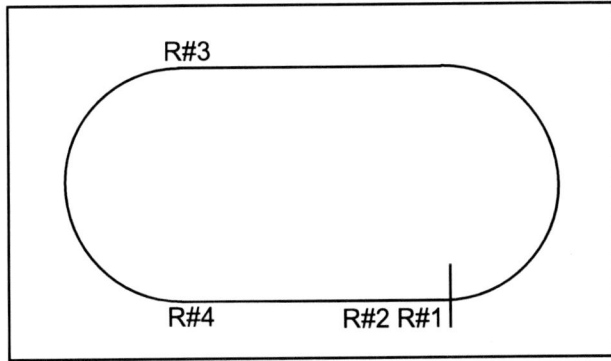

Figure 13-2. Track relay

❑ Relay #2

Set-up: Run this relay on a football field.

Directions: Team members must determine who will do the following:
- Run 50 yards
- Wheelbarrow for 50 yards
- Switch positions and continue for another 50 yards
- Crab walk for 50 yards
- Bear crawl for 50 yards
- Piggyback for 50 yards
- Switch positions and continue for another 50 yards
- Run 50 yards

❑ Relay #3

Set-up: You'll need 10 cones, 10 hurdles, 12 tires, and two soccer balls (and plastic for an optional water slide). The set-up for the relay is illustrated in Figure 13-3.

Directions: Run two teams at once and time them. Instead of using a relay baton, just have athletes slap hands.

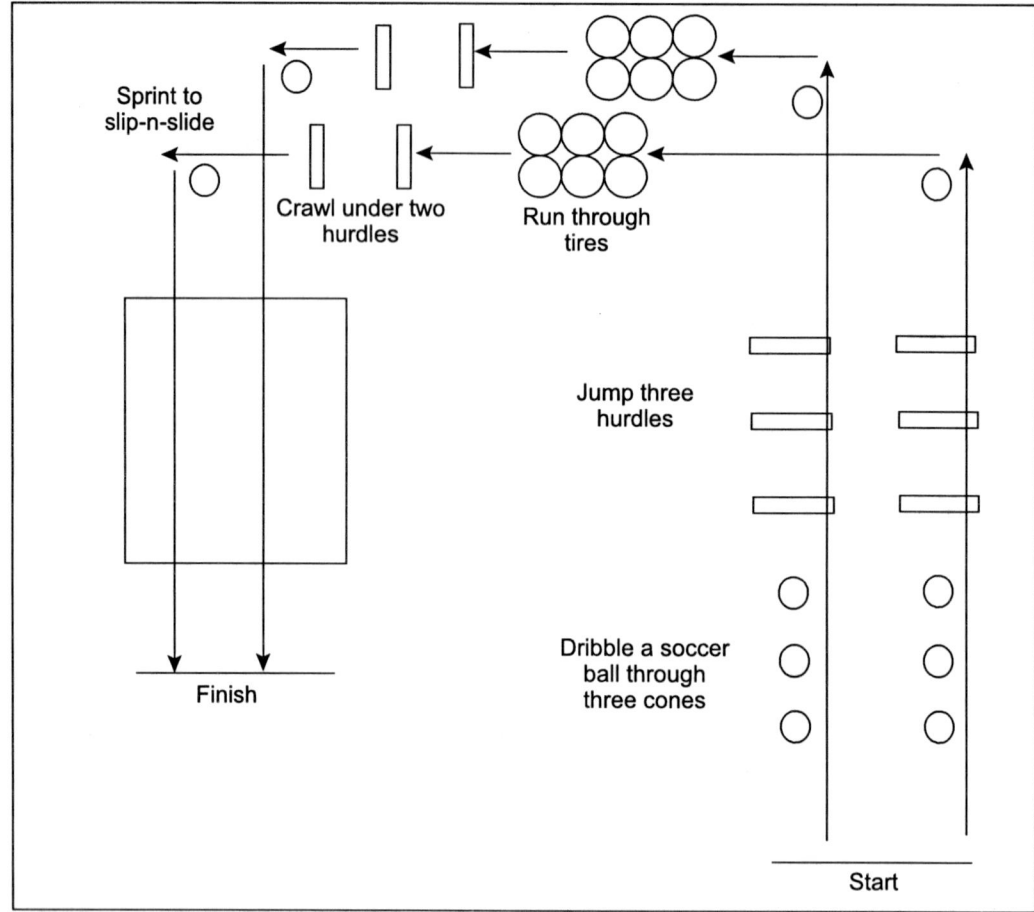

Figure 13-3. Obstacle course relay

Ultimate Football

Set-up: This game is played on the football field using the width but not the entire length. Use cones and the end zone as boundaries.

Directions: The ball may only be advanced by throwing or pitching it. An athlete may not run forward with the ball, only sideways and backward. If the ball hits the ground, the ball immediately goes to the other team. Play does not stop unless a touchdown is scored. A team scores by catching the ball in the end zone. If the ball is dropped, no points are scored and possession reverts to the other team. Play for four quarters or two halves.

Setting Individual Goals

General Goals

Since you have evaluated your team as a whole at the end of the season, each of your players should also spend time evaluating himself. You, along with each player, should individually fill out a form evaluating the player, and then compare forms. Figure 13-4 shows a sample form to use.

PLAYER EVALUATION SHEET

1. What are your strengths as a soccer player?

2. What do you need to work on to reach your potential?

3. What is your plan to improve in these areas?

4. What are your individual goals for the off-season?

Figure 13-4. Sample player evaluation form

Physical Goals

Have athletes decide how much they would like to increase their strength, vertical jump, speed, etc., during the off-season, and keep a record of their goals on their workout sheet. The goals should appear beside their test/evaluation performance for comparison. Test each athlete in the following areas:
- Strength—squat, hang clean, dead lift, bench press, dips, pull-ups
- Speed—40-yard run
- Quickness and agility
- Vertical jump
- Cooper test (explained in Chapter 2)

Off-Season Scoring Charts

Use the charts in Figures 13-5 to 13-13 to award point values. Instead of giving points for first, second, third, etc., assign points based on performance. This system allows your athletes to compete against themselves rather than someone else's best performance (as in the tryout evaluation). Consider it the off-season decathlon. Keep records in each event and total points for posterity.

❑ **Squats**

Weight	Pts.	Weight	Pts.	Weight	Pts.
300	1000	245	816	190	633
295	982	240	799	185	616
290	966	235	783	180	599
285	949	230	766	175	583
280	932	225	749	170	566
275	916	220	733	165	549
270	899	215	716	160	533
265	882	210	699	155	516
260	866	205	683	150	499
255	849	200	667	145	483
250	833	195	649	140	466

Figure 13-5. Point values for the squat. Note: multiply the amount of weight lifted by 3.3, if that weight is not on the chart.

❑ **Bench press**

Weight	Pts.	Weight	Pts.	Weight	Pts.
160	1000	125	781	90	563
155	969	120	750	85	531
150	938	115	719	80	500
145	906	110	688	75	469
140	875	105	656	70	438
135	844	100	625	65	406
130	813	95	594	60	375

Figure 13-6. Point values for the bench press. Note: Multiply the amount of weight lifted by 6.25, if that weight is not on the chart.

❑ **Dips**

No.	Pts.	No.	Pts.	No.	Pts.
15	1000	10	667	5	334
14	934	9	600	4	267
13	867	8	534	3	200
12	800	7	467	2	133
11	734	6	400	1	67

Figure 13-7. Point values for dips. Note: Multiply the amount of dips performed by 66.7, if that number is not on the chart.

❑ **Hang clean**

Weight	Pts.	Weight	Pts.	Weight
200	1000	155	775	110
195	975	150	750	105
190	950	145	725	100
185	925	140	700	95
180	900	135	675	90
175	875	130	650	85
170	850	125	625	80
165	825	120	600	75
160	800	115	575	70

Figure 13-8. Point values for the hang clean. Note: Multiply the weight lifted by 5.0, if that weight it not on the chart.

❑ **Dead lift**

Weight	Pts.	Weight	Pts.	Weight	Pts.
250	1000	205	820	160	640
245	980	200	800	155	620
240	960	195	780	150	600
235	940	190	760	145	580
230	920	185	740	140	560
225	900	180	720	135	540
220	880	175	700	130	520
215	860	170	680	125	500
210	840	165	660	120	480

Figure 13-9. Point values for the dead lift. Note: Multiply the weight lifted by 4.0 if that weight is not on the chart.

❑ **Pull-ups**

No.	Pts.	No.	Pts.	No.	Pts.
15	1000	10	667	5	334
14	934	9	600	4	267
13	867	8	534	3	200
12	800	7	467	2	133
11	734	6	400	1	67

Figure 13-10. Point values for pull-ups. Note: Multiply the number of pull-ups performed by 66.7, if that number is not on the chart.

❑ **800m run**

Time	Pts.	Time	Pts.	Time	Pts.	Time	Pts.
2:45	1000	3:00	850	3:15	700	3:30	550
2:46	990	3:01	840	3:16	690	3:31	540
2:47	980	3:02	830	3:17	680	3:32	530
2:48	970	3:03	820	3:18	670	3:33	520
2:49	960	3:04	810	3:19	660	3:34	510
2:50	950	3:05	800	3:20	650	3:35	500
2:51	940	3:06	790	3:21	640	3:36	490
2:52	930	3:07	780	3:22	630	3:37	480
2:53	920	3:08	770	3:23	620	3:38	470
2:54	910	3:09	760	3:24	610	3:39	460
2:55	900	3:10	750	3:25	600	3:40	450
2:56	890	3:11	740	3:26	590	3:41	440
2:57	880	3:12	730	3:27	580	3:42	430
2:58	870	3:13	720	3:28	570	3:43	420
2:59	860	3:14	710	3:29	560	3:44	410

Figure 13-11. Point values for the 800M run. Note: Add or subtract 10 points (depending on the time achieved), if that time is not on the chart.

❑ **Vertical jump**

Inches	Pts.	Inches	Pts.	Inches	Pts.
33	1000	26	788	19	576
32	970	25	757	18	545
31	939	24	727	17	515
30	909	23	697	16	485
29	879	22	667	15	454
28	848	21	636	14	424
27	818	20	606	13	394

Figure 13-12. Point values for the vertical jump. Note: Multiply the number of inches by 30.3, if that number is not on the chart.

❑ **40-yard sprint**

Time	Pts.	Time	Pts.	Time	Pts.
4.2	1000	4.9	720	5.6	440
4.3	960	5.0	680	5.7	400
4.4	920	5.1	640	5.8	360
4.5	880	5.2	600	5.9	320
4.6	840	5.3	560	6.0	280
4.7	800	5.4	520	6.1	240
4.8	760	5.5	480	6.2	200

Figure 13-13. Point values for the 40-yard sprint. Note: Add or subtract 40 points (depending on the time achieved), if that time is not on the chart.

A Sample Year-Round Conditioning Program

During the Season

Monday
- 120s and 40-20 sprints, or another sprint circuit covering anaerobic and aerobic components. Sprints are performed toward the end of practice with a shooting activity scheduled after the running.

Tuesday
- Practice

Wednesday
- Practice

Thursday
- Practice with no hard running

Friday
- Game

Saturday
- Light practice

Sunday
- Off

Winter

Monday
- Resistance training, with a concentration on the upper body and abdominals
- Wall circuit for ball skills

Tuesday
- Fitness (Fartlek or two- to three-mile run)
- Basic ball skill workout

Wednesday
- Resistance training with a concentration on the lower body and abdominals

Thursday
- Juggle routine or basic foot skills
- Agility

Friday
- Resistance training with a concentration on the upper body
- Fitness (sprints, stairs, or other anaerobic movements)
- Wall circuit for ball skills

Saturday
- Agility circuit or training

Sunday
- Off

Spring

Players may be playing club soccer, so they are getting touches on the ball. This part of the year is geared toward maintaining muscle mass.

Monday
- Agility training
- Basic foot skills or wall circuit
- Abdominal work

Tuesday
- Resistance training with an emphasis on the upper body (lower weight with higher repetitions)

Wednesday
- Spring workout or 120s
- Basic foot skills
- Abdominal work

Thursday
- Off

Friday
- Resistance training with an emphasis on the lower body

Saturday and Sunday
- Usually club game-days

Summer

Access to weight rooms tends to be limited, so players should concentrate on abdominal work and push-ups for strength maintenance.

Monday
- Cooper test or two- to three-mile run
- Basic foot skills
- Abdominal work and push-ups

Tuesday
- Sprint/recovery-type workout
- Wall circuit

Wednesday
- Agility training
- Basic foot skills
- Abdominals and push-ups

Thursday
- 120s or 40-20s

Friday
- Pick-up games
- Abdominal work and push-ups
- Agility training

Saturday
- Aerobic fitness

Sunday
- Off

As with any fitness program, it is best to have a professional trainer or doctor determine the type of program your players can handle. In the summer, as you and your team prepare for pre-season two-a-days, remember to make sure you outline the fitness tests you will run. Add the tests to your summer workout program so the players can practice them as one of the fitness sessions each week. The best teacher is the game itself, so always find ways to have your players play throughout the year!

A

Planning a Tournament

Three to Four Months Before the Tournament

Send letter to prospective teams. If your tournament is yearly, then you will probably already have a few teams that are regulars. For your open spots, get the coaching directory out and start addressing letters. Some schools may have already committed to a tournament at the end of last year's season, but it doesn't hurt to try and recruit them for the next year. Figure A-1 shows an example of a letter to send.

Dear Coach/Athletic Director:

We would like to invite you to participate in our annual soccer tournament. As in the past, Anywhere High School will be hosting the Toucan Soccer Classic on December 20th, 21st, and 22nd. Last year's tournament was very successful and, with the input we received last year, we plan on making this year's tournament even better. Once again, we will make every effort to give each team as many matches as possible.

The tournament format will be pool play followed by playoffs. There will be two varsity divisions: small school (under 1200 enrollment) and large school (over 1200 enrollment). If you wish to play up in the large-school division, you may.

The entry fee is $325 per varsity team. Entries will be taken in the order in which they are received. We can only accommodate a certain number of teams, so you must respond in a timely fashion to secure a spot for your team. Send your entry fee to: Stephenie Jordan, Anywhere High School, 1234 Somewhere Street, Anytown, TX 12345. Make checks payable to: Winter Soccer Classic.

Please send your information as soon as possible so we can set up the tournament without delay. We look forward to hearing from you. Additional information will be sent after we have your response. If you have any questions please contact either of the two tournament directors:

George Hageage
Work: (333) 555-1212
Home: (111) 123-4567
Cell: (876) 234-7654

Stephenie Jordan
Work: (222) 555-1313
Home: (444) 456-7890
Cell: (890) 123-1234

We hope to hear from you soon.

Stephenie Jordan
Anytown High School
Head Girls Soccer Coach

Figure A-1. Sample letter to teams

```
┌─────────────────────────────────────────────────────────────┐
│                    WINTER SOCCER CLASSIC                    │
│                  December 20th, 21st, & 22nd                │
│                                                             │
│                         Entry Fee:                          │
│                            $325                             │
│                                                             │
│                    Make checks payable to:                  │
│                      Winter Soccer Classic                  │
│                                                             │
│                          Mail to:                           │
│                       Stephenie Jordan                      │
│                      Anywhere High School                   │
│                     1234 Somewhere Street                   │
│                       Anytown, TX 12345                     │
│                                                             │
│  School Name: _____  Phone #: _____   │
│                                                             │
│  Coach's Name: _____  Phone #: _____   │
│                                                             │
│  (  ) Yes, we will participate.                             │
│                                                             │
│  (  ) No, we will not participate, but keep us on your mailing list. │
│                                                             │
│  Please check the division in which you would like to play: │
│                                                             │
│  (  ) Large school (1200 enrollment and above)              │
│                                                             │
│  (  ) Small school (Below 1200 enrollment)                  │
└─────────────────────────────────────────────────────────────┘
```

Figure A-2. Response card

You might want to include a self-addressed stamped envelope for the response cards. Figure A-2 shows an example of a response card.

Six Weeks Before the Tournament

Send another letter confirming participation in the tournament, with a list of the teams entered, an information sheet for the program, and a bracket. Figures A-3, A-4, and A-5 show a sample confirmation letter, information sheet, and tournament bracket, respectively.

Tournament Formats

At a minimum, try to get at least four teams to participate in the tournament, and construct a bracket similar to the one illustrated in Figure A-5. Figure A-5 shows the standard bracket most people use for an eight-team tournament. It can even be used with seven teams, with one team getting a bye.

Fortunately, if you need assistance in constructing a bracket for a tournament or you need more detailed information on pool play, there are plenty of tools (books, CD-ROM programs, etc.) available on the market.

Dear Soccer Coach,

We have received your response card and entry fee for the Winter Soccer Classic hosted by Anytown High School. We have your team entered at this time. You will receive your tournament information packet and bracket sheets in early November. If you have any questions, don't hesitate to call.

Sincerely,

Stephenie Jordan
Work: (222) 555-1313
Home: (444) 456-7890
Cell: (890) 123-1234

Figure A-3. Confirmation letter

**Winter Soccer Classic
Information Sheet**

School Name: _____   Coach: _____

School Colors: _____   District/Class: _____

No.	Name	Position	Class

Figure A-4. Information sheet

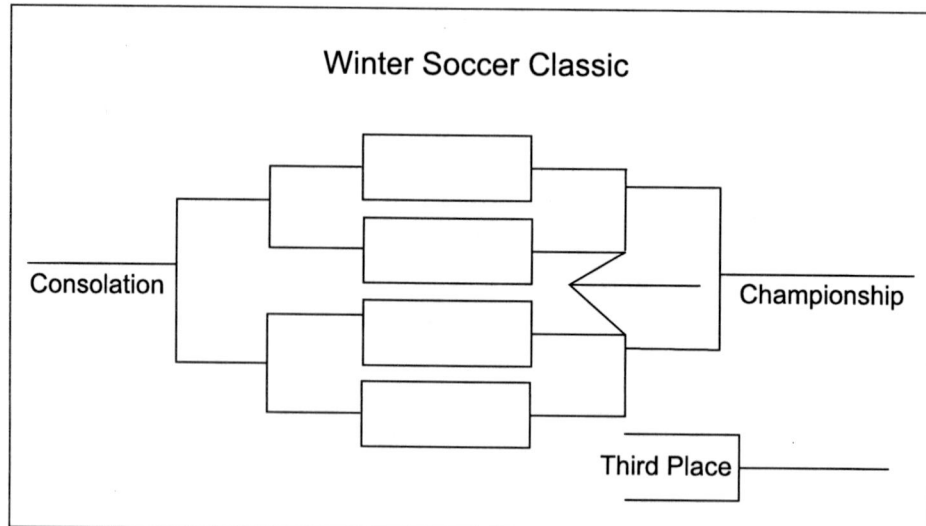

Figure A-5. Tournament bracket

One Month Before the Tournament

- Make sure you have officials scheduled.
- Assign coaches to run the clock and keep the score book for all games.
- Order trophies and plaques.
- Order or make programs.
- Find a gatekeeper.

Scheduling Officials

It would be wise to schedule at least four officials for the tournament. Then each set of two can alternate games. After watching them during early games, you could then choose your best two officials for the championship game.

Assigning the Score Book and Scoreboard

This might be the biggest headache you encounter in planning your tournament. You could go and ask each coach if they'd be willing to work, and you might get one to agree depending on the staff. It's much easier if your athletic director backs you and assigns coaches to do the job. Otherwise, you'll have to find parents to help, and they usually aren't knowledgeable enough about the game to keep either the score book or the scoreboard. Figure A-6 shows an example of a completed tournament assignment schedule.

Assignments for Tournament

December 20th

Field One
3:00 pm	Clock: Rebekah Jordan	Book: Scott Jordan
5:00 pm	Clock: Claire Scott	Book: Roger Scott
7:00 pm	Clock: Vicki Beard	Book: David Beard

Field Two
1:00 pm	Clock: Ramey Welch	Book: Jordan Beard
3:00 pm	Clock: John David Beard	Book: Wegi Talbert
5:00 pm	Clock: Grover Talbert	Book: Norma White
7:00 pm	Clock: Trevor White	Book: Teresa Janda

Figure A-6. Assignment schedule

Ordering Awards

Ask your athletic director for suggestions on a company to order awards from. You will need to order the following:

- First-place team trophy
- Second-place team trophy

- Individual trophies for champions (optional)
- All-Tournament trophies (however many you decide, but eight to ten are plenty)
- MVP award
- Outstanding Coach award

Getting the Programs Ready

You can either have the programs printed by an outside company or do them yourself. With the scanners and computers that are currently available, you can make a pretty nice program yourself. If you want to save some money, do it yourself. It doesn't have to be elaborate. Among the factors involving your programs that you need to address are the following:

Decide on a cover. Figure A-7 shows a sample program cover that could be used. Nothing very fancy, but it works.

Type an appreciation to go on the inside cover. It could say something similar to the sample text shown in Figure A-8.

```
23rd Annual
Winter Soccer Classic

December 20th, 21st, 22nd

School Logo Here
```

Figure A-7. Cover for program

The Lady Toucans take this opportunity to express our appreciation to the many people who help make our tournament possible. Our sincere appreciation and thanks to the following members of the athletic department: Jody Jordan, Athletic Director; Coaches Tamara Hageage, Chris Janda, Trevor White, David Martel, Teresa Janda, and Peggy White for their time and effort in making this a successful tournament.

Figure A-8. Appreciation for program

Include the tournament results from the previous year on another page. Figure A-9 shows an example of such an entry.

Get all of the information sheets from each coach and get them typed. If one team doesn't send you the information sheet back, call them and have them fax you one. If they don't get you one on time, they just miss out. As a general rule, allow one page per team. In fact, you can combine several teams on one sheet if you are short on paper or funds. Figure A-10 shows a sample roster.

Take a copy of the tournament bracket and reduce it to fit in the program. Now all you have to do is run it off! You can make the program with legal-size paper (8 x 14). Cut and paste your copies onto the legal-size sheets. You will need eight sheets to begin. Figure A-11 illustrates a sample eight-sheet program layout.

```
WINTER SOCCER CLASSIC
TOURNAMENT RESULTS

Championship Match: Katy High School 4, Katy Taylor H.S. 0
Third Place: Montgomery 2, Giddings 1
Consolation: Bellville 2, Sealy 0

ALL-TOURNAMENT TEAM

Most Valuable Player: Rebekah Jordan, Bellville
Winning Coach: Stephenie Jordan

Marnie Cordes, Katy HS              Elizabeth Williamson, Giddings HS
Elizabeth Rodriguez, Katy HS        Holli Sims, Bellville HS
Beth Blair, Katy HS                 Natalie Cashdollar, Cinco Ranch HS
Tracy Reding, Katy Taylor HS        LaDona Arbuckle, Katy Taylor HS
Cindy Burkhalter, Bellville HS      Christy Bilke, Sealy HS
Janet Willis, Bellville HS
```

Figure A-9. Tournament results

	Rockdale Tigerettes		
No.	Name	Class	Ht.
10	Shelly White	Sr.	5'6"
12	Tammy Shields	Soph.	5'3"
13	Cathy Booth	Jr.	5'8"
15	Dee Ann Poorman	Soph.	5'10"
17	Christy Thompson	Jr.	5'5"
20	Beverly Burch	Fr.	5'6"
21	Angela Milligan	Jr.	5'8"
22	Holly Strickland	Sr.	5'7"

Figure A-10. Sample roster

Page two should be copied onto the back of page one. Page four should be copied onto the back of page three and so on. Once you have made your two-sided copies, place page seven/eight on top of page five/six and so on. Then fold the pages in half, and you have your program. If you have a heavy-duty stapler, you can staple in the fold to keep it all together. If this is your first year to run a tournament or you don't have records of previous tournaments, Figure A-12 shows a basic program outline.

Finding a Gatekeeper

Your school may have someone who usually keeps the gate for the regular season games. If you don't have a regular gatekeeper, or that person isn't willing to sit for that long, then add that responsibility to your clock and book assignment list.

Figure A-11. Sample 8-sheet layout

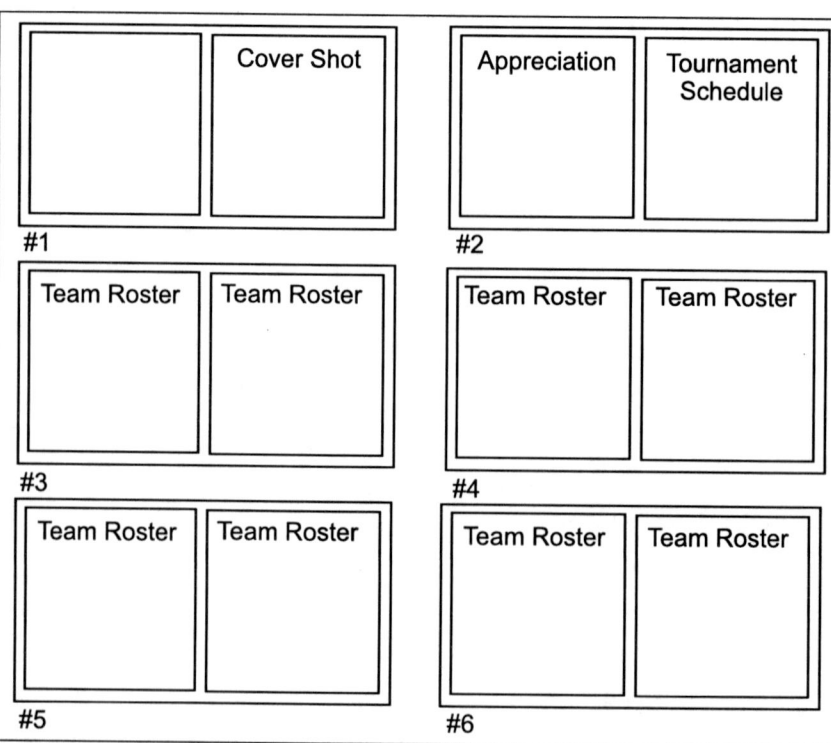

Figure A-12. Basic program outline

Two Weeks Before the Tournament

Have all athletes sign up to bring something for the hospitality area.

Hospitality Area

The coaches who attend your tournament are usually impressed by two factors: keeping on schedule, and what kind of food you have in the hospitality area. Have your athletes sign up to bring something, and then check to make sure there aren't too many desserts vs. real food. You will probably want to purchase cups and canned drinks (using tournament-fee money). If you can get them donated, it saves money. Set up a tent near the game field for opposing coaches so they can have a place to sit away from the fans.

One Week Before the Tournament

- Make a large bracket sign to post on the wall.
- Make signs with team names to post on the wall.
- Make packets for the coach of each team.
- Get large envelopes for packets.
- Order a sandwich tray for the hospitality area.
- Send information to the local paper.

Signs With Team Names

These signs will be used to designate the home team and the visiting team for the fans. Post them under the clock on the wall.

Packets for Coaches

The packets for each coach should include the following:

- Letter to the coach (refer to Figure A-13)
- All-Tournament ballots (refer to Figure A-14)
- A tournament bracket for the coach
- Programs for players and coaches

Information to Newspaper

Send your local newspaper any pre-tournament information that can be printed for a story (e.g., favored team, outstanding players, outstanding coaches, or any other tidbits of information). A finalized tournament schedule should also be included.

> Welcome to the Winter Soccer Classic. We hope that you enjoy the tournament and will return next year.
>
> Enclosed you will find the following items:
> - All-tournament ballots
> - Tournament schedule
> - Rules and information sheet
> - Programs for players and coaches
>
> At the completion of each game, please fill out an all-tournament selection ballot and give it to Stephenie Jordan. Don't forget to visit the coaches'/officials' hospitality room located behind the concession stand.
>
> If you need anything, please let me know.

Figure A-13. Letter to coach

> **WINTER SOCCER CLASSIC**
> **ALL-TOURNAMENT BALLOT**
>
> Nominate two players from your team and two players from your opponent's team. Indicate using the player's number.
>
> Your team name: _____ Opponent team name: _____
>
> Player # _____   Player # _____
>
> Player # _____   Player # _____

Figure A-14. All-Tournament ballot

The Day Before the Tournament

- Remind all athletes to bring food for the hospitality room.
- Buy cups, napkins, utensils, plates, and canned drinks.
- Prepare the ice chests.
- Put reminders in coaches' boxes for times they work.
- Make out an excuse list for your team if they play before school is out.
- Prepare the score book to be used as the official book.
- Pick up the sandwich tray.
- Set up the field.

The Day of the Tournament

- Make coffee for the hospitality area.
- Get ice, and cover drinks in coolers.
- Make sure the dressing rooms are clean.
- Set up the hospitality area as athletes bring food.
- Give programs to the gatekeeper.

- Give coaches the information packets as they arrive, and direct them to the dressing rooms.
- Have pencils ready for the score book.
- Set up the scoreboard.
- Have balls ready for pregame warm-ups.

After each trophy game, just hand the coach their trophy and get ready for the next game. All-Tournament selections should be announced at the conclusion of the championship game. Be sure to clean the dressing rooms and take care of the food in the hospitality room.

After the Tournament

- Call in results to the newspaper.
- Send a letter to participating coaches.
- Send thank-you notes to your helpers.

Results

Fax or call in the tournament results to your local paper as soon as the tournament ends. Include the MVP, tournament champions, etc. The sportswriter will ask you what he wants to include in the results.

Letter to Coaches

Send a letter to each coach who participated in the tournament and include the final results of the tournament. Figure A-15 shows an example of a letter that could be sent to each coach.

Letters to Helpers

You should jot a note to all those who helped keep the book, gate, etc. Figure A-16 shows an example of a letter of appreciation that could be sent to those individuals who helped run the tournament.

Dear Coach,

We hope that you enjoyed the Winter Soccer Classic and hope you will plan to participate again next year. We have had interest from a number of other schools, which will make this event even more exciting and competitive.

Enclosed are the tournament results. The coaching staff hopes you are successful this season and look forward to seeing you again next year.

Figure A-15. A sample letter to coaches

To:
From: Coach Jordan

The Lady Toucan Soccer Team and I would like to express our appreciation to you for your help and support during the tournament. Your efforts were a big part of making the tournament a success.

Figure A-16. Sample letter of appreciation

Terminology

A

Advantage rule: A special rule that allows an official to permit play to continue after a foul if it would benefit the team that was fouled.

Assist: The pass that immediately precedes a goal.

Attacking midfielder: The most forward-playing midfielder, who supports the offense by providing passes to forwards to set up goals; he plays right behind the forwards.

Attacking third: The third of the field that contains the opponent's goal.

Attacker: Any player on the team that has possession of the ball.

"Away": Instruction issued by a goalkeeper to teammates to tell them to clear the ball without attempting to control it.

B

Back: A defender. Also called a fullback.

Back pass: A pass made to a trailing player. Also called a drop pass or support pass.

Backside: The side of the goal that is away from the ball and is often poorly protected and harder to defend. Also called weakside.

Ball side: Refers to getting between the ball and the opponent.

Banana kick: A kick used to get the ball around a goalkeeper or defender that has a curved trajectory; usually attempted on a corner kick. Also called a hook.

Bicycle kick: An acrobatic shot by a player in which he kicks the ball in mid-air backward over his own head, making contact above the waist. Also called a scissors kick.

Block tackle: A standing tackle made with the inside of the foot; the most basic tackle.

Booking: Terminology used to indicate that a player has had his name/number recorded by the referee for receiving a yellow or red card.

Boot: The British term for a soccer shoe.

Box: The penalty area.

Break: When a team advances the ball down the field faster than defenders have a chance to retreat.

Breakaway: When a sole attacker is pitted against the goalkeeper in a one-on-one showdown.

C

Caps: The number of official international games a player has played in for his national team.

Cards: There are two colors of cards that the referee holds up to indicate serious fouls—yellow and red. When given to players, the referee will stop play, record the player's name and number (called booking), and will award a direct kick or indirect kick to the opposing team.

Caution: A disciplinary action in which the referee shows a player a yellow card.

Center circle: A circle in the center of the field with a 10-yard radius from which kickoffs are taken to start or restart the game.

Center mark: A painted mark at the center of the center circle on which the ball is placed for a kickoff.

Central defender: A player who is positioned in the center of the defensive line. If a team plays with a flat three in back, there is a center back. In a flat four, there are two. If they play behind the defensive line, they are called a sweeper and in front they are called a stopper; often considered the strongest defender.

Central forward: A forward who plays toward the center of the field.

Central midfielder: The midfielder most responsible for organizing play in the midfield area, creating scoring opportunities for the attackers, and often being the team's leader.

Challenge: When a defender tries to steal the ball.

Charge: Allowed intentional contact between players with the intention to gain possession of the ball; illegal against a player without the ball or from behind.

Chest trap: When a player uses his chest to slow down and control the ball in the air.

Chip pass: A pass lofted over the head of a defender from a player to a teammate.

Chip shot: A kick lofted into the air in an attempt to sail the ball over the goalkeeper's head and still make it under the crossbar and into the goal.

Clearing: To move the ball away from the penalty box by punching (goalkeeper only) or kicking it.

Combination play: When attacking players work together to execute a play; examples include give & go, overlapping run, etc.

Corner arc: A quarter circle with a radius of one yard located at each of the four corners of the field.

Corner flag: The flag located at each of the four corners of the field inside the corner area.

Corner kick: A type of restart awarded to an attacking team when the ball crosses the goal line and was last touched by the defending team; kicked from the corner arc.

Creating space: When a player from the attacking team moves without the ball to draw defenders away from the ballcarrier or other teammate and give him space to run into.

Cross: A pass from an attacking player near the sideline to a teammate in the middle or opposite side of the field; used to give the teammate a good scoring opportunity.

Crossbar: The horizontal beam that forms the top of the goal and sits on top of the two posts; it is 24 feet long and supported eight feet above the ground.

Cruyff turn: A turn used for change of direction; name for Johan Cruyff, a famous Dutch player who popularized it.

D

D: Abbreviation referring to the penalty arc.

Dead ball: A ball that has been whistled out of play.

Defenders: The players on the team that do not have possession of the ball and works mainly in the defensive third of the field.

Defense: A team's function of preventing the opposing team from scoring.

Defensemen: The three or four players on a team whose primary task is to stop the opposition from scoring. Also called fullbacks.

Defensive midfielder: The player positioned just in front of his team's defense and who is often assigned to mark the opposition's best offensive player. Also called midfield anchor.

Direct free kick (DFK): A free kick awarded to a player for a personal foul committed by the opposition; the player kicks a stationary ball with no opposition within 10 yards from his and may score directly from this kick without the ball touching another player. A direct free kick offense occurring in the other team's penalty box is a penalty kick.

Distribution: A term used to describe the various individual techniques used by a goalkeeper to pass the ball to teammates.

Draw: A game that ends in a tie.

Dribbling: The basic skill of advancing the ball with the feet while controlling it.

Drive: Typically a low, hard shot on goal taken with the instep.

Drop ball: A method of restarting a game in which the referee drops the ball between two players facing each other.

Dropkick: When a goalkeeper drops the ball from his hands and kicks it just after it hits the ground.

Dummy: To pretend to be about to receive the ball, but instead allow the ball to travel between your legs to deceive the opponent.

E

End line: The boundary line extending from corner to corner.

Encroachment: Being within 10 yards of the ball when an opponent is taking a free kick, corner kick, goal kick, or penalty kick.

F

Fake: A move by a player meant to deceive an opposing player; used by a ballcarrier to make a defender think he is going to dribble, pass, or shoot in a certain direction when he is not. Also called a feint.

Far post: The goalpost furthest from the ball.

Federation Internationale de Football Association (FIFA): The official governing body of international soccer since 1904; helps set and revise the rules of the game, called the 17 Laws.

Feint: A move by a player meant to deceive an opposing player; used by a ballcarrier to make a defender think he is going to dribble, pass, or shoot in a certain direction when he is not. Any of the step-overs and moves created by famous players constitutes feints. Also called a fake.

Field player: Any player other than the goalkeeper.

Finish: To score a goal.

Finisher: Any player who has the ability to score when opportunities are given to him.

First time ball: When the ball is received and propelled in a single movement; also called one-touch pass and first touch.

Flat back: A defensive shape in which the back three or four defenders move in tandem, maintaining a formation that is relatively straight across the field, as opposed to formations based on having at least one player stationed some distance behind the other defenders.

Flick header: A player's use of his head to deflect the ball.

Foot trap: A player's use of his foot to control a rolling or low-bouncing ball.

Football: Name for soccer everywhere except in the United States. Also spelled futbol.

Formation: The arrangement into positions of players on the field (e.g. 1-4-3-3 places a goalkeeper, four defenders, three midfielders, and three forwards on the field.) Also called system of play.

Forward line: The three or four forwards who work together to try to score goals.

Forward pass: A pass made toward the opposition's goal.

Forwards: The players on a team who are responsible for most of the team's scoring; also known as strikers and wingers who play in the attacking third of the field.

Foul: When the referee judges a violation against an opposing player; the team that suffers the foul is awarded a direct free kick unless the foul is committed by a defensive player inside his own penalty area, in which case the foul results in a penalty kick.

Free kick: A kick awarded to a player for a foul committed by the opposition; the player kicks a stationary ball without any opposing players within 10 yards. There are two types of free kicks—direct and indirect.

Fullbacks: The three or four players on a team whose primary task is to stop the opposition from scoring; play closest to their own goal. Also called defensemen.

G

Give-and-go: A pass to a teammate who one-touch passes the ball back into space for the player to run to. Also called a 1-2 or wall pass.

Goal: A point awarded for a ball that crosses the goal line between the goalposts and under the crossbar; also the name that represents the eight-foot high, 24-foot wide structure consisting of two posts, a crossbar, and a net into which goals are scored.

Goal area: A box surrounding the goal that is 20 yards wide and extends six yards into the field.

Goal kick: A type of restart in which the ball is kicked from anywhere inside the goal area away from the goal; awarded to the defending team when the ball is played over the goal line by the attacking team.

Goal line: The line that runs right across the front of the goal and which the ball must completely cross for a goal to be scored.

Goalie: Abbreviation for goalkeeper.

Goalkeeper: The player positioned directly in front of the goal who tries to prevent shots from getting into the net and the only player allowed to use his hands and arms—though only within the penalty area.

Goalposts: The two vertical beams located 24 feet apart that extend eight feet high to form the sides of a goal and support the crossbar.

H

Hacking: Kicking an opponent's legs.

Halfback: One of the two, three, four, or five players who link together the offensive and defensive functions of a team and play behind their forwards; positioned in the middle third of the field between the forwards and the defenders. Also known as a midflielder.

Halftime: The intermission between the two periods or halves of a game.

Handball: A foul in which a player touches the ball with his hand or arm; the opposing team is awarded a direct free kick for this foul.

Hat trick: When a single player scores three or more goals in a game.

Header: Passing, clearing, controlling, or shooting the ball with one's head.

I

Indirect free kick (IFK): A kick awarded after a player violation such as offside, delay of game, or misconduct. The player kicks a stationary ball without any opposing players within 10 yards of him, but a goal can only be scored on this kick after the ball has touched another player.

Injury time: Time added to the end of any period according to the referee's judgment of time lost due to player injuries or intentional stalling by a team.

Instep: The inside of a player's foot.

J

Jockey: To delay the forward progress of an opponent with the ball by holding a position close to, and on the goal side of, the opponent so that he can be tackled once support arrives.

Juggling: Keeping the ball in the air by using any legal part of the body; used to develop coordination.

K

Kickoff: The method of starting a game or restarting it after each goal from the center spot; a goal may be scored directly from a kickoff.

Keeper: An abbreviation for goalkeeper.

L

Laws of the Game: The 17 main rules of soccer as established by FIFA.

Lead pass: A pass sent ahead of a moving teammate to arrive at a location at the same time he does.

Libero: A position name given to a player playing in one of the positions normally associated with a stopper or sweeper.

Linesmen: The two officials who assist the referee in making decisions; they monitor the sidelines and goal lines to determine when a ball goes out of bounds and they carry a flag to signal their observations.

Lob: A high arcing kick.

M

Man-to-man: A type of defense in which each defender is assigned to mark a different forward from the other team.

Maradona turn: A turn used to change direction and elude an opponent; named for Diego Maradona, the famous Argentinian player who popularized it.

Marking: To cover an opponent with or without the ball to keep him from passing, receiving, or shooting the ball.

Match: A soccer game.

Midfield: The area of the field near the center line, or the middle third of the field.

Midfield anchor: The player positioned just in front of his team's defense and who is often assigned to mark the opposition's best offensive player. Also referred to as a defensive midfielder or holding midfielder.

Midfield line: A line that divides the field in half along its width; also known as the center line.

Midfielder: One of the two, three, four, or five players who link together the offensive and defensive functions of a team and play behind their forwards; positioned in the middle third of the field between the forwards and the defenders. Also called a halfback.

N

Near post: The goalpost nearest to the ball.

Narrowing the angle: When a goalkeeper advances to block an attacker, decreasing the size of the area of the goal in which an attacker can direct a shot. Also referred to as closing down the angle.

Nutmeg: Passing or pushing a ball between another player's legs.

NSCAA: National Soccer Coaches Association of America.

O

Obstruction: When a player impedes the progress of an opponent by using his body merely to prevent a play on the ball; penalized by an indirect free kick.

Offense: The function of trying to score goals.

Offside: The situation in which an attacking player on the offensive half of the field has put himself in a position where fewer than two opponents are positioned between him and the goal (usually the goalkeeper and one other defender); this positioning does not constitute a foul until he is involved in the play.

Offside trap: The act of defenders quickly pulling up in unison to place an opponent in an offside position, thereby creating an offside infraction.

On goal: A shot that will enter the goal if nothing stops it is said to be "on goal," "on frame," or "on target."

One-touch play: When a player redirects a moving ball with the first touch, either to pass to another player or as a shot, without using the first touch to control the ball.

Over the top: To send long, high balls forward into the attacking third so that they drop behind the fullbacks with the intention of creating opportunities for strikers or wing forwards.

Overlap: A tactic used by the attacking team in which one player runs past the ballcarrier to put himself in a better position to receive the ball.

Overtime: The extra periods played after a regulation game end in a tie; used in collegiate and championship international matches to determine a winner.

Officials: The referee and two linesmen who work together to make sure the game is played according to the rules of soccer.

Overlap: When a winger moves away from the sideline toward the center of the field to create space for a teammate to advance the ball undefended along the side of the field.

P

Passing: Kicking the ball to a teammate in an attempt to move the ball closer to the goal, to keep the ball away from an opponent, or to give the ball to a player who is in better position to score.

Penalty arc: An arc, the center of which is the penalty spot, that extends from the top of the penalty area.

Penalty area: A rectangular area surrounding the goal that begins and ends 18 yards to each side of the goal (from the inside of the goal post) and extends 18 yards into the field; the goalkeeper may use his hands to block or control the ball only within this area.

Penalty kick: A direct free kick awarded for a foul occurring in the penalty area. The ball is placed 12 yards out in front of the goal. Only the goalie and fouled player may be in the penalty area during the kick, but any player may play the ball once it is touched by the goalie.

Penalty spot: The small spot located 12 yards in front of the center of the goal line from which all penalty kicks are taken.

Pitch: A term used in some countries for the soccer field.

Punt: A goalkeeping distribution technique in which the ball is dropped from the hands and then kicked with the laces.

Q

Qualifying draw: The division of team into groups for World Cup qualifying matches.

Qualifying matches: Games played in the two years preceding the World Cup to determine which teams participate in the tournament.

R

Red card: Card held up by a referee indicating that a player has been ejected from the game; two yellow cards equal one red card.

Referee: The chief official who has been given full authority to enforce the Laws of the Game; he makes all decisions, acts as timekeeper, calls all fouls, and starts and stops play.

Restart: The use of a kick, throw, or dropped ball to restart play after it has been stopped because the ball goes out of the field of play or the referee stops play for any other reason.

S

Save: An action that stops a shot on goal from scoring.

Scissors kick: An acrobatic shot by a player in which he kicks the ball in mid-air backward over his own head, making contact above the waist. Also called a bicycle kick.

Score: To put the ball into the net for a goal; also the tally of goals for each team playing in a game.

Scrimmage: A practice game. Also called a "friendly."

Set piece (set play): A planned strategy a team uses when a game is restarted with a free kick, penalty kick, corner kick, goal kick, throw-in, or kickoff; similar to an inbounds play in basketball.

Shape: Refers to the characteristic placement of players in a given formation.

Shielding: A tactic that involves a ballcarrier putting his body between the ball and the defender who is marking him.

Shin guards: Protective equipment worn by players to aid in prevention of injuries to the shin.

Shootout: A tiebreaker that pits one player against the goalkeeper in either penalty kicks or a breakaway-type run from 35 yards away. In both cases, the winner is determined after a best-of-five round, alternating with each team. If tied after five, the contest continues with different players until a team scores and the other team doesn't.

Shot: An attempt by kicking, heading, or any intended deflection of the ball toward a goal by a player attempting to score.

Sideline: A line that runs along the length of the field on each side. Also called a touchline.

Sliding tackle: An attempt by a player to win the ball from an opponent by sliding on the ground feet-first into the ball.

Small-sided game: A game played in which the number of players involved is less than (usually much less than) the "normal" 11 per side.

Space: Used to define an area on the field that is free from opponents and pressure.

Stopper: Name of the defender who usually plays in front of the sweeper and marks the best scorer on the attacking team in a man-to-man defense; often the opposition's striker.

Strikers: The players on a team who are responsible for most of the team's scoring; also known as strikers and wingers who play in the attacking third of the field Also called forwards.

Strip: The uniform worn by all team members, consisting of a jersey, shorts, and stockings.

Substitute: Any of the team's idle players on the bench waiting to enter the field of play.

Sudden death: A type of overtime in which the first goal scored by a team ends the game and gives the team the victory; most overtime in soccer is *not* sudden death.

Support: A player on the ball is said to have support when he has one or more teammates in position and ready to receive a pass; a defending player, challenging the player on the ball, is said to have support when a teammate is ready to cover if he is beaten by the attacker.

Sweeper: The defender that plays closest to his own goal behind the rest of the defenders and is a team's last line of defense in front of the goalkeeper; responsible for "sweeping up" loose, through balls that are played behind other defenders.

System of play: A term used to describe the specific manner in which a given formation is implemented.

T

Tackle: A defensive technique used to take the ball away from an opponent using the feet.

Through pass: A passed ball that splits a pair of defenders.

Throw-in: A type of restart in which a player throws the ball from behind his head with two hands while standing with both feet on the ground behind the sideline; a goal cannot be scored directly from a throw-in.

Tiebreaker: A way to choose the winner of a match when teams are tied after overtime.

Timekeeper: The referee is the timekeeper and notifies the teams and fans when each period is completed.

Timeout: An official break in the action of a sport; the rules of soccer do *not* allow for any timeouts, but timeouts for television advertising breaks are permitted by NCAA collegiate rules.

Touchlines: The two lines marking the boundaries down the length of the field; commonly called the sideline in other sports.

Trailing: Running behind another player.

Trap or trapping: To receive the ball in a controlled manner, most often using the chest, thighs, or feet.

Two-touch pass: A pass in which the ball is received by a player with one touch and then played to a teammate with the next touch.

U

United States Soccer Federation (USSF): Organization formed in 1913 to govern soccer in America.

United States Youth Soccer Association (USYSA): The official youth division of soccer that organizes and administers youth league competitions, and establishes rules and guidelines.

V

Vision: The ability to see the happenings on the field of play; players with excellent "vision" have the ability to see and know where their teammates are located in relation to the defenders.

Volley: A technique used by a player in which he strikes the ball in midair.

W

Wall: A line of two to six defenders standing nearly shoulder-to-shoulder in attempt to defend a free kick near the goal.

Wall pass: A pass by a player who sends the ball to a teammate, then runs behind his own defender, and quickly receives a pass back; same as the "give-and-go" in basketball.

Wingers: The outside forwards who play to the sides of the strikers and whose primary task is to provide them with accurate crosses so they can shoot at the goal. Also called wings.

Wingback: A fullback playing in a wide position with responsibility for making attacking, overlapping runs down the flank.

World Cup: The official World Championship of soccer held by the FIFA every four years.

Y

Yellow card: A card held up by the referee that warns a player that any further misconduct will result in his ejection from the game. Also called a caution.

Z

Zone: A type of defense that assigns each defender to a particular area or zone in front of or around his team's goal; each player is responsible for marking any opponent that enters his zone.

C

Fundraising Ideas

If your program needs a few things, but you don't have enough money in the budget, you can arrange a fundraiser and generate up to $1000 per event. You can always resort to bake sales and car washes, or use one of the ideas presented in this section.

Powder Puff Football Game

Powder puff is a flag-football game played by the girls during the last few weeks of school against your rival school. The game is played exactly like a regular Friday night game (officials, announcer, down markers, etc.) and coached by varsity football players. You can even have a pep rally that day with male cheerleaders. If you can get your school's band to attend the game, it makes it an even better event. You need to get started by the first of May (or even sooner) if you want it to work.

How to Get Started

- Talk to your principal and get approval.
- Check with the football coach for use of the field.
- Have your principal call the opponent's principal and get a contact name.
- Put the date on the school calendar so it doesn't conflict with anything else.
- Have varsity boys sign up to coach or be cheerleaders.
- Have girls sign up to play.
- Check with PE teacher for football flags.
- Organize the concession stand.
- Arrange a time to meet with the other sponsor.
- Talk to the cheerleading sponsor and the cheerleaders.

Finding a Sponsor

The most difficult task may be finding someone from the other school to agree to sponsor such an event. After clearing it with your principal, call the principal from the other school and find out if they are interested in participating. If the other school's principal thinks it's a good idea, you can work together to find someone to sponsor the game, and you can go from there. If football is a big deal in your area, you can assure potential sponsors that they can make at least $800 to $1000, and even more if they have a concession stand.

Sign-up Day

Once everyone is in agreement (including the athletic director and head football coach), have a sign-up for varsity football players who want to coach. Once you've seen who has signed up, you can delegate who you want to be the head coach. He can then choose who he wants as his defensive coordinator, special teams coordinator, etc. You should also have a sign-up for cheerleaders. Let them know that they will be wearing skirts, wigs, and make-up and will perform a short dance at halftime (more on cheerleaders later). You will also need three people to take care of the down markers. You may or may not have to coax your girls into playing. Have them sign up, and if your best athletes aren't planning to play, find a way so they will! Be sure to make a team roster to hand out at the games once you've decided on positions.

Flags for the Game

Check with your physical education teachers for flag-football flags. You should have enough for both teams to use. See the rules section for guidelines on how to wear the flags properly.

Concessions

The most stress-free way to provide the fans with a concession stand is to let the pros take care of it. Whoever traditionally does the concessions at regular home football games would be your best bet. Call whoever is in charge and find out if they'll do it. They usually agree, but if not, check with another group in the school who'd like to do it (e.g., student clubs, athletic boosters, student council).

Meeting with the Other Sponsor

You'll need to meet with representatives of the other team to finalize rules and give them some flags to practice with. Be sure to count the flags you've given out so you get them all back. A set of rules needs to be agreed upon by both parties. (Refer to the sample set of rules that is included in the next section of this appendix). The game is designed to be an 11-on-11 game with kickoffs, returns, field goals, etc., which are not normally included in a traditional flag football game.

❏ Flag Football Rules

The playing rules for the powder puff football game are the same as those used for a regular high school game with the following exceptions:
- Rushing the kicker on an extra point attempt or a punt attempt is not allowed.
- A punted ball will be dead where it touches the ground, but not on a kickoff.
- All players of the offensive team are eligible receivers.
- Offensive blockers must have their hands clasped in front, as if setting a screen.
- Defensive players are not allowed to push or pull offensive players.

- Defensive players may not hold a ball carrier in order to grab the flag.
- A player is considered down when her flag is pulled or if a flag falls off while in play.

Keep the following equipment guidelines in mind:

- Shirts or jerseys must be tucked in so flags are clearly visible and accessible.
- Both teams will use a junior high football.
- Soccer-type cleats may be worn and are recommended.
- Both teams will agree on the type of flags to be worn.

Meet with the Cheerleaders

Have the cheerleaders take your group of boys who bravely signed up and transform them into polished cheerleaders. They should learn at least three cheers and a short dance routine for the pep rally and halftime show. Let your real cheerleaders do all of the planning for the pep rally (signs, introductions of players, etc.) and for the game. The football girls will need a sign to run through, too, as they come onto the field. The boys are really the highlight of the whole game, so be sure they are dressed accordingly (e.g., wigs, makeup). Instead of trying to stuff big guys into cheerleading tops, have them wear their football jerseys with cheerleading skirts so everyone knows who they are.

Organizing Practice

Saturday afternoons are really the best times to get everyone there for practice. You'll have to be present at all practices, of course. You'll need to give the individual who is serving as your head coach some direction on what to do during practice and who to play. Consider yourself the Jerry Jones of the entire operation since you want to win and you don't want anyone to be embarrassed on the field. That's not to say the coaches aren't competent, but since you had the training to be a coach, you should help. Once the game starts, however, let them call the plays. Just help with personnel decisions and practice organization.

Personnel Decisions

• Find a quarterback. You will be most successful if you have someone who can throw the ball well. Use junior high footballs since they are smaller and easier to handle. The main emphasis of your offense should be passing the ball and using misdirection plays (e.g., reverses), but more on that later.

• Find out who can catch the ball. Get someone who can throw the ball (your newly found quarterback if possible), line up the players, and have them run routes as illustrated in Figure C-1. Throw three to five passes at each route and have one of the coaches keep track of who makes a catch. Specify routes; some girls might catch an easy short slant pass but have trouble with the long ball (if you have a quarterback that can throw the long ball, that is).

• Find a center. You have to find someone who can snap the ball to the quarterback in a shotgun formation and then immediately block the player in front of her.

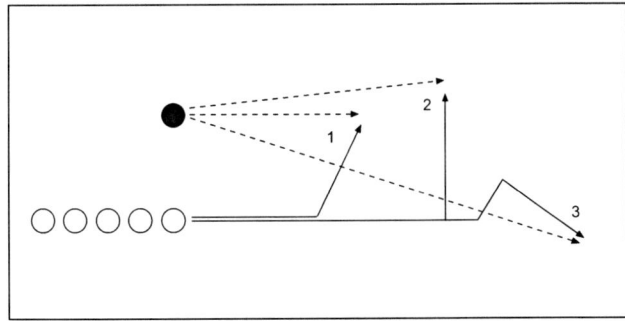

Figure C-1. Suggested passing routes

- Make your fastest four or five players your running backs. Since your running backs will not run right through the line in too many instances, you want quickness to run sweeps and reverses.

- Put anyone who is aggressive and not afraid of contact on the line (defensive and offensive). The line is usually a place for your slower girls to play and do well.

- Find a place kicker and punter. Ask who wants to try out for these positions and have them work with a coach. They might need some instruction from your varsity kicker and punter on technique, but usually you have a young woman who can just do it naturally.

- Put the rest of your players on special teams. If some players who want to be involved are not that talented at football, then they can be on the kick and kick return team or the punt and punt return team. They can also practice as back-up o-line and d-line players. You want to let everyone contribute—and still beat the dog out of the other team.

- Determine who will be your linebackers and secondary players. Linebackers stand just behind the defensive line and stop running backs, quarterbacks, and tight ends. The secondary players cover the receivers on pass plays and serve as the last line of defense on running plays. Because linebackers are generally quick players, use your running backs and quarterback in these positions. A common defense uses three linebackers (i.e., a 4-3) but your boys' team might do something different. Players in the secondary need to be quick as well, but should know how to play man-to-man coverage. Your coaches will tell them what to do.

Drills for Practice

The first practice should be spent finding the right people for each position. After that first day, each young woman should know what position she primarily plays. As a result, when you start practice, everyone knows which coach to report to. The following drills are recommended, although your coaches could and probably will add others that they think would be effective.

❏ Running Backs

Ball exchange drill—Players form two lines facing each other about six to eight yards apart; one player gets the ball. On command, the first player in each line starts running at the first player from the other line. When they meet, they execute an exchange of the ball, using the proper handoff technique. At that moment, the next player starts to get the next handoff, and then hands off the ball to the next player coming at her. Refer to Figure C-2.

Pitch drill—Players line up in a normal position behind the quarterback. Precise positioning will be determined by specific plays designed by the coach. On a signal from the quarterback, the first player receives the pitch in proper position and continues across the line of scrimmage. Players get reps going both ways. Refer to Figure C-3.

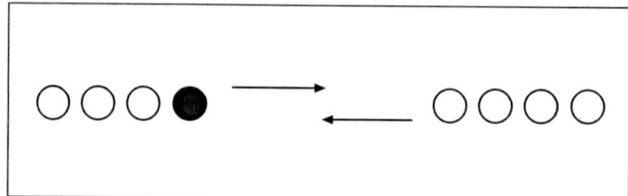

Figure C-2. Ball exchange drill

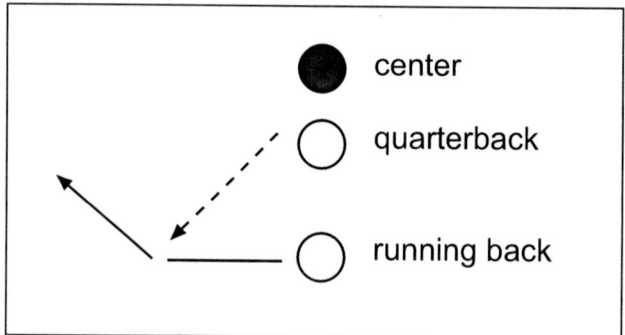

Figure C-3. Pitch drill

❑ Quarterbacks

Two-knee drill (20 passes) —Quarterbacks pair off about 10 yards apart, directly in line with each other, while both members of the pair are kneeling on both knees. The receiver will hold both of her hands up, giving the quarterback a target to throw to. Tell the players not to throw hard, and to concentrate on the target.

One-knee drill (20 passes)—The quarterback puts her throwing-side knee down. She places the ball on the ground, grips it with just the throwing hand, lifts it up with one hand, cocks it high with two hands, and throws to the drill partner. Players should exaggerate the follow-through.

Feet parallel drill (20 passes)—Players pair off 12 yards apart, directly in line with each other. They increase the distance as the drill continues. Tell the players not to exceed 20 yards, and not to step with the foot.

Circle toss (three minutes)—Players run in a circle, playing catch to simulate throwing on the run, then reverse the action.

Sprint out drill (20 passes)—Players sprint right and left. They throw to another quarterback or to a specific target, making sure shoulders and hips are square to the target.

Individual pass routes drill—Quarterbacks throw to a receiver running any of the individual pass routes. This drill is designed to teach timing.

❑ Receivers

Quick ball drill—Players line up about 10 yards from the quarterback or coach. They run across the field at half speed, catch the ball, and then line up on the other side. The drill can be repeated several times with variations on passes: low balls, high balls, and balls thrown behind the player. Refer to Figure C-4.

Tap-dance drill—Players line up about 15 yards from the sideline. On command, the receiver starts to run three-quarter speed toward the sideline. The coach or quarterback will throw the ball about five yards from the sideline, and the receiver will catch the ball and plant one foot inbounds before going out. Use this drill on the left and right side. Refer to Figure C-5.

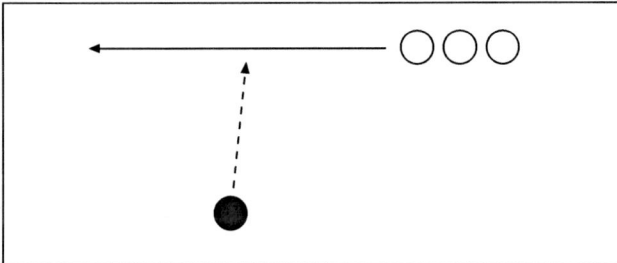

Figure C-4. Quick ball drill

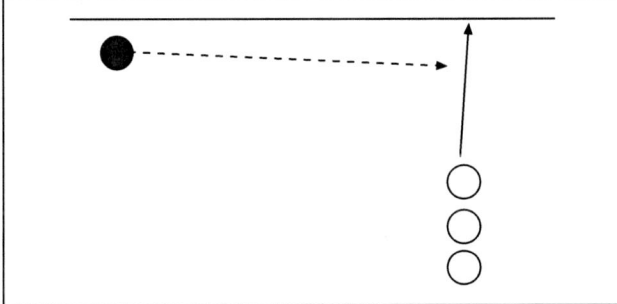

Figure C-5. Tap-dance drill

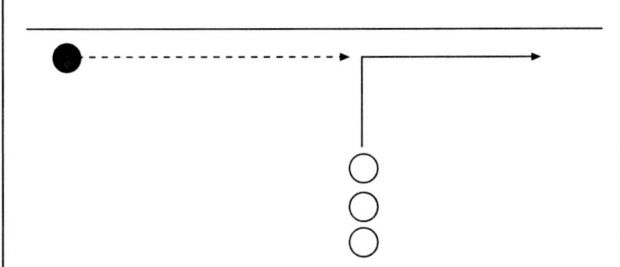

Figure C-6. Turn-and-up drill

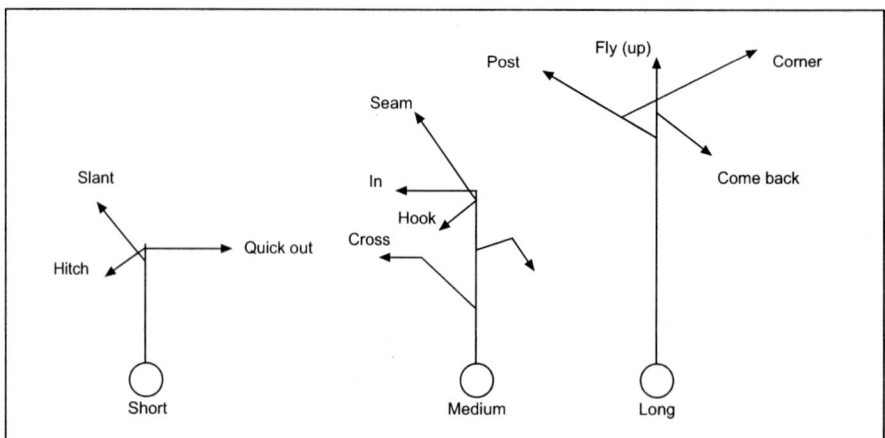

Figure C.7. Route-tree drill

Turn-and-up drill—Use the same procedure described for the tap-dance drill, but in this drill the ball should be thrown seven to eight yards in front of the player so she can adjust and turn upfield. Refer to Figure C-6.

Running routes—A universal wide receiver route tree that you can use to run individual routes is illustrated in Figure C-7.

❑ Defensive/Offensive Line

Playing on the line is tricky because the rules govern how much contact can be made, since no one is wearing pads or helmets. Both the offensive and defensive linemen should get down in at least a three-point stance and then come up with hands clasped in front of them, similar to setting a screen in basketball. This requirement needs to be the case for both teams, since the center has to get down to snap the ball. Otherwise, she is at a great disadvantage, having to come up and block someone who is already in a standing position. Your boys can teach the girls what to do: whom to block, where to block, etc., according to the play.

❑ Linebackers

Flag-grabbing drill—Players should form two lines in front of each other about 10 yards apart. All girls should be wearing flags. One player approaches the other, staying within a five-yard lane, while the other tries to grab the flag. Refer to Figure C-8.

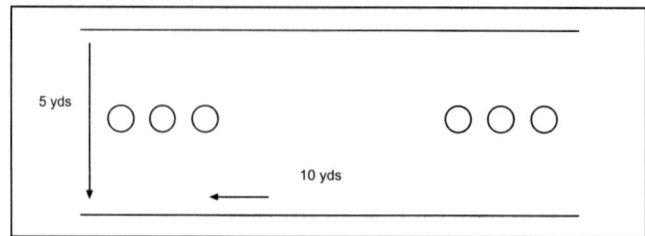

Figure C-8. Flag-grabbing drill

Live-action drill—While running backs are running the pitch drill, the linebackers can practice grabbing the flags.

Secondary drill—While receivers run routes, the secondary can practice covering the receivers. Mix up routes.

The Playbook

Figures C-9 through C-14 illustrate a few plays that should work well. Any misdirection play you run should fool the defense, since most girls haven't been exposed to football very much. Also, passing the ball will be your best bet offensively if you've got the athletes to handle the demands of the passing game. Run these plays to the right or left.

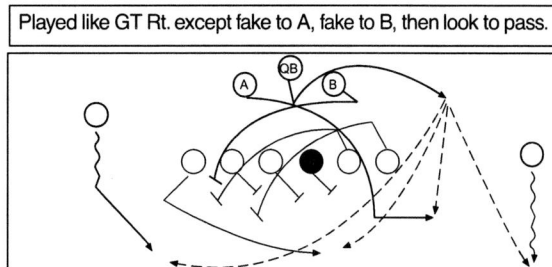

Figure C-9. G.T. right.

Figure C-10. G.T. right pass.

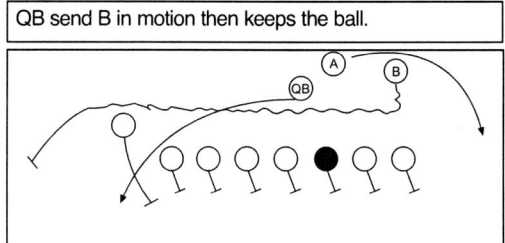
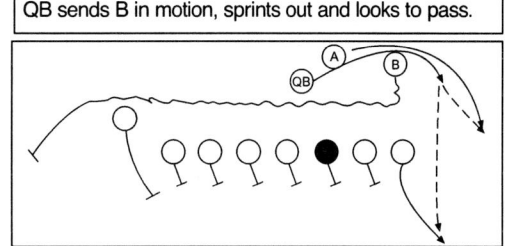

Figure C-11. Right, right, right.

Figure C-12. Right, right, right pass.

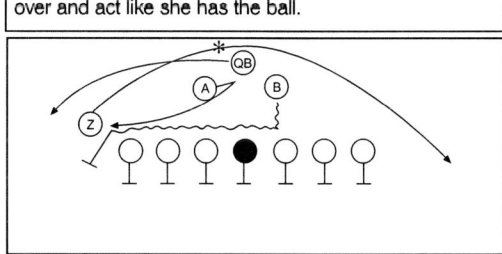
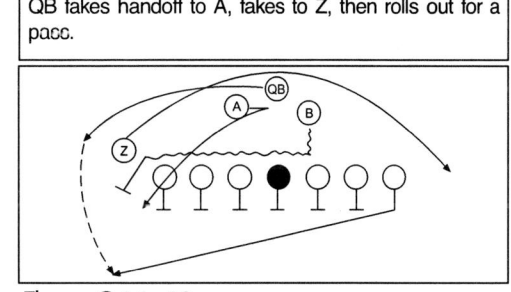

Figure C-13. 48 sweep reverse.

Figure C-14. 48 sweep reverse pass.

Practice Outline

Practice #1

60 minutes   Tryouts for positions

Practice #2

30 minutes	Individual skills in groups (a player should rotate after 15 minutes if she is playing more than one position).
15 minutes	Extra point
15 minutes	Punt

Practice #3

20 minutes	Individual skills (rotate after 10 minutes if a girl is playing more than one position).
30 minutes	Offense (learn plays using note cards)
15 minutes	Punt return

Practice #4

30 minutes	Offense vs. second-team defense
20 minutes	Defense vs. second-team offense
15 minutes	Kickoff

Practice #5

30 minutes	Defense vs. second-team offense
20 minutes	Offense vs. second-team defense
15 minutes	Kick return

Practice #6

Scrimmage vs. freshman boys

You can obviously have more than six practices. If you have the time and energy then, by all means, increase the amount of time devoted to practicing. The kids really enjoy it and will be there no matter how many times you meet. Have the cheerleaders meet at the same time, so you don't have to go another time to cheerleading practices too.

Preparations for Game Day

- Make sure the band will attend.
- Confirm availability of the concession stand.
- Get officials for the game.
- Hand out jerseys.
- Have a team meeting (coaches, cheerleaders, players, helpers).
- Get the down markers ready.
- Get an announcer, and another person to videotape the game, including halftime.
- Publicize the event.

Band Attendance

If the band can attend, great! If not, make a tape of both the school song and the fight song and play it over the loudspeaker.

Officials for the Game

You may try scheduling junior high football officials and explain the rule changes. Or consider using intramural officials from a nearby university.

Jerseys for the Girls

The day before the game, you should hand out jerseys. Hopefully your athletic director or head coach will be cooperative. Try to accommodate your players' desires for numbers, but that is not always possible. Get the jerseys and hand them out starting with seniors, then juniors, etc. If your girls have workout shorts, they can wear them for the game so everyone looks the same.

The Big Meeting

Your coaches should dress alike for the game. It looks sharp and professional. Most of the time, varsity football players have a travel shirt they can wear with khaki pants. It just adds to the atmosphere. Have the coaches, cheerleaders, and powder puff players wear their outfits to the meeting and take pictures and then go over the game plan (when to be there, what to wear, etc.).

Publicity

Put ads in your local paper and post signs all over town to encourage attendance. Be sure to mention the cheerleaders, as some people will attend the game just to see male football players dressed as cheerleaders. Make announcements at school and post signs in the opposing school's town, too.

Golf Tournament

To a great degree, the amount of money you raise from this type of tournament depends on how much the golf course is going to charge you to let everyone play. When it's to benefit a program in the school, it doesn't really matter to some people how much it costs. A $50 fee should include the greens fee, cart, and awards. You can move the fee higher and add amenities, if you prefer. You could also sell mulligans for $5 each (limit four). Provide refreshments and give out T-shirts for all participants. The T-shirts are optional if funds won't allow the expense.

The format of the tournament should be a four-person scramble with a shotgun start (everyone starts at the same time but at different holes). Try to sign up at least 10 teams. You may have to limit the number of teams depending on how many carts the golf course will have available. Give awards to the first-, second-, and third-place teams. Individual awards should be presented for longest drive and closest to the hole. You can give certificates for other awards such as last-place team, slice king/queen, and slowest team. Make up more if you feel so inclined.

Eight Weeks Before the Tournament

- Call the golf course, strike a deal (carts included), and set a date.
- Publicize the tournament at both the course and around town.
- Send entry forms to potential golfers (see Figure C-15).
- Line up volunteer helpers.

	1st Annual Golf Tournament
WHEN:	April 24th, shotgun start at 8:00 a.m.
WHERE:	Community Golf Course
FOR:	Taylor High School Girls' Athletics
COST:	$50 per person (includes cart, greens fee, "goodie bag," and awards)
PRIZES:	$200 first prize, four Wilson golf bags, $100 longest drive, $100 closest to the pin, and others

Mulligans available for purchase on the day of the tournament ($5 each — limit two per person).

Make checks payable to Anywhere H.S. and return the entry form and fee by March 30th to Coach Shaver.

Team captain: _____ Number: _____

Team members: _____
_____
_____

Entry fee: _____ (# indiv's X $50 each)
_____ (# of mulligans X $5 each)

Amount of $ enclosed: _____

Figure C-15. Entry form

Four Weeks Before the Tournament

- Order plaques and T-shirts.
- Ask businesses to help sponsor the tournament.
- Pay golf course required fees.

Order Plaques and T-shirts

The school may have someone it deals with for plaques and trophies. Ask your athletic director who it is or if he has any catalogues you might find useful. He also might have worked with a printer who will give you a relatively good deal on shirts.

Sponsors

You can earn more money by selling sponsorships for each hole. Charge $50 to the sponsor in exchange for a sign on that hole, advertisement, etc.

One Week Before the Tournament

- Get drinks.
- Pick up T-shirts and plaques.
- Make "farthest drive" and "closest to the pin" markers.
- Make a poster to record all scores.

T-shirts

Put a nametag in each T-shirt, and then alphabetize the T-shirts to speed up handing them out.

Making the Markers

The markers should have a piece of paper with at least 10 lines for 10 names (more if the tournament is really large). Secure it to a piece of wire and stick it in the ground.

Scoreboard

Put team members' names in one column and leave a space for their score underneath. As each team finishes, record the scores on the board for everyone to see, as shown in Figure C-16.

John Smith Susan White Steve Scott Joe Garza	Sheryl Ham Lisa Porter Marge Frank Cindy Hall	Joseph Smith Danny Long Chris Lopez Al Johnson
72	69	75

Figure C-16. Scoreboard

The Big Day

- Ice down the drinks.
- Put out the markers and signs for hole sponsorship.
- Post the names of team members on carts, along with the specific hole where they will start play.
- Arrange the plaques on a table.
- Set up a table for purchasing extras and a table for registration.
- Meet with everyone at 7:50 a.m. to get organized.

Putting the Markers Out

Put the longest drive marker on a par-five hole that is somewhat wide open. The closest-to-the-hole marker should be placed on a short par three. Let teams know at the meeting which holes you've chosen.

Purchasing "Extras"

- Mulligans – limit four per person.
- Tiger Woods Drive – participants can purchase one automatic 250-yard drive.
- The String – a 12-inch long string to be used for assistance with short putts.

After the Tournament

Once every team has finished, send someone out to pick up the markers and gather everyone for the awards presentation. Depending on the number of people who will be involved in the awards presentation, it can be extremely informal. If it's a large gathering, you may want to seat everyone in the clubhouse and use a podium for the presentations. Be sure to clean up all trash and park the carts in the appropriate place afterwards.

Co-Ed Softball Tournament

Use the same format for the golf tournament, with the following changes:
- Get permission for use of the boys' baseball field.
- Go to neighboring towns and recreation centers to recruit teams.
- Charge at least $100 per team.
- Require each team to provide two softballs (check the size of the softballs).
- Hire three to four umpires.
- Get an official scorekeeper and clock/scoreboard keeper.
- Mail a bracket sheet to the coach in charge of each team.
- Organize a concession stand.
- Present T-shirts for the first-, second-, and third-place teams.

Using the Baseball Field

A baseball field is more appropriate than a softball field since it is a coed tournament. Technically, the fence should be between 275 feet and 300 feet, and the bases should be moved to 60 feet or 65 feet instead of 90 feet. The pitching distance should be 46 feet, using a 12-inch ball. The day before the tournament, mark the baseline/foul lines and the batter's box. Each side of the plate should be a 3' x 7' rectangle.

Recruiting Teams

Go to neighboring grocery stores and churches to publicize the tournament. If you live in a larger city, you may have a city softball league where you can solicit teams during their games. Post a flyer in each dugout, and you will have plenty of teams interested.

Getting Umpires

If your baseball and softball coaches are not participating in the tournament, you could ask them to call the games for you. If they are playing, you can do one of two things. Either call the recreation center in your city and ask them for some names of umpires that call city games, or call some umpires from the local baseball or softball chapter your school uses. Check to see what they usually earn for games and offer them the same level of compensation.

The Bracket

If you only have one field, it must have lights. The maximum number of teams you should allow is eight, which means a total of 11 games. Each game should have a time limit of 50 minutes, except the championship game. Each game is a seven-inning game with the normal run rule of 10 runs after five innings or 15 runs after four innings.

The Scorekeeper, Time Keeper, and Scoreboard Keeper

Three people or just one can do these jobs. A scoreboard is not necessary, but a neutral scorekeeper and someone to keep the time for each game is important. These jobs could be done by the coaches who are helping you put on the tournament, or you could pay people to fill these positions.

Concession Stand

If you can get someone to grill hamburgers, you can make quite a bit of additional money. Provide a meal of a hamburger, chips, and a drink for around $3.00. This idea will be especially successful if you are a small community without the convenience of a fast-food option. Have bottled water available as well.

T-Shirts

If possible, specify first, second, or third place on the shirts. Or, for convenience, you could print one design for all the T-shirts. Order at least 45 shirts (10 players and five subs per team).

Adhering to the Scheduled Time

Stay as close to the schedule as possible so that the teams know when they will play. However, make each team aware that if a game ends unusually early, the next game will start immediately. Allow 10 minutes for a team to show and then call it a forfeit.

Other Ideas

Garage sale—Use items donated by community members.

Spaghetti supper—Get merchants to donate ingredients and have the dinner before a home football game.

Potluck supper—Have parents of players bring dishes for the supper and have a set charge per plate. Seconds are allowed, but individuals are charged for another plate. Set up a silent auction with items such as old uniforms, cakes, pies, donated gifts from area merchants, season tickets to your home games, booster wear items, etc.

Road race—This event can be similar to a cross-country meet. Give participants T-shirts and prizes for winners in each age division (you decide on the age groups).

Baked potato supper—Again, try to get food donated and include different toppings such as chopped meat, nacho cheese, etc.

Baby-sitting service—Reserve the gym and advertise a Parents' Night Out some Friday or Saturday. Have the girls baby-sit from 6:00 to 11:00 p.m. and charge $10.00 per child.

Car wash—Consider selling tickets beforehand. You might generate more revenue this way.

Bake sale—To put a twist on this one, have the girls spend the night together cooking—an all-night baking party. You might want to check into using the school cafeteria or a church fellowship hall rather than someone's house.

"Meet the Team" dinner—Use any of the supper ideas listed previously and turn it into a "Meet the Team" dinner. Include a silent auction and a raffle, sell your team's booster wear, and sell advertising space on place mats.

Club Team Information

As a high school coach, your better players will probably be members of a travel soccer club. You should encourage their involvement in club soccer and understand the importance these clubs play in the recruitment of players. You should also help educate your players and parents about what to look for in a club, including the club's reputation, club costs, the reputation and qualifications of the coaches, and how many players actually receive scholarships after playing with the club.

Reputation

The first question to ask is whether the club has any pending disciplinary action. You can check with the local association to determine if any action is pending and, if so, the player should look for another club. A club that is in consistent trouble with the local district for bending or breaking the rules will probably treat the players with the same level of respect with which they treat the rules, which are supposed to protect the children.

Club Philosophy or Mission Statement

Every reputable club should have a club philosophy or mission statement, and possibly a curriculum that is given to each coach in the club. Ask to see these documents so you are fully aware of the environment the player is getting into.

Time Commitment

Committing to a club and fulfilling that commitment is important. A player must be fully aware of the commitment before signing on with a team. Before joining a club, a player should ask some of the following questions:
- How often does the team practice?
- Are their extra "skill" practices or position-specific practices that are mandatory?
- How often does the team go to tournaments?
- Does the coach frown upon players playing more than one sport?

Fees

Club costs will vary, and more does not necessarily mean better. Ask for a breakdown of the club dues. Every reputable club will be able to account for every penny of your money.

Coaches

The best way to determine if a coach is qualified is to watch him run a practice and conduct games. Parents and players should pay attention to the types of activities the coach presents to the team and how well the coach conveys to the players the skills involved for the activity. Tell them to look for the following when watching a training session:
- Does the coach present a challenging environment?
- Does the coach lead practices that allow for the development of individual players?
- Does the environment allow players to be successful?
- Are players developing character and good sportsmanship?
- Is a lot of whistle-blowing and yelling taking place?
- Does the coach spend lengthy parts of practice with players in long lines and dribbling through cones?

Coaching Director

Most clubs have a coaching director. If they have a director, parents should find out what his qualifications are and what his role may be in the club.

Scholarship Opportunities

A good question for a parent or player to ask is how many players actually receive scholarships each year and whether those athletes spent all of their youth development with that club. Knowing if the players spent their youth development with the club will give you an idea of whether the club places its priorities on recruiting developed players or on developing good players. Players should not settle for just a number of players who received scholarships. They should be sure to ask for a list of names and institutions attended.

About the Authors

George Hageage is the head women's soccer coach at Eastern Washington University. In 2004, he led Eastern to its first-ever Big Sky Conference title with a 4-1-1 record (7-9-2 overall), and was named the 2004 Big Sky Coach of the Year. In his five seasons at EWU, Hageage has produced 11 All-Big Sky players, 17 all-conference honorable mentions, three All-Big Sky Tournament players, and 81 Big Sky All-Academic team honorees. In 2000, Hageage took over an Eagle team that was 1-17 overall and 0-7 in the Big Sky Conference and turned it into the sixth most-improved team in the nation in 2001 by winning more games (seven) than in the previous two years combined. Hageage has also helped continue the growth in youth soccer in the region with soccer camps and clinics at Eastern.

Since 1988, Hageage has coached at the club level and in 1998 and 1999 was appointed as a head coach for the Ohio-North Olympic development program. Hageage has been coaching at the Division I level for nine years and in the NCAA Collegiate level for 12 years. He is currently the regional technical director for the NSCAA for Region 12 and is in charge of all nonresidential coaching courses throughout the Pacific Northwest. Recently, Hageage was added to the Washington State Youth Soccer coaching staff and serves as an instructor for nonresidential courses in Northeast Washington.

Before going to EWU, Hageage spent three seasons as an assistant under Rj Anderson at the University of Toledo in Ohio. Toledo was 26-26-2 in those three seasons and qualified for the first-ever Mid-American Conference Tournament in 1998.

Beyond being recognized for his on-field achievements, Hageage was honored in spring 2001 for earning his Premier Coaching License with distinction. This honor was presented by the National Soccer Coaches Association of America.

Hageage received his bachelor's degree in biology from the University of Richmond in Virginia in 1988 and obtained his master's degree in education from the University of Toledo in 1998.

Hageage is married to Eagle assistant coach Tamara Browder and they have a two-year-old son, George.

Stephenie Jordan earned her bachelor of science degree in mathematics from Southwest Texas State University with a minor in physical education. There she earned varsity letters in volleyball and track and field and was a two-time Southland Conference Champion. As of 2005, she was still the school record-holder in the heptathlon. Before attending SWTSU, she was recruited to Western Illinois University as a freshman pentathlete/heptathlete and earned All-Conference honors in the javelin for the Gateway Collegiate Athletic Conference. She also earned a varsity letter for volleyball at WIU.

During her high school athletic career, Jordan was a varsity letterman in volleyball, basketball, tennis, and track and field at O'Fallon Township High School. She qualified for the state track meet in the discus and 300 m hurdles, played on the number-one doubles team in tennis, and was Athlete of the Year in 1987.

Jordan began her coaching career in the summer of 1991 at Camp Ozark, where she was the head coach for all team competitions and later became the girls' sports director in 1993. Her first teaching job was at Bellville Junior High School, in Bellville, Texas, where she coached 64 girls in seventh grade. The following two years, she assisted the varsity Bellville High School Brahmanette volleyball team to a 3A state title in 1993 and to the state finals in 1994. Also at Bellville, Stephenie was the JV volleyball coach, the JV basketball coach, an assistant varsity track coach, the JV cheerleading sponsor, and director of the Fellowship of Christian Athletes. She was also the tournament director of the 47th Annual Basketball Tournament and helped supervise the Little Dribbler's program.

After her marriage to Jody, they both accepted teaching and coaching positions in Arp, Texas. Jordan was the head track coach when 14 of 16 girls qualified beyond the district meet. In addition, she assisted the volleyball team as they advanced to the area finals, coached the JV and freshman volleyball teams, and again sponsored the Fellowship of Christian Athletes.

The following year, Stephenie and her family moved to Garrison, Texas, where she became the first softball coach at Garrison High School. After starting the program, the team went 8-4 and played in the first round of the playoffs. She also coached the junior high girls' basketball teams, assisted the varsity team, was the boys' and girls' cross-country coach, acted as Little Dribbler's program coordinator for two years, coached two high jumpers to the regional finals, and also sponsored the Fellowship of Christian Athletes.

Jordan is also the author of *Developing a Successful Girls' and Women's Basketball Program* and coauthor of *Developing a Successful Volleyball Program*, *Developing a Successful Softball Program*, and *Developing a Successful Cross Country Program*.

Stephenie and her husband, Jody, have a son, Scott, and a daughter, Rebekah. She has temporarily given up full-time coaching to raise their family.